The Chronicle of the Good Duke Louis II of Bourbon

JEAN CABARET D'ORVILLE

TRANSLATION AND COMMENTARY BY

STEVEN MUHLBERGER

The Chronicle of the Good Duke Louis II of Bourbon

Jean Cabaret d'Orville

Translated and with commentary by
Steven Muhlberger

Freelance Academy Press, Inc.
www.FreelanceAcademyPress.com

Freelance Academy Press, Inc., Wheaton, IL 60189
www.freelanceacademypress.com

Printed in the United States of America
by Publishers' Graphics

22 21 20 19 18 17 16 15 14 13 1 2 3 4 5

ISBN 978-1-937439-54-5

Library of Congress Control Number: 2020947900

To Briar, Gavin, and Heloïse

Acknowledgements and translator's note

The challenge that all translators face is preserving much of the flavor of the original text while producing a final text that is reasonably accurate. I benefited from the help of a number of scholars during this project, but first and foremost from the advice of my long-term collaborator, Phil Paine.

I decided to use personal and geographic names primarily as they appear in the Chazaud edition of the *Chronicle* except when doing so would be ridiculous. As a result, there are some usages that one does not usually find in English-language accounts of the fourteenth century. I felt more comfortable writing (inconsistently) King Jean (II)/Jean de Châteaumorand /Jehan/St. John's Day rather than use one version of "John."

Scholarly institutions that reproduced valuable materials on the Web include ATILF, which hosts the Dictionnaire Moyen Français, and Google Books, which provided me with the electronic version of Chazaud's edition of the Chronicle.

I delivered a preliminary treatment of the Chronicle in a special lecture sponsored by Boydell and Brewer and *De Re Militari* at the International Congress of Medieval Studies; it was later published in the *Journal of Medieval Military History* as "Chivalry and Milit*ary Biography in the Later Middle Ages:* The Chronicle of the Good Duke Louis of Bourbon." I am grateful to the editors of JMMH and particularly Kelly DeVries for the opportunity to present that paper before members of the Society of Military History, an ideal audience.

Thanks to Ian Hargrove for reading an early version of the translation. Thanks, too, to everyone who listened me praising the excellence of this source, whether they liked it or not.

Introduction

Two dukes of Bourbon, factual and legendary

Duke Louis II of Bourbon was a leader of the French in the Hundred Years' War (1337-1452). He not only took part in every aspect of that war, from battlefield to high level politics, but came out of it as a hero. At least, that is how his friends saw it.

What his friends thought of him is preserved in *The Chronicle of the Good Duke Louis of Bourbon*, which not only gives us a dramatic account of Louis as prince and warlord, but also shows his friends observing him in action. The resulting *Chronicle* is as much a portrait of Louis' circle of friends as it is of Louis himself. The book, very like a collection of legends, gives us modern readers a striking picture of the Hundred Years' War. This is the first translation of the *Chronicle* into any modern language. I hope my work will provide a vivid picture of the war camps, courts, and battlefields of the late fourteenth century. Whether this is the story of a hero is a separate matter.

Duke Louis was a descendant of the French King Louis IX (Saint Louis, d. 1270) and of the first Duke of Bourbon (a position created in 1327). As a royal cousin of Kings Charles VI and Charles VII, and the ruler of a key French duchy, Louis was (along with the other French dukes) a major player in the Hundred Years' War. He was a general, a diplomat, and considered a pious Christian by the standards of his day. In particular, he was a successful warlord, first in his campaigns against the English, then later in the campaigns launched by the French into the Baltic region, Muslim North Africa, and the Iberian peninsula. He also was an important participant in the civil strife among the French royal dukes in the latter years of the 14th century. The records of Duke Louis' constant activity are preserved through numerous archival documents and contemporary histories. But we know more about Duke Louis than the simple facts. As the subject of a biography, and as a legend, he is a literary character. *The Chronicle of the Good Duke Louis of Bourbon,* which was commissioned in 1429 by his descendants, is a remarkable portrait. Although there is much accurate historical fact in the *Chronicle,* it also contains many perhaps less accurate anecdotes as told by those who loved him. As a result, we can appreciate him—as many of his followers did—as an inspirational general and a good lord who was larger than life. We can understand why they called him a "good duke," and what that entailed. Finally, we can catch the echoes of gatherings where members of his family and household remembered his victories and virtues and his occasional defeats. We learn not only what he was like (through sympathetic eyes) but also about some of his closest associates.

How Cabaret portrayed his Good Duke and the role of Jean de Châteaumorand

To understand the portrayal of this Good Duke, we begin with those responsible for the biography, the author Jean Cabaret d'Orville and Sir Jean de Châteaumorand, Cabaret's chief informant. Not much is known about Cabaret except that he was commissioned by Duke Charles I of Bourbon in 1429 to write about Duke Louis. Cabaret borrowed substantially from the writings of a veteran knight and diplomat, Sir Jean de Châteaumorand, who was considerably better known. Châteaumorand's contribution to the *Chronicle* shaped it in important ways.

The *Chronicle* shows that Duke Louis excelled in a variety of roles, but the intended, chivalric audience was keenly interested in the large number of campaigns Duke Louis fought between 1367 and 1392. Cabaret was too young to have witnessed these military feats, or to have known the people involved, but he nevertheless was able to find Châteaumorand, an aging member of Duke Louis' military household. In 1429, Châteaumorand was in his 70s and was able to provide details of the campaigns, the sieges, and the personal interactions between the leading French generals and captains of the previous century. His own career was substantial and was closely identified with that of Duke Louis. Châteaumorand began as a young man fighting the duke's wars against those referred to as English brigands (who were actually freebooters from all over Europe) who were devastating central France. He was later given more responsibilities at court (such as guarding King Charles VI at his coronation) and diplomatic roles of great importance. He became a key figure in French campaigns in the Mediterranean and in Spain.

Many of the campaigns are described in such convincing detail, and the military narrative is so central to the *Chronicle,* that modern scholars have sometimes argued that Châteaumorand the soldier rather than Cabaret the scholar should be considered the author of the *Chronicle*. That conclusion likely overstates

Châteaumorand's contribution, but there is no doubt that many facts and observations came from the older man. For instance, the *Chronicle* tells us that when the Good Duke's men landed in England in 1369, they fought against an English leader "who was armed in a cuirass covered with vermilion velvet." Surely this little touch of local color came from Jean de Châteaumorand – who else? Similarly, who in the late 1420s would remember Sir Jean d'Aye as being the best knight of the 1380s except someone who was there—someone like Châteaumorand!

Châteaumorand's value as a source for Cabaret was due to his extensive service with Duke Louis and his respect for his patron. The knight had fought for and with Louis in such places as England, Germany, Castile, Tunisia, the Baltic and Mediterranean coasts, and most importantly, various provinces of France, where Louis and his followers campaigned to expel English garrisons and plunderers who had overrun and wrecked the country. Châteaumorand was able to give Duke Louis's biographer details of various raids and sieges and ambushes: an informed account of how siege engines were built and used; how invasion fleets were stocked with supplies; and how practical soldiers (including both Duke Louis and Châteaumorand) sometimes felt compelled to take part in chivalric deeds of arms and ostentatiously courteous behavior toward noble ladies.

Thus, the *Chronicle* goes beyond providing us with a vivid picture of the techniques of late 14th-century warfare, fine as some of those passages are. It also tells us much about the relationship between an important princely warlord and one of the captains who made his power a reality. Châteaumorand's family was a noble landholding one whose members had been active warriors for generations. Their willing, loyal, and competent service acted as an important foundation for the Good Duke's position as an advisor to King Charles VI; indeed, at some times Louis' influence was so great that he practically acted as a viceroy. Duke Louis' leadership benefited his followers. His patronage made it possible for a military man attached to him to take part in campaigns in many parts of Europe and Africa, to win renown and profit, and to gain practical experience in diplomacy as a deputy of the Good Duke. The military account contained in *The Chronicle of the Good Duke* radiates Châteaumorand's pride in, and even reverence for, the man who was his beloved commander and patron.

The *Chronicle* allows us to see the mutual love of a lord such as Louis, and military followers such as Jean de Châteaumorand, as well as many other companions that Châteaumorand named in the account. Such love was the traditional glue that made war and government possible. The strength of this bond can be seen in a number of episodes, beginning with Cabaret's account of Duke Louis' return to France in 1363. After the terrible defeat at Poitiers and the death of Louis' father Pierre de Bourbon, Louis succeeded to the ducal title, but he remained a captive in England. Like many other French nobles, Louis was saddled with the obligation to pay not only his own ransom but a hefty share of King Jean's. While

Louis waited for the ransoms to be collected and paid, his family holdings, like most parts of central France, suffered badly from the depredations of disbanded English soldiers. Once his ransom payments had been made, Louis returned to Poitou and called upon the nobles of his region to meet him at Molins. There he urged them to follow him in cleaning up the countryside. Although he had good reason to be dissatisfied with how his lands had been defended in his absence, Louis took a diplomatic approach when addressing his followers. He told them that he meant to rely on his "chivalry and nobility," forgiving their deficiencies and receiving in turn the rededication of his nobles. He openly rejected the alternative strategy of allying with non-noble officials against the rather ineffective nobility. The "commoners" of Louis' duchy were, like many elsewhere, angered by the nobles' failure to protect them. One ducal bureaucrat had gone so far as to prepare a dossier (a book called *Peloux* ["hairy"]) that recorded the misdeeds of the nobles during Louis's absence. Louis rejected this attack on noble families, seeing it as being motivated by the hatred of social inferiors for the nobles. *Peloux* was tossed in the fire and Louis turned to his traditional followers and affirmed their status as respected junior partners, saying:

> Herewith, I request your affirmation that you will help me to make up the time I have lost, and to restore my place in the house from which I have been cast out. I have the heart and will to act forcefully, and because of this, I pray that, along with the other boons you have granted me, you will help me in this. For I want to live and die with you, and I suspect that you feel the same towards me.[1]

And they responded, weeping with joy: "God be blessed! For we have our lord and master."[2]

This is simply one example of the strength of the bond between people like Châteaumorand and the princely warlords of the military aristocracy. The fighting men (meaning the legitimate men-at-arms, excluding bandits and rebels) shared the values of Louis, and drew much of their identity from their membership in a group of warriors. Such men as Châteaumorand shared the duke's renown and identity. In 1375, when Duke Louis' forces took the formidable strong point of Roche-Senadoire, Châteaumorand not only carried Louis' pennon or war banner but also assumed its identity and became himself a symbol of Bourbon. The *Chronicle* makes this clear in its account:

> During this melée, the pennon of the Bourbon continually

1 Below, p. 4.

2 P. 4.

> carried by Jean de Châteaumorand passed through the breach in the palisade, with those who followed. Then the English who saw this did not know what to do, outside of retreating into the fort and while they retreated the pennon rushed forward with the valiant men; and in this retreat of the English, who ran away, there were killed and taken a good fourscore of the better men-at-arms ....the pennon of the Duke of Bourbon and the people of his household charged them so close that as they entered the tower, the pennon of the Duke of Bourbon rushed among them very well accompanied, so that those Englishmen were not able to close the door of the tower, and so they surrendered to the one who carried the pennon of the Duke of Bourbon ... five or six others of the household of the Duke of Bourbon, with his pennon, headed over to one of the other towers ... But when the English saw the pennon of the Duke of Bourbon approach them, the captain Nolimbarbe surrendered with all of his companions to the Duke of Bourbon. So was La Roche Senadoire taken without a word of a lie.[3]

The duke and his men benefited from their respective reputations and prized their reciprocal relationship. On one occasion, when members of Louis' household were allowed to accompany other commanders fighting pagans in Prussia, Châteaumorand refused to take money or gifts from other French crusaders. When the duke's men took part in a raid across the English Channel in 1377, they did so under the command of Sir Jean de Vienne, Admiral of France, but they remembered to whom they belonged. They asked that word of their accomplishments be passed on to the duke, who was still engaged in France. On other occasions (such as at a formal deed of arms at Vannes in Brittany in 1381), men such as the Duke of Brittany were so impressed by the behavior of Bourbon's men that they offered them expensive gifts (and implicitly a new patron-client relationship). The men of Bourbon refused monetary reward because, they said, Duke Louis rewarded them more than adequately, and they would not care to look like they were motivated by greed. The renown gained by Louis' followers similarly added to Louis' reputation. In the *Chronicle* account of Châteaumorand's expedition to Prussia, their worthy ambition was noted by people who fed and housed them along their journey; their behavior on the part of his *gens d'armes* led Louis' princely allies to compliment him in turn. Likewise, the men of Bourbon were grateful to the Good Duke for bringing them up well in the ways of chivalry.

---

3 P. 53.

Why the *Chronicle* was written

During the Hundred Years' War, French historians quite naturally were drawn to write about the most dramatic events and personalities of their time. It was a time of battles and ambushes, of intrigue at court, of divisions in the church and crusading expeditions to fight the infidels. French writers, like most historians, had a particular interest in the great leaders; a favorite genre was what we might call "chivalric biography."

The Chronicle of the Good Duke Louis of Bourbon is one of the best of these biographies. It was commissioned in 1429 by Duke Charles I of Bourbon, to remind its audience of the excellence of Duke Louis and his wise, courageous leadership during the decades following the French defeat at Poitiers (1356; d. 1410). Although the author, Jean Cabaret d'Orville, was an obscure character, he had access to the ducal court of the Bourbons which included a few survivors of the period he wrote about. He also worked to order; what Charles and his court wanted was spelled out very clearly. Cabaret's account was a family history—better yet, a dynastic political history of the Bourbons. Duke Louis was cousin to the kings of France and a lord of extensive fiefs. He was a prince, with extensive military, economic, and political resources. He was, in fact, just one of several royal dukes (those of Berry, Burgundy, and Orléans, King Charles V's brother and cousins) and others slightly less exalted by birth (Brittany and Bar). As a group and as individuals these nobles were the key political actors in the French kingdom. When these princes were cooperative, they provided the best troops and experienced leaders for the armies of the king. Their efforts during the late 14th century allowed the monarchy to recover territories lost to England in the 1340s, and extend French influence through campaigns in Africa, Spain, Italy, and Germany. However, when the dukes and princes fought each other, the monarchy itself was endangered.

When Cabaret wrote the *Chronicle* in 1429, France was in terrible shape. King Charles VI, who had died in 1422, had been an ineffective king; in fact, he had had fits of insanity off and on since 1392. He had left his son and successor, Charles VII, in a severely weakened position vis-à-vis the dukes, who fought harder against each other than against the English. Thus, for the second time since the outbreak of the Hundred Years' War, the once-mighty kingdom of France was in danger of being overrun by the English king and his French collaborators. The *Chronicle* was written with this crisis of leadership in mind—Cabaret called 1429 "the year of the Maid" (Joan of Arc) —but he had nothing to say about her eccentric role in the ongoing war. Cabaret was interested in the conventional type of leadership appropriate to a royal duke. He shows Louis as an aristocratic warrior-prince of the best sort, a Good Duke in an era which, like the one in which Cabaret himself lived, had a great shortage of good dukes.

Duke Louis' wars

Louis' involvement in the defense of France from English invasion, and the recovery of territory from the English and English allies may well have been the most important military and political achievement of the Good Duke's fighting career, and no doubt led him to be called upon to participate in more distant conflicts. The duke loved war, despite its high cost. Although the kingdom of France suffered severely from English aggression, anytime the French kings and their generals attained victory and a period of peace, they plunged almost immediately into new wars against their neighbors. In 1377, following victories in Normandy, Louis not only provided some of his best men to support a raid on the English coast, but also prepared for a major invasion of England. This was not merely a riposte against an enemy that had many times in the preceding decades invaded France; it was a major and worthy enterprise, the kind of preparation a monarch should undertake when the opportunity arose. (In this case, the invasion never happened.) Similarly, the French on two occasions during Louis's career mounted royally sponsored incursions into the Iberian Peninsula—partly to keep the English from combining with the Castilians and attacking them, and partly to prevent the Castilians from attacking the French. Louis was involved in these campaigns.

Toward the end of his active fighting career, when the English threat diminished, Louis was a major player in efforts to expand French power into the Mediterranean. This effort was based on an alliance with the rich merchant city of Genoa, which the French considered to be a somewhat unsteady ally. Cabaret portrays Louis as the foremost and most effective leader of the Crusade expedition against the Muslim-ruled city of Tunis, even though there was certainly doubt even among the Crusaders themselves that the effort was worthwhile. (Tunis, after all, was not taken.)

Yet Cabaret and his prospective readers of the Chronicle would have been keenly interested in Louis' early campaigns in France to restore the power of the monarch. The weakness of French princes in the 1360s and 1370s was echoed in the 1410s and 1420s. Thrilling stories of castles taken from foreign brigands and of Louis' role in crushing the communal movement of the 1380s would have resonated with his aristocratic fellows. They faced a violent response to an issue that had repeatedly come up in French politics: the failure of so-called fighting men to adequately defend the community, which had led to the rise of independent-minded urban governments (communes). These popular movements were repugnant to the military aristocracy which Louis championed. The commoners were equally contemptuous of their so-called lords. Some of the most gory scenes in the Chronicle are depictions of savage attacks or the use of torture by outlaws or brigands on the French population, or of retribution by ostensibly loyal Frenchmen such as the Duke and his men on those who perpetrated atrocities in the ungoverned countryside.

The orderly duke

An important characteristic of the *Chronicle* is that it gives us, as modern readers, a sense of how professional and hereditary warriors, i.e., "those who fought," thought about their role in society. It's worth pointing out that these warriors were by no means restricted to those called "knights." All men-at-arms, including knights and squires and some who had no title, considered themselves members of a universal God-given community of fighters. Long before the 15th century, theorists had divided the Christian people into three orders: "Those who pray, those who fight, and those who work." This division emphasized the superiority of the clergy, and the necessity of both powerful and weaker lay people to follow clerical leadership. But the idea of a division of society into orders, established by God to accomplish His work, did not remain restricted to the original three orders. In the Middle Ages, any organized community might come to think of itself as an order. Such orders had names and symbols, duties and privileges. The most influential clerical orders were monastic orders, whose organizations were far from being only theoretical. Monastic leaders legislated in detail how members of a monastery or a whole order of monasteries should live. When the crusading movement provided "those who fought" a newly important role, chivalric orders of monk-warriors (such as the Templars and the Hospitallers) provided a structure based in large part on the institutions of monks. By 1300, orders of lay (nonclerical) warriors were being founded by kings and princes, who by their actions and by traditional Christian teaching laid claim to an important role in organizing a pious society.

Among these leaders was Duke Louis of Bourbon. We have already seen in his meeting with the Bourbon nobility at Moulins that Louis created an order to bind his duchy—or at least one very important group within it—close to him. The Order of the Golden Shield formalized the idea that his "chivalry and nobility" were brothers who would "live and die" together. The members of the order would take the lead in works of honor, specifically in the service of God, the defense of their country, and the honoring of ladies (especially by avoiding poisonous gossip directed at them). It was a beautiful act, which his nobles—says Cabaret—enthusiastically accepted and made their own. It is worth noting that Duke Louis, who had just burned the book *Peloux* that had recorded the misdeeds of the nobility, had by that act shown his allegiance to the traditional social order that gave privilege and leadership to the military aristocracy. At the same time, Louis carefully maintained a conventional piety by supporting religious causes:

He was devoted to the local martyrs Mayeul and Odile and honored their relics, a style of religious practice as old and important as any used in the Middle Ages; he built a beautiful chapel in his town of Souvigni; he secretly did penance for his sins by wearing harsh clothing; and finally, he spent much of his later military career fighting and otherwise supporting the worthiest of causes: Crusades in Spain, the Baltic region, and North Africa. In other words, Duke Louis, a rich and influential layman, spent a great deal of his wealth on religious causes, selecting many of the possible devotions from the extensive menu available to late medieval Christians. His founding of a high-minded religious order was just the most ambitious expression of his religious respectability.

His upholding of order in general did not stop there. In describing the duke's adventures, Cabaret and Châteaumorand had much to say about the practical organization of Louis' war band. Even away from the battlefield and the campaign trail the Good Duke was a beacon of organization. If Cabaret built his depiction of the Good Duke as a general largely on the informed account of Jean de Châteaumorand, Cabaret also seems to have had access to the expertise of Louis' chief financial officer, Pierre de Norris, (called Lord Norris in this translation) who for many years made the most of the duke's landholdings, rents, and other taxes so that the duke was able to maintain his princely status, his military support for the king, his generosity to churches, and other adventurous policies. Norris not only collected large amounts of money with great efficiency, but he also successfully encouraged Duke Louis to keep his expenditures within realistic limits when his patron was liable to overspend on the support of religion, largess to royal officials, and the kind of luxuries men of his standing had to surround themselves with. Cabaret explained what Lord Norris did in some detail, and with no small amount of pride. In a chaotic period in French history, Duke Louis was able to live an orderly Christian life, whether it was a matter of seating dinner guests according to their rank or preparing for his own death in his last days through prayer and penitential practices.

If the *Chronicle* presents a largely military picture of a military career, it is hardly the biography of an average "man at arms," or even an average prince. Louis is an exemplar of perfection, showing how a successful warlord, a graceful courtier, a prudent ruler, a faithful Christian, a dutiful vassal, and family man should and could excel. Indeed, it is hard to identify any flaws in this portrait of perfection. This positive view is a natural consequence of the fact that the *Chronicle* was commissioned by Louis' family during a time of great crisis to present him as a hero whose reputation could reflect glory on the Bourbon dynasty and remind France of the sterling leadership of that dynasty in an earlier era of crisis. The memory of those crises was strong; if not so much was said about them as was said about the English wars, they were not neglected. Likewise, readers who remembered the long papal schism (when rival pontiffs fought and schemed for control of the western church, 1378-1417) would understand from the *Chronicle* that Louis had been faithful to the papal claimants recognized and supported by France, and by undertaking his African crusade, advanced a cause dear to at least one of the popes. Even more important was his role in defeating the communal movement of the 1380s, when some of the largest and most prosperous urban communities of the kingdom rose up against the nobles. The devastating defeat that Duke Louis and his fellow nobles inflicted on these rebellious commoners is reported almost with a sense of glee. This incident, like others in the *Chronicle,* shows the traditional military aristocracy as under challenge, but also as the essential "order" that preserves the Christian society of the 15th century.

The Chronicle of the Good Duke is an example of the use of history—or legendry—to justify claims to dominion. By no means was this a new form of literature, or a new role for it. The Frankish emperor Charles the Great (Charlemagne) generated vast amounts of legendry, and the great French king of the 13th century, Louis IX (Saint Louis), inspired an impressive saint's life and Crusading history. The physical books, like the text, had political and cultural roles quite different than they have today. Important books were luxury items, aimed at a restricted readership. One of the three surviving manuscripts of the *Chronicle* belonged to Queen Anne of Bourbon, regent of France in the late 15th century, and it is of a quality fit for a queen. One gets the impression that the *Chronicle* was a product of such fighters as Châteaumorand but designed to teach the princes of the Bourbon branch of the French royal dynasty. *The Chronicle of the Good Duke,* too, has the potential to teach us some aspects of that royal and chivalric education. One of the lessons that should be learned is that when Louis and his followers said "chivalry" they did not usually mean something vague; rather, they saw chivalry as their way of life, very much focused on the use of weapons that defined *chevaliers.* They and their brothers in arms practiced arms (= weapons) bore arms (= armor), even wore and flew arms (= coats of arms and heraldic banners). When they gathered together they were chivalry. *The Chronicle of the Good Duke* gives us some idea of how that felt in the era of the Hundred Years' War.

Important dates relative to the career of Duke Louis

1356 Battle of Poitiers; the English Prince of Wales captures King Jean of France and holds him for ransom. Death of Peter, Duke of Bourbon, (father of Louis).

1356 Louis is one of the prominent hostages held by the victorious English after the battle of Poitiers.

1363 The Good Duke returns to his duchy, Bourbon.

1364 The Good Duke founds the Order of the Golden Shields; *Peloux* burns.

1367-70 French campaigns against "English" garrisons in France.

1372 French campaigns in Poitou/Guyenne/Gascony/Sainte-Sévère/Brittany.

1373 French campaign in Brittany.

1374 Duke of Lancaster's chevauchée in northern France.

1375 Louis II's campaign in Auvergne; his march to Spain.

1376 French campaigns in Spain cancelled.

1377 France attacks Rye (in Sussex) and Normandy.

1380 Earl of Buckingham's chevauchée in northern France and Brittany.

1380 Death of du Guesclin, Constable of France and Charles V of France.

1381 Brittany: Charles VI's siege of Nantes; Jousts at Vannes.

1382 Three rebellions of the Communes against the royal government in Flanders, Paris, and Ypres.

1385 Louis appointed as royal lieutenant in the march along the Dordogne River.

1386-7 The French campaign with the Portuguese against Castile.

1388 French war with Guelders and Juliers (Germany).

1390 Crusade in Africa; France allies with the Republic of Genoa in the central Mediterranean.

1392 French campaign in Brittany; Charles VI goes mad.

1407 Assassination of the Duke d'Orléans by the Burgundians.

1409 Invasion of Genoa by Bresse and Boucicault.

1410 Death of Louis.

Louis II of Bourbon in a 17th century portrait.
Gallica Digital Library.

THE CHRONICLE OF THE GOOD DUKE LOUIS OF BOURBON

Prologue

To the very noble lord Charles, Count of Clermont, oldest son of the puissant prince Jean, Duke of Bourbon and Auvergne, Count of Forez and Lord of Beaujeu, who has the care, direction and administration of his seigneuries in his absence, and who is lieutenant of the King of France and his wars, because you know rightly how to use your dignity well, you evoke the prowess and valiances of your predecessors, and for the great desire that you have to follow in their ways, you have pleased to command that a book of their deeds be compiled and written, and especially the deeds of arms and chivalries, virtues and good manners, beautiful life and good end of the high and excellent and well renowned prince, Duke Louis of Bourbon, your grandfather. As for me whom I consider to know little, you have condescended to order this description, and it was one of the singular pleasures that I have had to be able to do for you and your household. I have willingly obeyed your command although it has been a difficult thing for me to undertake so high a deed, because of the inadequacy of my small talent and also my rough language. But so that the reading should please readers and listeners I have put the history in sufficiently common speech according to the decision and recollection of the honored knight Sir Jean de Châteaumorand, who at my advice and according to the truth spoke more about what he had seen than what he had heard; and I took singular delight in hearing in his words the honorable life of Duke Louis, the very great benefits which the knight told me he had received from him, and also the honor which he had had in his company. There would have been little profit in this volume if the valiant knight who had frequented the deeds of battle had not helped me in this matter. Most assuredly I, Jean D'Orville, Picard,[1] called Cabaret, a poor pilgrim, after having gathered his memories and the notes I made, undertook to describe and engross in chapters the praiseworthy deeds of the duke and very noble baron, on Tuesday 29 March, 1429, after Easter, and willingly commenced and continued the material of the book, such as it is.

1 A person from Picardy, a province north of Paris.

The battle of Poitiers resulted in the capture of King Jean by the English, the death of Louis's father Peter, and Louis's subsequent sojourn in England as a hostage.

The image shown here is an early depiction, though still a generation later) of the battle of Poitiers in 1356. This image is very iconographic, showing the two kings charging each other lance to lance rather than representing an actual event from the battle. Jean likely never faced Edward directly amd his capture came during the climactic attack of the English mounted reserve against the left flank of the last French remaining battle (the French army had been organized into four "battles" of which only the first, which had made the intial attack, was mounted) led by King Jean while it was engaged by King Edward's counterattack.

From a Grandes Chroniques de France c. 1375-1380. Gallica Digital Library.

I. How Duke Louis of Bourbon went as a hostage for King Jean in England.

This is the history of the very excellent, mighty and very noble prince, Duke Louis of Bourbon, Count of Clermont, Grand Chamberlain and Peer of France, of excellence and nobility I consider according to the right line of generation or degree of consanguinity. He is descended genealogically from the very glorious St. Louis, former king of the earthly kingdom of France, as you have heard. This lord St. Louis had of the queen his wife many sons, one of whom, named Robert, was Count of Clermont, who married the Baroness of Bourbon; and from Robert issued Louis, first duke in the Bourbonnois. For St. Louis elevated this barony to a duchy, after his return from Damietta. Duke Louis took as wife Lady Marie de Hainault, sister to count William. From Louis and Marie descended Duke Peter, who married the sister of King Philip of France and from Peter and Isabel, his wife, came a son, Louis de Bourbon, the third duke, about whom this book is made. That duke was required to go to England after the capture of King Jean, who was taken at Poitiers in battle, which the Prince of Wales won against him, in 1356. So Duke Louis of Bourbon obeyed, and went there, (as did many other princes of the kingdom of France, of the royal blood, such as the dukes of Anjou, Berri and others), and raised the pledge of the duke according to his hostage status, the sum of 100,000 francs. The Queen of England who lived at that time, the wife of King Edward, of the house of Hainault, was his kinswoman through the duke's mother, and also was of the lineage of Hainault; the queen saw the valiance and youthful beauty of the Duke of Bourbon, her kinsman, who was very handsome and gracious, and who loved honor before everything, regarding also the good manners of which he was replete. He was a very passionate knight, in the first instance towards God, next towards all the ladies and demoiselles, full of gracious speech, and he was not able to stay anywhere where he heard slander of the ladies or demoiselles, and this he did all his life, as plainly is said in some books which are written about him. His virtues were so agreeable to the Queen of England, and to the ladies of the country, and to all other knights and squires of honor, that Duke Louis went through the whole kingdom at his pleasure, and often came before the queen at court, where he amused himself sometimes at dice, at which the queen willingly passed the time. Duke Louis received this favor of going and coming to all the celebrations and amusements because of her courtesy, joyous speech and good life which no one holding the hostages had, and in the kingdom of England the ladies and demoiselles, knights and squires called him the King of Honor and Joy. Duke Louis of Bourbon remained as hostage, at his own costs, fees and expenses for his sovereign lord, for the space of seven years paying for expenses the sum of forty thousand gold francs without the principal, which amounted to 100,000 gold francs; which 100,000 francs his country of the Bourbonnois and

Beauvoisin paid on the spot with all his expenses; for in this time King Charles [V] of France who then lived, the son of King Jean [II] who had died in England, had so much to do in his kingdom, as much because of the revolts of some of his communes, called Jacques and Maillets (or Maillotins), as of the King of Navarre, and other grand companies, who opposed him. The king had hardly helped the duke even though the King of France had married his eldest sister, and King Peter of Spain [Castile] had married the other; and the other of his sisters was married to the Green Count of Savoy, a great and valiant lord. The fourth sister married the Count of Harcourt, the fifth the lord of Labreth, and the sixth was the prioress of Poissy; and Duke Louis's aunt had as her husband the King of Bohemia.

II. How Duke Louis of Bourbon set off homeward from England to his Duchy of the Bourbonnois, and what he said to his knights.

The Duke of Bourbon, after the death of King Jean, paid all the ransom which he had pledged, and had a full quittance from the King of England. Then he crossed the sea and returned to France, and conducted a great knight of England, Hugh de Calverley, to Clermont in Beauvoisin, and there the two remained for the space of two months, to pay some debts outstanding, which he owed in England. Bichat de Nade and Lorin de Pierrepoint came, who always had well and duly served Duke Louis in England, and afterwards in great affairs; he carried the payment which the duke owed to England, and also the money for coming to the Bourbonnois. Duke Louis left Clermont and came into his duchy at Souvigni, where he arrived two days before Christmas in 1363 at the age of 28. For he felt great devotion for the relics of two saints, Mayeul and Odile, who were honored by two recumbent effigies in its priory, and there he sojourned gladly, because Souvigni was one of the best cities in the country.

Knights and squires who were well-informed of his coming, were very happy and joyous about the return of their lord on the day of the celebration. There came Griffon de Montaigu, and Sir Gui his brother, Sir Guichart Daulphin, the lord of Châteaumorand, and the lord of La Palice, the lord of Chaseuil, Sir Guillaume de Vichy lord of Busset, the lord of Chastel de Montaigne, Sir Lordin de Saligny, Sir Regnault de Baserne lord of Champroux and many other knights and squires of the Bourbonnois country, and they came at a good hour. On Christmas Day, and on the morrow and the next, he led the grandest life that could be at the city of Souvigni. The duke was overjoyed and pleased with the beautiful noblesse which he saw in his company who had come there out of such great affection and willingness, splendid and in a great state of magnificence. On the fourth day of the celebration the duke said laughing to the knights, "I would not offer you thanks for the boons you have bestowed on me, for in the event that I should thus thank you, you would then desire to depart, and that would be among the greatest displeasures that I could have, since for seven years I have never been so happy as when I was with you, for I am now in the company with whom I would prefer to live and die. I pray that you will wish to be with me on New Year's Day, in my town of Molins, and there I would bestow upon you, from my heart, a pledge of goodwill. I would hope that you, also, would bestow the same pledge, and such will be rich gifts, pleasing to God. For I hope to be guided by you, and your good counsel, in things that relate to my lands and the welfare of this kingdom, so as to advance my position, with your kind help. Herewith, I request your affirmation that you will help me to make up the time I have lost, and to restore my place in the house from which I have been cast out. I have the heart and will to act forcefully, and because of this, I pray that, along with the other boons you have granted me, you will help me in this. For I want to live and die with you, and I suspect that you feel the same towards me. And for the good hope of which I have in you, after my hope in God in advance I will carry for a device a belt where there will be written a joyous word: ÉSPERANCE [=HOPE]." At the end of this beautiful speech, the baronage present, and knights and squires, wept with joy, saying "God be blessed! For we have our lord and master."

The "great knight" Sir Hugh Calveley depicted in a modern statue. The armor shown is drawn closely from Sir Hugh's effigy at Bunbury.
Wikimedia commons, public domain.
Man vyi Photographer.

III. How the Duke of Bourbon gave many knights his Order of the Golden Shield, on New Year's Day; and how Huguenin Chauveau, with whom the duke was lodging, presented to him the book called Peloux, *which he had written against the nobles, and what the duke did with it.*

In that year, 1363, it came to pass that on New Year's Eve Duke Louis was in the city of Molins and his chivalry with him; and he lodged in the said town in the home of one of its bourgeois named Hugenin Chauveau who was Chief Magistrate of the Bourbonnois. On New Year's Day early in the morning the gentle duke rose to receive his knights and gentlemen and to go to the church of Notre Dame de Molins. Before the duke left his chamber he wished to confer on them a beautiful badge for an order which he had devised, which he called the Golden Shield. On this Golden Shield was a band of pearls where he had written ALLEN ["We go together"]. The first of this order was received by the lord of the tower, Sir Henri de Montaigu, son of Sir Gille Aicelin. The second was Sir Guichard Daulphin; the third Sir Griffon de Montagu; Sir Hughes de Chastellus lord of Châteaumorand; the lord of castle de Montaigne; the lord of la Palice; Sir Guillaume de Vichi, lord of Busset; Sir Phelippes de Serpens; Sir Lordin de Saligni; the lord of Chantemerle; Sir Regnault de Baserne, lord of Champroux, the lord of Veaulce; the lord of Blot; Sir Guillaume de la Mothe; Sir Pierre de Fontenai, of the country of Berry, and many other knights, who received the order of the Golden Shield, and not without cause. In giving the said order, the Duke of the Bourbonnois commenced to say to each one: "My lord, this order of the Golden Shield which I have created symbolizes many honorable things for all knights and others, about which I will tell you after divine service and we have dined, in order that we should swear and promise altogether." For this they thanked him most humbly. Responding for all the knights, Sir Guillaume Dames, lord of Vichy, said in part: "Very high and puissant prince and our very dread lord, see here your knights who very humbly thank you for the beautiful order and great gifts which you have given them. Concerning these they don't know what to give you today except that they should offer their bodies and goods, and that which God has given them; may it please you to receive them as a good present on this New Year's Day notwithstanding that they are obliged to do it; but their hearts are firm and their will the same." Duke Louis, having heard the words of the knight, thanked them very dearly for their very good will and plainly told them: "Today I have received the most beautiful gifts that a lord can receive, when I received the hearts of such noble knights. For I hold that you will come to the purpose which I desire." Then they left, and the duke went to hear mass, and in his company were eight barons and as many as forty gentlemen of name. After mass the duke held court with his barons, and when he had come back to the hall where there was a good fire lit, Huguenin Chauveau presented himself and brought a book half a foot tall, which he had secretly made to denounce the nobles of the Bourbonnois' knights and squires. Chauveau came before the duke saying, "Most dread lord, when you were in England, where you have been a long time I myself kept watch over your justice and the business of your country, and I have put in writing all the crimes and bad behavior which the knights, squires, and nobles of arrière-fiefs[2] have committed, men who were so great that they have had all their goods confiscated while other lesser men lost parts of their bodies. Therefore on this New Year's Day I give it to you and make you the most beautiful gift that has been given to you since you have left England. I have put seven years into making it, and call my book *Peloux*. So I ask you my most dread lord that you have it put into effect and that it will be a treasure for you." Duke Louis of Bourbon, who had heard the words of his host Chauveau and reflected on his malice, wisely and moderately answered him in this way: "Host, you have put in long study and great effort during the seven years I stayed in England, in order to undermine my chivalry[3] and the nobility of my country. In this way, you have done the work of a wicked serf, and it well demonstrates the nature of your birth. For when a lord takes you into his service, seeing the status you have, you forget your place, and come in the end to ignore your beginnings; forgetting that you are nothing, if not for the prince who has chosen you for the office where he put you. As for that, Chauveau, since you tell me that your book *Peloux* should be put into effect, it will be done before you immediately. Certainly it appears to me that you have written nothing at all in your book about the good things done by my barons, who have freed me from prison, but in order to bait my temper, you have filled it with the great hatred that your sort carry for all gentlemen.

The duke having finished talking took the book *Peloux* from Chauveau's hands and into his own, called to his barons and said "My friends, come close and see what I will do with this book which this host has presented to me." They came over, and then he hurled the book in the fire, where it burned before Chauveau, who had sought to obtain a hearing against the nobles to destroy them. The knights and squires humbly thanked the duke for the great franchise[4] which they saw in him, and he did that so honestly that the renown of it lasted as long as he lived, and will endure a hundred years after his death. Great joy for all his barons, for many there were afraid of being charged.

---

2 i.e., nobles who could be called up as a reserve by the king.

3 As in "order of the chivalry."

4 Here, noble character.

A fifteenth century depiction of Louis II and his wife, Anne of Auvergne, Dauphine d'Auvergne, (1358-1417). Wikimedia Commons, public domain

IV. How the Duke of Bourbon explained the significance of the Golden Shield to the knights, and how Sir Philipes des Serpens spoke for all, and how the duke answered him.

Because of the solemnity of New Year's Day, after the solemn Mass, the duke sat at table and there was a great dinner and one that was full of the joy of the noble chivalry and squirearchy present. After dinner, by the grace of God, Duke Louis of Bourbon, while he was wearing a fine green hat on his head, announced to his barons and knights the Order of the Golden Shield, saying: "My lords, I thank all of you concerning my order which you have taken after my coming from England. So I wish to say what the order signifies and supports; the said order signifies that all nobles who have it and bear it should be like brothers and live and die with each other in all their affairs. It is known that in all good works that knights of honor and noble men ought to lead. And beyond that they should not be in a place to hear people blaspheme God, which they ought to refrain from. He requested that those of the order should be willing to honor ladies and damsels and not suffer to hear evil of them. For those who speak evil of them diminish their honor. They say about a woman, who cannot avenge herself, what they would not dare say of a man, which increases their shame. For from ladies, after God, comes part of the honor this world. The second article of this order thus is, that those who bear it should not gossip or argue or slander one another, which is a shameful thing for all gentlemen. They should keep faith with one another, as it belongs in all honor and chivalry. And my friends," said the duke, "across my Gold Shield is a bend where it is written 'ALLEN.' 'Allen' is to say: we go all together in the service of God, and we are all one in the defense of our country, and there we are able to find and acquire honor by deeds of chivalry. For that, my brothers, I have told you what the order of the Golden Shield signifies, which I have given each of you, who wants to swear and promise to keep it, and I the first." Then all the knights knelt before him, and they told him that this was the most beautiful order which they had heard or spoken of, and they asked him most humbly what had pleased him to place them in the number of this order and they all swore in his hand. When the oaths had been made, Philip des Serpens, a knight of the Bourbonnois spoke, one of the best knights of the realm, who said to the duke "Most puissant prince and our most feared lord, see here your chivalry which is as happy and joyous as it is possible to be in this world, from the grace that God has given them, which has removed from them the darkness in which they have remained for fifteen years; and they thank God who has given them the way of honor and light." Duke Louis responded to this: "Sir Philip des Serpens, I give thanks to my good and loyal servants for the things they have said to me, but despite the sadness and anger which they have had in my arrest they have shown themselves to be good and loyal subjects. For I have in my country more than a dozen places which destroy my men which you have delivered from my enemies, for which I am very happy with you, those places being Verrières, Bleth, Veros, le Bourg des Barres, Saint Amande l'Aillier, Montrond, Saint Gerand-le-Pui, Puifol, Les Borbes, Bor-le-compte, Baignols, and Chantemerle. To these places you all, my loyal servants and subjects, have so devoted yourselves in my absence that the greatest part of them have been surrendered while I was a prisoner to which deliverance you, my good cousin Sir Guichard Dauphin, and Sir Griffon de Montagu, the lord of Châteaumorand, Sir Erard de L'Espinace, Sir Lordin de Saligni, Dames de l'Espinace, the lord of Griffe, the lord of Blot, and Sir Guillaume de la Mote, have powerfully aided; to which you others here named have always men in your houses to guard yourself and for the defense of the country, and the other knights and squires at your command who follow you, because of your valiance. You have done so much that I am bound to you." These words made the knights ashamed and they said that what he commanded they were quick to obey.

V. How the Duke of Bourbon ordered his people and armed himself, first to take certain places in this country which the English held; and how for the honor of God he followed the custom of making a boy king and how he organized his household.

The duke who saw and recognized the good will of his nobles, spoke to them again: "My friends, I have found in my country only three places which to me are very much in my heart. One is Roche-sur-Allier, which makes such great evil as you know, for it holds the river from one side to the other. The second place is Beauvoir, where the English have built a dungeon called 'Hell'; and there they throw the people who they can't or don't want to ransom. The third is indeed Montescoth, where there is but a league and a half from one to the other and the English who hold the places are captains Le Bourg, Camus, and Guillaume Pot who there have dwelt from the time that the prince of Wales passed through France. So I require you," said the duke, "my very good servants and subjects, that on the fifteenth day after the Feast of the Kings you will be assembled with all the power of Bourbonnois, knights and squires and other men of war, to go someplace where I may wish to go in your good company and I will distribute to you certain goods that God has given to me." Then the knights thanked him humbly and told him that they were ready to accomplish his good will, and to live and die by his good command and that they had plenty of goods to expend in his service; so they commended the duke to God, and taking his leave from him, left and gathered in their assembly. Duke Louis remained at Molins, and had made secret devices, and gathered a great multitude of people and vessels to go besiege the Roche, which was in the middle of the river Allier, and ladders, and he prepared three vessels with mast platforms. The people who had left the court came on the day of the kings, when the Duke of Bourbon made a great celebration and good cheer, and made his king a child eight years old, the poorest he could find in all the city, and had him dressed in royal costume, and gave him all his officers to rule, and they made good cheer for this king in reverence to God. On the next day this king ate at the table of honor; afterwards his master of the household came, who had made the search for the poor king, whom Duke Louis of Bourbon habitually gave forty livres to keep him at school, and all the knights of the court gave a franc each, and squires each half a franc. So the sum amounted at a given time to nearly a hundred francs which he gave to the father and mother, for the children who were kings in their turn, to learn at school without other work, and many of these came to great honor from this, and this beautiful custom Duke Louis of Bourbon kept as long as he lived. The day after the kings, Duke Louis of Bourbon chose the officers whom he wished to have in his household. First of all concerning his body. Among others he took

Sir Jean de Demoret, who was a wise old knight. He retained him as master of the household, and Sir Gousset de Thoury as his counselor; and he wished that Barberie, who had served him in England, should be declared to be a squire, and that he should carry his pennon, and the lord of Champropin squire of the stables, and his pannetier[5] a squire named Jean de Confès. Then he made for every one of these officers a counterpart and raised up his estate to be beautiful and grand, not at all as one makes it today but by good order and measure. He retained a knight whom he much loved, for his good disposition and for the great and good things that the duke had heard said about him, and summoned him and made him his marshal; he was Sir Jean de l'Aye, who served very long and honorably, and this was not a large retinue of people for this time.

5 Supervisor of the bread supply.

VI. How La Roche d'Allier was taken by the duke, and by his captains, Beauvoir where Hell was, and Montescoth, and the arrangement which the duke made.

The Duke of Bourbon had prescribed to his people to come to him after fifteen days and they did not fail to do it. On that day they were all mounted and armed most excellently. So one party went to Molins, another to Villeneuve-es-Breschars, and another to Belleperche and Baignols. On the second day the Duke of Bourbon had his Marshal Jehan de l'Aye, and Sir Lordin de Salingy, Dames de l'Espinace, and Gomin Buret, sent before, in vessels with mast platforms, and on the land side, Sir Griffin de Montagu, the lord of Châteaumorand, Sir Guillaume de la Mote, the lord of Blot, and Sir Erard de l'Espinace. On the other side of Baignols was Duke Louis with his banner, and the great multitude of chivalry, who had ships to go to the place as they wished, and the duke had stayed with him no more than three days before the Rock of Allier was taken by force, and the English who were on top of it were killed and captured, and the place was razed; the walls are still there. On leaving there they pulled back to Villeneuve-es-Breschars, and all those who had gathered were very happy and joyous about that which had been accomplished, and they said to the duke their lord, that he made for them a beautiful deliverance. Then the duke replied, "My lords, we haven't done anything, if we don't do yet more. We have still two other places here, Beauvoir and Montescoth, which the Bourg Camus holds, and they have made a pit at Beauvoir which when they have taken someone who they do not wish to or cannot ransom, they say 'Put them in Hell' and they are thrown into this pit full of fire." Everyone was so terrified of this pit, that when anyone became a prisoner, he gave out that he was rich for fear of being thrown in Hell. Therefore Duke Louis required that all of his company should take part. They all replied "Most redoubtable lord, we are ready to go where it pleases you and we desire nothing else. But we pray you humbly, that it please you that you personally should not go there; for it would be granting too much of honor to such people as they are, that such a prince as you would go there. For they are excommunicated by the sentence of the Pope, and are men of the companies, and without absolution;[6] but if you please, order us to go there." Therefore the duke agreed with them suffering greatly, as one who always wished to be with them. So it was ordered that Sir Lordin de Saligni who always had people, the lord of Châteaumorand, Sir Erard de l'Espinace, and many others should go there, and that the duke should retreat to Molins, together with Guichart Dauphin, Sir Henri de Montagu, Sir Griffon his brother, Sir Guillaume

6 Penance and excommunication.

de Vichi, Sir Guillaume Dames, Sir Philip des Serpens and other knights of his household, to have advice and counsel on the great affairs that the duke had after his coming into his country; and the others named above came before the places, and so things were organized so as to not lose time. The duke went to Molins, and the captains with their men went before those places, and besieged them, which were taken by force in eleven days, and all those at Beauvoir were killed except the captain, Le Bourg Camus, who was taken to Molins, and the others were thrown into their hell. The news came to the duke, who was overjoyed by it as was the entire country, by the way that it appeared that God had done it. After the taking of the places, the captains went to Molins, before the duke, who received them gladly, and in their presence made some good ordinances. First of all he retained four knights for the management of his affairs and those of this country. Chosen first were Jean the Bastard of Bourbon, lord of Rochefort, Sir Phelibert de l'Espinace, Sir Pepin Chailleu; then the duke arranged the marriage of Sir Jean the bastard and the daughter of Sir Pepin, who afterwards was called the Lady of Rochefort. The fourth knight was Sir Goussaut, lord of Thoury, and these knights were very old, and no longer followed arms. He retained Sir Lordin de Saligni who was a skilled and valiant knight, for his companion at arms, and all the other knights he retained for himself. Some part went in arms who after that never failed to be in his company, in all his deeds, which have been grand.

VII. How the Duke of Bourbon went to Paris, to King Charles, and the duchess his wife.

King Charles of France, son of King Jean, when he had found out how Duke Louis of Bourbon (whose sister he had as wife) had after his arrival from England recovered his places by deeds of arms and had a very fine company of knights and squires, was overjoyed by this news, as one who had real need, and the king ordered Philippot de Santueil, one of his squires from his office of the horse, whom he ordered newly that on top of all the favors which the Duke of Bourbon had been able to do for him, that he should be with him on Candlemas. So the duke excused himself, for he was not able to do that, because he had actually affianced (as the king knew) the daughter of the Count Dauphin, who by right ought to be Countess of Forez, notwithstanding the fact that Sir Reginaud de Forez had sold the county to the Duke of Anjou; but nevertheless Duke Louis of Bourbon did not abandon his promise of marriage, and the duke recovered, later, the county of Forez, by the good services which he performed for the king and for the Duke of Anjou his brother. Duke Louis of Bourbon left to go marry the duchess his wife, and the marriage celebration and wedding party were in Dauphiné of Auvergne, in the city of Ardres, and the duke greatly hastened to go to the king. But after the third day of his wedding a knight came from the king bringing him letters and the duke having heard the credentials of the knight, and seen the letters, in which the king to him had prayed and required of him that he hasten to come before him at court and that he should have the duchess his wife accompany him and remain with the queen, he did as the king commanded them. The king was very happy about that when he saw them in his hostel, and the duchess remained a long time with the queen, notwithstanding that the duke always was in arms for the good of the realm.

VIII. How Sir Louis de Sancerre said to the Duke of Bourbon that he should speak to the king to go before Saint-Sévère.

While the Duke of Bourbon remained in Paris with the king his sovereign lord, it happened that Sir Louis de Sancerre and Sir Jean de Villemur, who thought Duke Louis was most chivalrous, asked him that it would please the king to command him to Saint-Sévère, which destroyed Poitou, Berry, and Bourbonnois and them with him. But the king did not wish it, responding that he awaited his Constable of France, who was in Spain, whom he had sent to be fetched and extricated from prison. But to them the king said that it appeared good to place the country under protection to repair the evil which the English at Saint-Sévère had done. So the king ordered that the Duke of Bourbon should give Sir Louis de Sancerre a hundred men-at-arms, knights and squires, to go man the frontiers of Berry, and so it was done. So Sir Louis de Sancerre left Paris and went to garrison the frontiers and sent forty men-at-arms from the army to the Duke of Bourbon at Bomiers and at Orsan, which is a priory, and put another forty in Berthenous, and ten in Pruniers; and Sir Louis de Sancerre sent some of his men in a squad to Puy-agu, of the best that he had, because of whom those of Saint- Sévère did not care afterwards to ride out in the countries mentioned above, except for a great English adventurer called Michelet la Guide, who went riding out from wood to wood through seven forests as far as Souvigni, right up to the gates. One fine morning about the hour of Terce Michelet encountered outside a gentleman of the Bourbonnois, brother of the prior of Souvigni, mounted on a beautiful courser, with another equally well mounted namely the squire Launcelot de Chenillat, father of Regnaulde, both of whom were taken; but returning with his captives he had encountered some of the Duke of Bourbon's men, who went from one garrison to another, and there were eight of them, Sir Guichart de Châteaumorand, Jean his brother, a squire, Perrin d'Ussel, Odin de Rollat, and four other gentlemen who plundered Michelet la Guide, and indeed Jean de Châteaumorand took him.

IX. How there was a little quarrel between the Constable and Sir Louis de Sancerre about the capture of the Marshal of England.

At this time the rumor ran in Berry about how the good Constable of France, Sir Bertrand du Guesclin (alias Claquin) came from Spain to the king in France, and there were great heaps of men available to come with him. He came back to fight the English who had been before Paris, and the captain was Sir Robert Knowles. Sir Louis de Sancerre, who knew the Constable ought to fight against the English, dismantled all his frontiers, and led them after him, the Duke of Bourbon's men and all the others, and he did not stop until he came to Vendôme. When he was dining there, news came that the English had not dared to await the good Constable at Point-Valain, but fled, one party, that of Sir Robert Knowles to Derval, and the Marshal of England Sir Fitz Walter thought to retreat to the Abbey of Saint-Maur-sur-Loire. But he encountered Sir Louis de Sancerre with the Duke of Bourbon's men and his own near the Abbey of Vas, and the marshal pushed himself inside, thinking to save himself, and there were beautiful deeds of arms to take it. So all the English were killed or taken, to the good number of three hundred combatants, and the Marshal of England taken prisoner, who was captured by Sir Jean d'Azay, seneschal of Toulouse. Around three hours at Vespers, the Constable of France arrived in battle order who chased them away and saw the rout of the English. He was very enraged that he had not been there, and demanded that he be given the Marshal of England. He was told that he was a prisoner in the hands of Sir Louis de Sancerre. So the constable commanded Sir Louis through the lord of Mailly to send him the Marshal of England for he pertained to him, he said, on account of his office. To this speech Sir Louis de Sancerre responded that the marshal was the prisoner of a very gentle knight, and that he would not do him any injustice. The lord of Mailly answered arrogantly saying that the constable would have the prisoner and abused the one who had taken him. So Sir Louis repeated his words to Mailly that this is not any reward to pay such men as the knight was and promptly said to Sir Jean d'Azay with the lord of Mailly present that he should lead away his prisoner. For this reason they did not speak to each other for some time.

X. How the English were defeated before Bressuire in Poitou by Sir Louis de Sancerre, and how the Constable took the bastide of Saint Maur-sur-Loire.

A knight named Jean de Troux, who had harassed the English, and knew where they had retreated, came to Sir Louis de Sancerre, and said to him, "My lord," said he, "if your people were not tired and worn out, I would show you the finest adventure that you have had for a long time. For I have seen a good three hundred combatants who have escaped from Point-Coursillon, and it isn't even four little leagues from here." Sir Louis asked him if he could guide him well. "Certainly, my lord, yes!" said the knight. Then Sir Louis de Sancerre commanded the captains of his company to mount their horses secretly and come to a place he would show them, where they would find him and his standard. So they obeyed his commands. Then they took to the road all night, and found themselves, after midnight, at Coursillon, where the knight led them, but did not find the English, who had already been gone from there for two hours, having fled like people who knew well that they were pursued. They were in Poitou in a town called Bressuire to which town the English came thinking to enter it. He bargained hard with those of Bressuire who received him. During the bargaining Sir Louis de Sancerre came with his people to the Cross before Bressuire, which is three arrow flights long. When the English saw the French approaching them, they strongly implored the people of the town, who wished to have no part in the fighting, to go inside. Seeing this done, the English retreated together into the enclosed space in front of the gate. Then Sir Louis de Sancerre with the people of the Bourbonnois and his own, dismounted and surrounding the enclosure fought hard, and there were beautiful deeds of arms performed there, because the English defended themselves strongly and they were strongly attacked. But the French took the affair so definitely in hand that they gained the enclosure which they entered by force, and they fought each other hand-to-hand. But in this battle all the English were killed with no more than four escaping. After this annihilation, three hours did not pass before the Constable of France appeared, with many great men, at the place from which Sir Louis de Sancerre had already left—that is to say, at the cross in front of Bressuire—and he was disappointed and angry that he had not been at this plundering. So he and his men at once turned around to go capture the fortress of Saint Maur sur Loire, which the English held, who were perhaps four hundred combatants, and were destroying the country. When the constable appeared before its battlements, the English offered to make treaty with him saying that they would go away, and quit the region, but he did not wish to do so, because of his wrath over twice failing to find them. He attacked the fortress from all sides, and he was the first in the forward charge, and so inspired his people that he won the fortress of Saint Maur by force of arms and assault, and thus the country was delivered from these men, who too often bewailed their defeat. Sir Louis de Sancerre, who had no wish to be idle, went with the people of the Bourbonnois and others, straight to Ferte Sainte Fosse (between Berry and Orléanois), where there were also English who had done many evil things, and were perhaps two hundred combatants. So bitterly did Sir Louis fight, with the help of his own people there, that it was taken by force; and Sir Louis made some fine roast meats for them, for he was a good master.

Louis Sancerre. Basilica Saint-Denis.
Robert Charrette photographer, use by permission.

XI. How the King of France made some good ordinances concerning the affairs of his wars and his countries; and how the Duke of Bourbon and the Constable loved each other.

King Charles, who well knew the fine deeds of arms which his Constable of France and Sir Louis de Sancerre with their men accomplished every day, thus augmenting his honor, and that they had taken many places from the English, and they had killed and routed them, commanded them to make and draw up some fine and good ordinances on the affairs of his wars and his countries, which since have lasted a good long time. It was the wish of the king to give to each the responsibilities which he ought to have. First, he gave to the Constable of France, when he had come, fifteen hundred men-at-arms and two hundred arbalestiers [=crossbowmen], of whom he had in this number one of the marshals and the Master of the Arbalestiers. It was ordained that Duke Louis of Bourbon should have eight hundred men-at-arms and two hundred arbalestiers, a total of a thousand combatants; and the Count of La Marche was with the duke. Sir Louis de Sancerre had in charge five hundred men-at-arms. The king also ordered five hundred men-at-arms to the frontier of Calais, which the lord of Sempy had under his command. Further the king made an ordinance that Duke Louis of Bourbon and the constable should together have charge of the duchy of Guienne. Furthermore the king ordered that on Christmas Day upcoming all the lords, captains and officers should appear before him on the feast; to be greatly accompanied with chivalry and also to hand over the ordinances, which each one ought to make for the year. The king ordered that all the men were to be present at the end of March, and ordered the war treasurers to pay each of them their monthly due. So it was that treasury agents were assigned to the Duke of Bourbon, to the Constable le Flament, and to other commanders. It was decided that men-at-arms would thus be paid monthly for the next five months, until winter came, the border could be secured, and the great power withdrawn.

The ordinances having been completed, Duke Louis of Bourbon looked favorably on Bertrand de Claiquin [=du Guesclin], Constable of France and loved him well, because the constable had returned from Spain, where he had avenged the death of the Queen of Spain, Duke Louis's sister, whom King Peter, her husband, had killed, which lady had been very devout and holy. The duke loved him also for the great chivalry with which the constable was replete; likewise the constable loved the duke and so they loved each other with a good love. For the Duke of Bourbon loved honor and all valiant knights.

XII. How Saint-Sévère in Limosin was won and taken by the Duke of Bourbon and the constable Sir Bertrand and Sir Louis de Sancerre.

In A.D. 1372, King Charles held in Paris the feast of Christmas grandly and solemnly. For the captains of war and officers came before the king just as it was ordered, and each day the Constable of France served the king at table, staff in hand and chaperon on his head and so did the marshal, the Master of the Arbalestiers and each one according to his place. When New Year's Day had passed, the aforesaid ordinances were proclaimed so that each captain ought to go where he was assigned. It pleased the king that the Duke of Bourbon, the constable Sir Bertrand, Sir Louis de Sancerre, and all the troops should go to Guienne, before the city of Poitiers, chief city of Poitou, which the English held. This understood, Duke Louis of Bourbon, agreeing with what the king had proclaimed, responded that, in his view, it would seem to him that their first journey should be to Saint-Sévère, and then onwards to Poitiers. The reasons the duke gave for this were that no commanders of war should leave behind them anything that they have not put in order, and Saint-Sévère sits within eighteen leagues of Poitiers. It would be best to go there first, to clear the way, wasting no time at it. To this, the Constable of France added "As God wills, my lord of Bourbon speaks the truth. For all valiant captains ought not to leave something to be taken behind them, and in going to Poitiers we will see what the fellows at Saint-Sévère wish to say." Then they decided to ride before Saint- Sévère, and then to Poitiers, and each captain was to go and hold his assembly. On the assigned day they came to find all the lords and captains on the marches of Berry and Montluçon, and after they assembled they went before Saint- Sévère, numbering as many as three thousand men-at-arms and some eight hundred Genoese arbalestiers. When they had come before Saint-Sévère at the hour of Prime, the Constable of France spoke to the English inside, telling them they should surrender, to which they were not willing to respond at all. Now the Duke of Bourbon, the constable and Sir Louis de Sancerre deliberated over what they should do. So the constable said: "As God wills, Sir de Bourbon, since these fellows won't say a word I advise that you and your people should go and hold one part of the town near the walls, and my brother of Sancerre should do the same with his people on another side and me with my Bretons and the other people I have, on another; and these fellows will be attacked." The discussion finished and the plan determined, the Duke of Bourbon went on his side, a constable on his, and Sir Louis de Sancerre on his, and listening to a common cry commenced a great and strong assault. Hence the English holding Saint-Sévère, seeing the French besieging them, and already approaching the walls to begin the assault, were yet confident of their strength. And to be assured of their strength, the said English swore, before their commanders, this oath: that they would defend themselves with vigor, that they would not move from the positions they held, and that they would rather die than relinquish them. So the French assault was strong and orderly, and from the Duke of Bourbon's flank, his pennon came forth right up to the wall itself, for it was carried there by Jean de Châteaumorand. Quickly rallying to the pennon was a bastard named Louis Verd, the fair squire Ploton de Chastellus, and Sir Guillaume de Vichi. What remained of the ditch was full of the duke's men-at-arms. Four of these men attempted to mine the wall from below, making a tunnel suitable for three armed men, but none dared to enter it, for fear of the repelling action of the English lances; and the constable's attack was mounted from there to the corner of the town, which was a beautiful thing to behold. For they fought at six places with ladders, and there were six more mines, but nevertheless on the side of the Duke of Bourbon were his people, who entered the town first, and many men at arms entered by way of the mines of the constable and Sir Louis Sancerre, since none could enter by means of the ladders, by reason of the valiant and strong defense, and some fine fighting by those within. The assault being of such considerable duration for all three parties, it seemed to each of the lords, in the midst of their attack, that it was their men who were the first to enter. For in each place, they could see strong attack and fierce defense, and could not be aware of their other men, who were climbing the walls. These had reached the point where they could see the duke's men, up to two hundred of them, entering and heading for the high ground of the castle, to which a party of English had retreated. Hence, the pennon and the Duke of Bourbon arrived pell-mell, slaying the English in disarray, and so all the English who had reached the castle were killed. And at same the time, the constable's men who fought in their own section, as well as those of Sir Louis de Sancerre, when they saw the aforesaid pennon of Duke Louis above the castle, hastened to surmount the walls of the town, where the English still were, each and every one standing firm, as they had sworn. And this is a marvelous thing to recount, for the French within were fighting hand-to-hand with the English, who would not leave their positions except by death, but right there would employ fine fighting and defend their place proudly. This melée lasted more than an hour, but the English could then resist no more, and so died valiantly, each on his guard. And it is true that, of all the company of English holding Saint-Sévère, only five escaped: the captain named Hennequin Foudringay, three others, and Robin de Nieuton whom Châteaumorand took, which said Robin declared himself for the Duke of Bourbon, affirming that he had served him in England, while he was a hostage, under his benefices. So Jean de Châteaumorand presented him to the duke his lord, who looked kindly upon him, and saved his life. And Sir Louis de Sancerre had Foudringay killed for some offensive words which he had made to him at the Tower of Vesvre. And everyone knew that one of the most beautiful assaults which had been seen in this realm for a long time, or anywhere else, for that matter, was the taking of Saint-Sévère, best attacked, but best defended.

An illustration of a mid-fourtennth century crossbowmen (arbalestiers). Bodleian Library, Ms. Bodel 264 folio 156.

XIII. How many places in Poitou were taken by the Duke of Bourbon, and how the Duke of Berry came to the country.

Saint-Sévère having been taken, early the next morning the lords decamped to make their way to Poitiers; but they heard it said that there was a place near the route to Poitiers called Bellabre which Poqueron held and was very strong. When they came before it, they demanded entry. Those within hesitated briefly, but after deliberation, decided that they would deliver the keys of their fort to the lords and surrender the place. That accomplished, the lords rode on to Chauvigny, which is a castle of great renown, where they remained five days, for the Duke of Berry had written in a letter to them that they should await him. And so they did. The Duke of Berry arrived on schedule, with a company of notables. And during this wait, they yearned so much for the surrender of Chauvigny that they dared to take it by assault, and the Duke of Berry found it surrendered when he arrived. The dukes of Berry and Bourbon, the constable, Sir Louis de Sancerre and their people decamped from Chauvigny and went unto Poitiers. It seemed likely to the Duke of Berry that people of Poitiers would obey him, but they did not do so, and so they confronted them for a day and a half, fully four thousand men-at-arms. And the lords deliberated as to what should be done. So they decided that they should go before a great town called Vivonne to camp there. So they did that, and the next day they went to a beautiful castle named Mortemar. So it was attacked and taken by assault; and the first who got inside was a squire of the Duke of Bourbon named Huguenin de la Terrasse; and this Huguenin took the nephew of Sir Aimery de Rochechouart, who was lord of that castle and of Vivonne. After the taking of the castle it was arranged to go before Niort on the belief that they would be able to take it. So they decamped in the morning at Fontenai-l'abbatu, which is very close and was taken by assault.

But a knight-captain of the English named Sir Walter Spurton who had fully three thousand combatants was sent into Niort, awaiting the arrival of the French lords. This Sir Walter and his Englishmen made a stronghold in the marshes in anticipation of battle. So all the lords and the men-at-arms went there to fight: but there is no remedy in which there is not great danger, for the English were in a very strong place and the French were not easily able to get at them: so the French and English remained a day and a night before each other. While the lords were in such a risky position, not able to attack the English, news came to them that the Duke of Brittany was coming in great force to engage the English and fight them. So the lords concluded, on deeper reflection, that they should leave there and go forth to confront the Duke of Brittany, for they had much rather face him than the English. The lords went to camp before Fontenai-le-conte, one of the most beautiful castles of Poitou and one of the strongest and when they were before it, it was proclaimed that one party of the garrison of Fontenai should be delegated to go and defeat the French. So the lords promptly rode out there, only to find the place unprepared, and so that was that, for it was taken by assault and much treasure was gained inside.

XIV. How the Duchess of Brittany was taken, and the Duke of Bourbon rescued her; and how some Breton barons allied themselves with the king; and how the constable defeated the English before Chisech.

When the lords had taken Fontenai-le-conte the same night, they decamped to go day and night to encounter the Duke of Brittany who was lodged at Breschesac where there is the beautiful pond. But when he became aware that the French lords were coming, he decamped in great haste, and the lords failed to find him, and the Duke of the Bretons divided his people among various places; and the French who always had news of it left the marches of Poitou and continued day and night in Brittany to Rennes, the city of the duke; and when the lords reached there, they found that the Duchess of Brittany had left a little before they had arrived to go to Vannes. So the Duke of Bourbon and the constable sent a good five hundred men-at-arms after her and took her four leagues from there. The duchess was taken—her carriage, too—by people of the Duke of Bourbon's household who were well mounted. They led her to the Duke of Bourbon and the constable. She was very happy when she saw the Duke of Bourbon, and the lady said to the duke, "La, good cousin, am I your prisoner?" The Duke of Bourbon replied, "Not at all, my lady, for we do not make war on ladies, but we have indeed a war with the Duke of Brittany your husband, who behaves in a contrary manner towards the king, his rightful lord, and launches a foolish enterprise, which he will not be able to finish." And then the Duke of Bourbon, and likewise the Constable of France, proclaimed that all men who had taken anything from the duchess, should return everything to its place, on pain of the noose. So each one obeyed that command and soon enough everything was given back to the Lady Duchess of Brittany, all of which she could have lost, except some letters of alliance of the English and Duke of Brittany which were found there, which were useful to the King of France, but bad luck for the Duke of Brittany, for such perfidy was demonstrated by the letters that none of the barons of Brittany were then willing to serve him. And after the Duke of Bourbon gave leave to the Duchess of Brittany, and to her and the Constable, and assigned people to safely conduct her and her goods five leagues from there to her castle of Loheach. With that, she thanked the Duke of Burgundy most humbly for the honor which he had done her, and that God had given her good grace when she had fallen into the hands of such a knight as he. So the duchess took herself away, and the next day the Duke of Bourbon and the Constable together with Sir Louis de Sancerre decamped and went before Redon, which belonged to the lord of Rieux, of valiant bearing, a knight and prudhomme [7]of Brittany, who came to speak to

---

7 *Prudhomme*: here, noble man.

the lord in security before his place. Immediately they showed him the letters of alliance which the Duke of Brittany had with the English king, and he was much dismayed; and the lord of Rieux said openly that he would never serve the Duke of Brittany his lord, as long as he held to this course against the king. After a time, the Duke of Bourbon, the constable and Sir Louis de Sancerre sent to the Count of Penthièvre the copy of the letters, which the count was exceedingly dismayed to see, and the Count of Penthièvre sent back towards one of the best knights of the Duke of Brittany, Roux de Piédreuch, to assure them that he would not serve the Duke of Brittany in holding the course that he was taking; and just so did a baron, the lord of Hunandoie. And during all this, news was brought to the Duke of Bourbon, and to the constable, from the king, since it was not yet the season when the duke would come before the king, that the constable should consolidate the places that had been taken by some of the duke's men.

So it was done, and the Duke of Bourbon was summoned to appear before the king in Paris, with his retinue, by the lord of Rieux, who afterwards was to be Marshal of France. And also summoned were Le Roux de Piédreuch, and the Count of Penthièvre and the lord of Hunandoie, all at surety. The king made great festival and cheer for the Duke of Bourbon, when he saw him, for the good things which he had accomplished, and the king indeed averred that the duchy of Brittany was half conquered. The constable went into Poitou to stake out his boundaries and came upon a place named Chisech, which had inflicted much harm on the country, and he personally laid siege to it. He was there nearly a month, and at the end of that very same month, the English gathered themselves from their neighboring garrisons and came to join battle with the Constable of France, who was in the last stage of his siege. So when the constable saw them drawing up before him to fight, he commanded his people to set aside their closing attack [on Chisech], and [instead] attack [the arriving English] in well-arranged sorties, and they did it just so. The constable and his people went in fine array, to attack a greater distance than a crossbow shot, and he was victorious. There were dead and taken before Chisech a good eight hundred English from the garrison of Niort, and the country of Poitou was relieved of enemies. And the constable set his frontiers, then went to Paris, because it was close to Christmas, when there was very great cheer, and he was welcome and joyfully celebrated by the king and other lords: for it was the common talk at court that he and the Duke of Bourbon had greatly damaged and pushed the enemy out of the country of Brittany and from Guienne and especially the county of Poitou.

XV. How Sir Louis de Sancerre was made Marshal of France; and how the Duke of Bourbon and the Constable went into Brittany to make war, by the command of the King, and what places they took.

The King of France, as was the custom, solemnly held the Christmas holiday; after the holiday he ordered what should be done in the coming season; and his orders were that the Duke of Bourbon and the Constable should go to conquer in the Duchy of Brittany, which the king had much to heart. At this feast of Christmas Sir Louis de Sancerre was Marshal of France after the death of Marshal d'Audeneham, which Marshal Sancerre was ordered to go to Poitou, on the frontiers to carry on the war for the season. The other lords left in the month of March to complete the conquest of Brittany. Their assembly at Angiers and at Pont de Sez, amounted to two thousand knights and squires, and eight hundred projectile men. And at Angiers the Constable of France said to Duke Louis of Bourbon, "As God wills! There is a castle, one of the strongest and most beautiful that exists in the duchy of Brittany, which belongs to the duke and is called Jugon, and if it can be taken the duke will have suffered a great loss, for in Brittany there is a proverb: who has Brittany without Jugon, has a cloak without a hood. And I think," said the constable, "that the duke, who is unnerved, will not have the judgment to foresee that, so we have plenty of time to take it." They left, and went before Jugon, where they found nobody outside of the people of the town, and the captain named Robert de Guitry who had a son who was the best reader that one could find. Robert was shown the letters of conspiracy. The lords made so much of this that he surrendered Jugon to them, for even had he wished to defend it, it could yet have been taken by but little force, for it did not have any defenders. The lords left Jugon, and went before the Tower of Broon, which without delay was surrendered to the Duke of Bourbon and the Constable, and from that tower the lords proceeded to besiege Tinteniac, a good little town, which belonged to Sir Olivier de Mauny, who was inside, and it was said of him that he was one of the most valiant knights of Brittany; and by the judgment of arbitration which they had together, Sir Olivier surrendered the place and made obeisance to the king and submitted himself to the Duke of Bourbon and his might. From Tinteniac the lords went onward to Fougières-la-Rons, where they make cloth. Upon the arrival of the first messengers of this army, the townsmen came out, which turned out badly for them, for a good six score of them were killed and the army followed the remainder into town. And so Fougières was taken, and right away lords rode up to Dinan, which is the entrance to Breton Brittany, and inside Dinan was Sir Morice de Terriguedis, the most valiant knight of Brittany, for he was one of the chiefs at the Combat of the Thirty, and with him was his nephew the lord of Prustallet. And the lord sought from Sir Morice the opening of Dinan, and showed him the letters. And Sir Morice de Terreguedis, who had a great part of the town, he and the Prustallés surrendered the town of Dinan, in the name of the King of France, to Duke Louis of Bourbon, who retained Sir Morice and his nephew de Prustallet, who thereupon served him honorably all their lives, everywhere the Duke of Bourbon went; and the duke, considering himself well served, eventually pensioned Sir Morice de Terreguedis.

After Dinan had surrendered, the lords left and went to Saint-Mathieu de Fineterre, a great town on the coast facing England. Coming before it, they saw that it was somewhat badly fortified, so they quickly assaulted it, and it was taken. There the companions were well refreshed and the next day they left Saint-Mathieu and went before a fine castle called Cons whose captain was an English squire called Jennequin Pel who did not want for any consideration to surrender the place. So it was eagerly attacked, and there was a beautiful assault and Himbert de Couture, squire to the Duke of Bourbon, fought on the ladder with the same Jennequin Pel, and the attackers and defenders performed some fine fighting; but notwithstanding their defense the place was taken by force of arms and Jennequin Pel was made prisoner. Then the lords left and headed for a beautiful castle and demi-ville named Quimpernay, which was speedily surrendered to the lords, and from there they transferred to Quimper Corentin quite near Brest. The lords asked them to open up, but they did not wish to, because the Duke of Brittany, their lord, was at Brest, near them, and on account of this they held themselves arrogantly. When the lords saw this they went to attack the place, and a great part of the people of the town died.

XVI. How the Duke of Bourbon, the Constable and the Marshal took the isles of Jersey and Guernsey by Brittany, and how they besieged Brest, and what words Sir Robert Knowles declared to the constable, and how they left Brest.

The duke of Brittany who knew how many of his places had been lost, and saw the lords followed him so closely, hastily left Brest, him and the duchess his wife (sister of King Edward) and passed over to England, and left Sir Robert Knowles in Brest. The lords, believing that he was still inside, left Quimper Corentin to Brest, wishing to give battle to the duke, and when they got there they found that he was gone. So the men-at-arms attacked the harbor, and captured four vessels, and then returned to Quimper Corentin which was a place from which one could see the islands of Jersey and Guernsey which are adjacent between England and Brittany and did great harm to the French lords who were not able to pass by them. On account of this the lords started to arm the four vessels taken in the harbor of Brest and others which they had from Saint-Mathieu, to pass over to the Isles of Guernsey and Jersey, where the lords intended to command their people of the isles to outfit the vessels. But the Duke of Bourbon said to the constable, the marshal and others, that this would not be an honorable thing if they did not go themselves, to which the constable answered "As God wills, my lord, it happens that you are right." Having said this, the lords entered the vessels with two thousand men-at-arms and six hundred projectile men at some risk for the vessels were not worth much. They arrived at the Isle of Jersey, which had two castles before which the Duke of Bourbon and his men placed themselves before one, and the constable, the marshal and their people before the other. And the next day at Matins they attacked, and the Duke of Bourbon took his men where he had pitched the siege camp through the energy of his men, and the first to get in was Barberie. After the place was taken, the duke left and went to the constable and the marshal, who had not taken their place; but when those inside saw the Duke of Bourbon coming in his power, they surrendered to the constable. The lords passed from the Isle of Jersey to the Isle of Guernsey, where there was a castle which could not be held, when those who guarded it saw the others taken, though it was the strongest. The people of the islands of Jersey and Guernsey promised to be good and loyal to the King of France, which they did as long as the good Admiral of Vienne lived. Sir Jean de Hangest and Thibault his brother were put in charge of Jersey and Guernsey, surrendering them to the king or his admiral. From there the lords went back to Quimper Corentin, and to Hennebon where they had left their horses and their carriage,[8] and the lords decided with some of the barons of Brittany, that it would

8 A group of wagons.

be a fine thing to go and besiege Brest. For as they affirmed Sir Jean de Montfort, Duke of Brittany, had hardly anything on the coast of his country besides Brest, and had gone to England. On this the lords were in agreement, and besieged Brest, where Sir Robert Knowles remained in garrison with a few men. In that place there was not very much in the way of provisions, as it was said, and the lords should take the environs of Brest by land for they did not have any fleet to besiege by sea. The Duke of Bourbon, the Constable of France, Sir Bertrand and the Marshal Sir Louis de Sancerre remained before Brest for forty days. In that time it rained continually so hard that no one had ever seen so much rain fall, and in the country of Breton Brittany there was no provision for horses, from which the lords had a great loss, and the same Sir Robert Knowles had nothing to eat in Brest except his horses, and spoke to the Constable of France about how he was unhappy that he was not able to raise the siege which the Duke of Bourbon, himself, and the marshal held before Brest where they had besieged him. But he counted it for little, because he knew that the horses and the army were much weakened by the rain and he was consoled by the fact that the lords also had very little to eat, just like him, and that he was not at all afraid of their assault. He sent a further message to the constable: "You have made me eat my horses here at this castle of Brest, as I made you eat yours at the siege of Rennes; so go the changes of fortune and war." During the siege the lords saw six vessels furnished with provisions come from England, which the Duke of Brittany had sent to his castle of Brest, which was depleted. They deliberated among themselves [and concluded] that they would not be able to take the castle by force, and neither would it succumb to famine, because of the provisions that had come to them, and also that their own army had very little to eat. So the lords—the Duke of Bourbon, the constable, and the marshal with the barons of Brittany—decided and were in accord that they should hie themselves off to the king, for nothing remained in the marches of Brittany except Brest, which was not able to cause damage. And so, given that they agreed on that state of affairs, some of the barons warned the duke that if the Duke of Brittany should pass over to England, he could later return to France with all the power of his realm, and that which they said, he did, just so, the year after.

XVII. How the Duke of Bourbon left Brest and led to Paris some Breton barons, whom he kept at his hostel, and they gave an oath to the king.

The barons of Brittany having said this, the Duke of Bourbon, the constable and the marshal left to go to the king, having passed a great and honorable season, and the Duke of Bourbon took with him to Paris, as retainers to his household, the lord of Rieux, the lord of Loheac, the lord of Piédreuch, the lord of Carsselio, Sir Herve de Manny, all save for Sir Olivier, who wished to go with the Duke of Anjou to Gascony, with the good leave of the Duke of Bourbon. And together with the barons named above, the duke brought along Sir Morice de Terreguedis, the lord of Prustallet, and the lord of la Suze, whom he kept in his house for their well-being. And the Duke of Bourbon, the constable and the marshal being in Paris, God knows what cheer was made for them. And those who came to see them were born on a lucky day, because these men had brought low the arrogance of Brittany. And the barons of Brittany were well received and celebrated by the king, and they were given great gifts, and they made an oath which they kept for the rest of their lives. In these days news was reported to the king that the Duke of Brittany, Jean de Montfort had gone to England to recruit a great army to invade France, in the coming year, which turned out to be true. And all the while that these lords were with the king, a marriage was being arranged and consummated between the Duke Philip of Burgundy, brother to the King of France, and the daughter of the Count of Flanders, a thing much desired, for it was held that this alliance would guarantee the conquest of England and much good was anticipated to follow. After Christmas, around Candlemas, news came to the king that the English had assembled a great army to invade France, and this army should be ready and arrive around the Feast of Saint John—the largest ever to be seen arrive in France. So the King of France took counsel with his barons that he should send his brother the Duke of Anjou, with all the forces he could find in pursuit of them, and also the dukes of Berry and of Burgundy, his other brothers, and all other knights marshal and constables, and that all should be by the week of St. John at Troyes in Champagne, where the king should be before the army. And it was ordered by the considered counsel of all the captains that they should not fight the English at all, because of the dangers that might occur. To this the Duke of Bourbon asserted that that it sufficed to follow and harass them in such a way that where they passed they would not find any provisions, and that this was the surest way by which their departure would be hastened. This counsel was praised by all, and as scheduled, the assembly of the king at Troyes took place on the assigned day, as had been ordered, and sojourned there for some days.

XVIII. How the Duke of Bourbon sent some of his people to Plancy, and how they did against the English at their "Barrier of Love."

Jean de Montfort, Duke of Brittany, who very much took to heart the loss of his lands, having gone to England, beseeched King Edward, whose sister he had wed, much and often for his help to recover them, in defiance of the power of the French. And in his aid King Edward chose his uncle the Duke of Lancaster, to cross to France to help the Duke of Brittany, and immediately afterwards the army of England left, passing to Calais which perhaps, what with English, Hainaulters, Germans and Bretons, numbering six thousand combatants, and took their path right to Troyes in Champagne, where the King of France was, with the lords of his blood and his power. And two days before the English came before Troyes, a gentleman named Jean de Nedonchel, captain of Plancy, spoke to the Duke of Bourbon, saying "If you my redoubtable lord wished to grant me fifty men-at-arms, gentlemen, I will make for you a fine adventure, for the English ought to pass by this town along the river." Hearing this, the Duke of Bourbon immediately had those of his household whom he loved the most mount up to go there. These were Jean de Châteaumorand, who carried his standard, his brother the lord of Espinasse, the Borgne de Veaulce, the lord of Montaigut, the lord of Chaugy his chamberlain, Himbert de Couture, Bertrandon Ernaud, Baulseurre, and many other people of his household, and they went to Plancy where they remained two days before the English king, and the Duke of Bourbon's people built before the gate the most beautiful barrier that one had ever seen, and they called it the *Barrier of Love*, and it so happened that the English passed through it very tightly. So it happened that the English came to pass by Plancy, and all the companions were armed outside their barrier, and the English seeing them dismounted to come to fight. Seeing this, the garrison of Plancy, because there were so many English opposed to them, withdrew inside their barrier where they were well stocked with shot. Immediately the English advanced thinking to take the barrier, and the men of Plancy and the Duke of Bourbon's people vigorously defended against them with their shot and their lances, and the most beautiful arms were performed there lasting nearly two hours; for when those inside the barrier saw their advantage, they came out all at once, and charged in among the English, and their charges succeeding to their honor, they withdrew inside, and these charges which those of the barrier made killed seven English men-at-arms and a large crowd were injured by shot, and in supporting this tumultuous attack, some of the Duke of Bourbon's men died at this barrier, Himbert de Couture and also Baulseurre and Jean Foucault; and Bertrandon Ernaud was struck by an arrow under the breast, and as a result he lost his eyes and lived for a long time thereafter. Because it was already night, the English withdrew on one side and the duke's men back to Plancy, and then around three hours into the night the Duke of Bourbon's men left Plancy to meet up with him; and along the way they encountered some Englishmen who were scouting between the army of Troyes and their own. So the men with the duke attacked them and put them to flight and killed fifteen Englishmen and took seven of them, whom they led into Troyes to their master. And that was very reliable news that the lords of France had from the people with the Duke of Bourbon; for the English had not been so upset up till that time since Calais.

Siege of Troyes in a 15th century miniature depicting the English army at the wall of Troyes, showing two heralds at the barriers surrounding the besieged city. British Library, Royal ms. 14 E IV folio 57r. Public domain.

XIX. How the Duke of Lancaster offered battle before Troyes.

The year of grace was 1373 and it was the month of June when King Charles of France was in his city of Troyes, with the dukes his brothers and others of his rank. In this season the Duke of Lancaster -- leader of the English at the incitement of the Duke of Brittany who was with him, accompanied by many Bretons-- prepared himself in good battle formations and presented himself before Troyes. So the King of France and the lords wanted no one to sally out from Troyes, except for some people who were ordered to, mainly fifty of the Duke of Bourbon's men and fifty of the lord of Clisson's, who sallied out to skirmish, just as was ordered. When the Duke of Lancaster, who always held himself in battle order, saw that these French lords who were at Troyes with a good four thousand men-at-arms would not come out at all, he had his people advance and rush forward at the ditches of the faubourgs of Troyes which were not at all enclosed, and when they perceived that none would come out to defend the ditches they entered the suburbs in undisciplined groups, so then, at the direction of the king and the lords, a good two thousand men-at-arms sallied out of Troyes against them there; and the French repulsed the English valiantly from the ditches, so that a good six score were killed at least, and four score were taken and remained as prisoners, among them an English captain named John Bull and three Bretons who had their heads cut off. And that night the English withdrew and camped a half league from Troyes, and the next day decamped early in the morning to head toward Sens in Burgundy. Inside Troyes the king gave orders in the presence of the lords that each of the dukes, Anjou, Berry, Burgundy and Bourbon, should send a hundred men-at-arms to ride every day to keep the English from provisioning and the valiant knights said that the English couldn't have been more effectively obstructed. And it was ordered that the great captains, such as the constable and the marshals, should go to the side one day to prevent anyone from reassembling on the marches of Limosin and Poitou and that thus nothing would be lost.

XX. How the lord of Clisson destroyed a party of the English in the faubourgs of Sens, and how the English rode through the Bourbonnois.

The English went so far that they lodged in the faubourgs of Sens, and when they were camped, the lord of Clisson, with some of the men of the Duke of Bourbon and of other lords, made an undertaking and went to set a great ambush, two leagues from Sens, of a thousand men-at-arms and close to Sens, at one league distance, another one of two hundred men-at-arms, and the lord of Clisson sent his scouts so that they should make a semblance of fleeing up to the large first ambush, and so it was done. So it happened that the English chased the scouts right into the first ambush, and those in the first ambush seeing them coming began to flee. Looking at this the English mutinied and followed the path of flight, without thought of being ambushed; and the first ambush of two hundred combatants came back at speed, with them digging in their spurs, into the ambush of the lord of Clisson, where there were a good twelve hundred combatants. The lord of Clisson leapt from concealment with his company and ran to attack the English, who yet came on in mad disorder. The lord of Clisson, by force of arms, drove them right back to where he had originally been, and there they killed as many as six hundred Englishman, and had some good prisoners, and it was the biggest setback which the English had on this voyage. For never, after this defeat, did the English go on the offensive, for no one confronted them directly, but they lost people on the way, by the action of small parties, never massed together. And when the dukes of Lancaster and Brittany saw their men decrease every day, they rode by their daily stages up to Brive-la-Gaillarde in Limousin, where they were welcomed by the people of the town, who were traitors to the King of France. And there the English estimated the number which they were able to have there since their descent from Calais, where they were sixteen thousand combatants, and at Brive they found themselves to be not even eight thousand, of whom half were on foot, for the others had been killed or taken along the way. And when the subjects of the lords of France beheld the treason of Brive, even though it was nearly Christmas, each one headed towards his master, namely the marshal, the Duke of Burgundy, the Duke of Berry, and the Duke of Bourbon who were still in pursuit of the English; these knights each reported to his master the treason of Brive, which had welcomed the English.

XXI. How the Duke of Bourbon, with his people and the Angevins, took Brive-la-Gaillarde and other places.

Duke Louis of Anjou, brother of the King of France, who heard the reception which those at Brive had given to the English, was unhappy, and in order to recover it as soon as possible, he sent without delay one of his own knights, Sir Jean de Bueilh, to the Duke of Bourbon praying and requesting, on the basis of the closeness of lineage, that it should please him to be in March following, with eight hundred or one thousand men-at-arms, for the lands of Anjou and Maine ought to join under Sir Jean de Bueilh with the Duke of Bourbon all of whom should assemble in mid-March at Busençai without the Duke of Anjou who felt a little disheartened, and from there the Duke of Bourbon and the Angevins, in 1373, should go to Limousin before Brive-la-Gaillarde, from which the English had left a month before. The Duke of Lancaster had gone to Bordeaux, where the few men he had with him remained and the Duke of Brittany to Derval, in its marches, and they had left in Brive but fifty combatants, twenty-five men-at-arms and twenty-five archers. Duke Louis of Bourbon—who perceived this—made to besiege Brive and he likewise established the men in their places and he went to lodge in Cordeliers before the gate, and the duke said to those of Brive that they should surrender the town, and they should hand over the traitor who had given it to the English, those who did not wish to obey the duke. During this negotiation of the treaty, the English shot arrows and wounded some of the duke's people; and because of this he commanded the assault which commenced strongly and bitterly on the side of the Duke of Bourbon and the other side of the Angevins. This assault was strong and grand, and lasted three hours and there was a very valiant man, the lord of Chalencon, and the Angevins did well, likewise the Bourbonnois, and fiercely the people of Brive defended themselves; but the fortified bridge was taken. This brought them to the foot of the gate, where they did some fine fighting, and the duke had a table spread thereupon, since it had been broken by force, Jean de Châteaumorand, who carried the Duke of Bourbon's pennon, climbed up on a false braye where he did not have to climb over the wall more than five feet, and there a falconer of the duke brought a ladder, which was put on the false braye to climb the wall, by which the Duke of Bourbon's pennon entered, and he who carried it, and many others after him. The English seeing this put themselves on defense, but they saw well that there was little for them to hold, and they were so discouraged that they were no longer able to defend themselves: then to safeguard their lives they fled into the church. Then from all sides the men-at-arms entered by force, and so Brive-en-Gaillarde was taken, and all the English found there were put to the sword. And the gate of Brive was opened, and the Duke of Bourbon entered and had it proclaimed that no one should pillage the churches, and that the traitors should be brought to him, and would have their heads cut off. The next day the Duke of Bourbon and his company left to head to Martel, and he left behind some of his men in Brive, which had not been pillaged, and he went away with his knights leading three hundred men-at-arms, to repair a league from Brive while awaiting his people. And in going they encountered the Anglo-Gascons, who rode up thinking to enter Brive-la-Gaillarde, and the duke and his people charged among the English at will, and the Duke of Bourbon who was mounted to good advantage on a beautiful courser, was the first to charge among them, and knocked to the ground two men-at-arms in the chase, from whom the lord of Prustallet took their faith for the Duke of Bourbon. Whereof Sir Morice de Terreguidis, Sir le Barrois, Sir Guy de Baveulx, Sir Gauchier de Passac, and Sir Jehan de Bueilh, who followed the duke with all speed in this chase, when they had caught up with him, very strongly reprehended him, saying that this should not be done by such a lord as he, to so pursue and overtake his enemies alone at speed, and that if a lowly captain had done it he would have been disciplined. And these words the good knights said to the duke despite the risk, but they knew well in their hearts that it was an act of great daring for any knight. From there they rode straight to Martel, which surrendered bit by bit, and which the Duke of Bourbon wished to be put into the hands of the Duke of Anjou. So he gave it into the hands of Sir Jean de Bueilh to guard it for he for whom it was intended. And Martel having been surrendered, they went to lodge at Chastel-Cervis and there Sir Arnoul de Marle came to the Duke of Bourbon, in the name of the Duke of Anjou, to thank him for his coming and the fine company which he led, and the fine works which he had accomplished on the way to Limousin, and inviting him to Aguilhon on a given day, where he would find the Duke of Anjou. So the Duke of Bourbon hastened and hied to those parts, and arrived two days before the Duke of Anjou came. And as the Duke of Bourbon approached, those of Aguilhon gave him the keys even before the Duke of Anjou came, and made a great celebration for him and cheered his coming; and the company was a beautiful thing to see: for so many were gathered together that they were estimated at three thousand knights and squires and one thousand projectile troops.

XXII. How the Duke of Bourbon aided the Duke of Anjou with his war in Guienne, and the places which they took, and the gifts which the Duke of Anjou gave to the Duke of Bourbon.

After Aguilhon surrendered to the dukes of Anjou and Bourbon, they left and went to Port Sainte Marie and with their men attacked a faubourg which they had fortified, which was taken and one of the young men of Nades died there, and on this the town surrendered and the Duke of Anjou put a garrison there. From Port Sainte Marie the dukes left and rode to La Réole, seven leagues from Bordeaux, which was besieged, and it was one of the strongest places in the country. And the Duke of Anjou had brought forth before La Réole one of the biggest bombards that had ever been seen anywhere, and the dukes were on the siege for nine days. And the Duke of Bourbon with his people were lodged by the Cordeliers monks amid their vines, right at their gate, and the Duke of Anjou camped on the riverbank where his battering rams and bombards were. And one day the English sallied from La Réole, unluckily, directly into the ambush of the Duke of Bourbon, who resisted them so strongly that pell-mell they were brought back captive by him to the Cordeliers, into the town; and by this capture, those who might have replenished the castle with victuals could not do so. And the castle held out for but three days before surrendering to the Duke of Anjou, which is one of the greatest joys the duke could ever have, for this is the place he desired the most. To make a long story short, the Duke of Anjou, along with the Duke of Bourbon, in this year took Penne d'Agenois, and Penne d'Albigeois, and Saint Makaire, Langon, the city of Condom, Florence, Jenne, all

in Gascony, and then the dukes together with their company went to Bigorre before the castle of Lourde. So often was the town attacked that it was taken and the castle was handed over to the Duke of Anjou, according to the promise which there was between them. And thus passed the season, and winter began, and the Duke of Anjou gave his people permission to go home, and went to Toulouse to winter over; and then the Duke of Bourbon asked permission to go home, notwithstanding that the Duke of Anjou really wanted to keep him. He thanked him for his service. Also the Duke of Anjou made the Duke of Bourbon many beautiful gifts, giving him thirty thousand gold francs that he owed to the Duke of Anjou for the county of Forez, which formerly he had acquired: this right he gave to the Duke of Bourbon for the fine, good and agreeable services which he had done him in the wars where he had been continually in parts of Guienne and Gascony for the king and the Duke of Anjou. Further he paid his men for a month, and the Duke of Anjou gave some beautiful gifts to knights who were with the Duke of Bourbon, some vessels of silver and silk cloths, and he gave to the lord of Beaujeu, who was with the Duke of Bourbon, a courser and two thousand gold ecus. The Duke of Bourbon and the lord of Beaujeu and their company left the Duke of Anjou and went to Montpellier, where the lord of Beaujeu caught a bad case of diarrhea from which he died; about which the Duke of Bourbon was very angry and sad and it was a great loss, for he was one of the finest knights of the realm.

XXIII. How the Duke of Bourbon went to Savoy to visit his sister the countess, and how some of his men went to Prussia.

After the funeral celebrations and the interment of the lord of Beaujeu were done, the Duke of Bourbon left Montpelier, and went to Savoy to visit his sister the countess, and gave leave to go to the men-at-arms and did not retain any people outside of those of his household, of whom he always had a great company, and passed by Nissy, which belonged to the Count of Geneva, where he found the cardinal of Geneva, who afterwards was Pope, and a fine company of ladies and damsels. The cardinal kept him for four days, and he feasted him joyfully, and the cardinal gave the Duke of Bourbon one of the most beautiful destriers[9] of that time. From Nissy the Duke of Bourbon went to Chambery in Savoy to his sister who awaited the Feast of All Saints, where the duke remained six days with the Green Count of Savoy, husband of his sister, where there was a great joyous festival, and the Duke of Bourbon sojourned in Savoy so long that the King of France was dismayed that he did not come to him, for he knew when he had left from the Duke of Anjou: so he sent him many messages that he should come quickly to him at Christmas or before. The Duke of Bourbon obeyed and on the departure from Savoy some asked him to please give them leave to go away for the winter, namely to Prussia, to fulfill and follow the *Reise*, on which many knights from many countries had gone. The Duke of Bourbon was very happy about the worthy ambition which they had, and asked them with a smile "Do you have money?" "Yes," they said, "plenty, for we have done well in the expeditions on which you have gone, and my lord the Duke of Anjou has given us some of his money and vessels." Hearing this the Green Count said to the Duke of Bourbon, "Good brother, you have good people, for they don't hide what goods they have in the least, but wish to employ them honorably." Those members of the household of the Duke of Bourbon who asked for permission were Jean de Châteaumorand, Sir Aymard de Marcilly, Sir Odin de Rollat, Sir Ouldray de la Forest, Sir Jehan de Saint-Priest, Sir Pierre de la Bussière, Saint Porgue, Perrin d'Ussel, Guyon Gouffier, and Jehan Goudelin, Breton. The companions took the authorization of their master the duke, who stipulated above all that, as much as they feared to anger him, they should be back very soon after Easter. At their departure, the Countess of Savoy, sister of the Duke of Bourbon gave to each of the companions going to Prussia a diamond, and they were overjoyed about the gift of the ladies. The companions left Savoy passing through Lorraine and Germany, and continued on to Bohemia to Prague, where they found the queen, the Duke of Bourbon's aunt, who saw them gladly and out of the goodness of her heart gave them some gifts; and in the city were

9 A warhorse.

many knights from the household of the King of France and his, who reciprocated their great joy because they had taken the road to Prussia. The first, Sir Hutin de Vermeilles, Le Borgne de la Heuse, the bastard d'Aussy and others, and they traveled so much by their daily stages that they entered into the frozen ice of the swamps of Prussia, and travelled often by sled, as is the custom there. And so they came to Marienburg,[10] the great religious house of the knights of Prussia, where the High Master of the order gladly received them. The duke's people found Sir Jean de Roye, Sir Patroulhart de Renty, Sir Robert de Chalus, Sir Jean Le Maingre called Boucicault, who for his chivalry was later Marshal of France, and, for his good sense governor of the city of Genoa; Sir Jehan de Bonnebault, Sir Gaultier de Passat, Sir l'Hermite de la Faye and many others from nations which I can't name who had come as if by miracle. For the King of Letho, a Saracen, had made strong undertaking to injure and conquer the order of Prussia, and so as to be stronger, recruited the King of Norgalles, who from the sea fought the master of Niffelant, defender of his religion and protector of Prussia, which is all one. And, at the risk of unduly mixing this history of the Duke of Bourbon with those of others, it must be said that the high Master of Prussia by the help of knights and other noblemen of the nations which he had in his company, carried himself so valiantly that he imposed the castle of Endrach upon them, and chased them into the great forests of Prussia, which extend more than eight days' journey, in which are the ermine beasts, snow weasels, gray and sable martens whose rich furs are exported to the provinces of the world. And the Christians made an agreement with the Saracens that they might return to their lands, understanding that, from that time onward, the Saracens of Letho and Norgalles would not pillage the churches of Christians, nor burn them, just as the Christian Knights of the Faith, whether from Prussia or Niffelant, should neither in Letho or the Marches burn the holy pine trees (as they are called), where they cremate the dead and make sacrifice. Both sides agreed to this, and so peace was proclaimed throughout the provinces. And the high Master of Prussia, seeing how much this Reise had brought him honor, one day, the feast of Our Lady at Candlemas, banqueted with the knights who were with him most splendidly. And in honor of that day, after mass, he had a table of honor laid out in his castle of Marienburg, meant to seat twelve knights from many kingdoms; and from the realm of France, prominently seated there at the high table, Sir Hutin de Vermeilles and Sir Tristan de Magneliers, whom everyone acclaimed a good knight, and from other realms from two up to twelve, by order of the master, who were served for the eminence of the day, as was befitting them. And thanks be to God, a way was found to set this table in proper order! And then, one of the knightly brothers in religion gave each one a motto, written in letters of gold, to be put upon

10 Now known as Kaliningrad.

their shoulders, "Honor conquers all!" The next day the knights took their leave of the high master of Prussia and each returned to his country.

A banquet with King Charles V, in the center wearing his crown and the heraldry of France. At the right of the image the evening's entertainment, a reenactment of the siege of Troy, takes place. The reenactors are obviously not dressed as ancient Greeks and Trojans but as soldiers contemporary with this manuscript of c. 1400.
Les Grandes Chroniques de France de Charles V. Ms Français 2813, fol. 473v.
Gallica Digital Library.

XXIV. How King Charles ordered the Duke of Burgundy and the Duke of Bourbon to make war in Normandy against the King of Navarre.

While these men of the household of Bourbon were traveling in Prussia, the duke left Savoy and went to the king who strongly urged him to hurry and who had a great desire to see him on account of the great good things that the duke had done that year, and when the king saw him, he welcomed him and said: "Good cousin, I am happy and joyous at your coming, for we are informed that the King of Navarre wishes to put the English in the places which he has Normandy, and you know which they are, and this will be the destruction of our realm. Thus it is our intention, as soon as Candlemas is past, that our brother-in-law of Burgundy and you, the Constable and the admiral, will go in arms to these places; for this is one of the great affairs that we have in which we wish to put all our power, in order that we finally bring this to an end, which we desire more than the English themselves."

Then the Duke of Bourbon responded that he was ready to go according to the order which the king had given and he did it. The following month of March the dukes of Burgundy and Bourbon, the constable and their company left to ride through Normandy near the county of Evreux, territory of the King of Navarre before Mortaigne, a strong fine town, and after they had besieged it thirteen days they took the town by assault and the castle too, where they gained many goods. The lords left and went to the city of Evreux, where there was one of the King of Navarre's captains named Farrandon, who did not dare to remain at Evreux, when he saw the lords approach with all their host to besiege the city. He left everything and fled hastily to Gavre, the castle where the treasure of the King of Navarre his master was. Those in the city saw the captain leaving them so they made obeisance and surrendered the city to the lords for the King of France. The Duke of Burgundy left Evreux and went away because of the army he was going to build in England. The Duke of Bourbon, the constable and the admiral went with their people to Gavre, the finest castle in Normandy, and they set their siege, and before them was Ferrandon, who had left Evreux, who held himself inside the castle. It happened one day that he went to inspect the powder for the cannons and artillery in one tower, and when he inspected it a lit candle fell on the powder which burned Ferrandon's whole face, from which he died and two others with him. Because those within were completely overwhelmed and during this extreme fear to those in the castle the Duke of Bourbon had his people take a false brayes in front of a gate beneath the castle, where he lodged a hundred men-at-arms. The constable and the marshal were lodged on the other part of the mountain and every day the Duke of Bourbon negotiated with them, that they should surrender, which they would not do for anything, if the treasure the King of Navarre was not taken and turned over to him, for he had three very rich crowns, gold and precious stones which had belonged to the kings of France and more than 60,000 gold francs and so those inside thus recognized it. Immediately after three days, the lord de la Rivière came in the presence of the lords in haste to escort out of greed the said treasure. De la Rivière pushed strongly for a treaty by which he would remove the money, but the Duke of Bourbon, the constable and the marshal did not want him to go forward, because they held the place for the good of the king. Thus did the lords by assault and strong war, that inside of three days those in the castle surrendered to the Duke of Bourbon and the constable and gave the lord de la Rivière the treasure which he desired so much. Then they razed the castle as they had done at Mortaigne, just as the king had commanded to the lords if they took it by force. After taking Gavre, the Duke of Bourbon, the constable and the marshal went to Reineville, which was well forward in Normandy, which surrendered when they knew that the other places were taken and razed. Then the inhabitants' lives were saved, but they all went elsewhere to live, and the lords had the town razed like the others.

The battle of Cocherel (1364) depiccted in an early 15th century manuscript in the collection of the Bibliotheque National de France. The battle was fought between the French, led by Bertrand du Guesclin, and the forces of Charles II of Navarre under Jean de Grailly. Alamy Stock Photo.

XXV. How the admiral of Vienne took Ponthieu from the sea with the help of the Duke of Bourbon's men, Rye in England, and the prior of Léaux.

The Duke of Bourbon, the constable and the marshal left Normandy to deal with some business that the King of France had at that time but in order that no place should remain intact for the King of Navarre, (who was allied to the English), the Duke of Bourbon wished to complete that which he was sent to conquer; and to do this Sir Jean de Vienne, Admiral of France, sent him and the constable to Ponthieu-de-Mer which he held for the king of Navarre, which was a beautiful town and a large castle, and the Duke of Bourbon gave the greater part of his men to the admiral, and likewise the constable, and the admiral led a large army which was to go to the frontier of the English sea. It was sent to Sir Renier de Grimaud of Genoa, who was at Rouen, where he was having galleys made for the king so that he should lead four galleys down the Seine to besiege Ponthieu-de-Mer, in case relief arrived there from England. And so he did, and Ponthieu-de-Mer was besieged by sea and by land, and the siege lasted six weeks, where some fine deeds of arms were performed both by the attackers and by the defenders: for the Duke of Bourbon's and the Constable's men desired that their lords who weren't there should hear good news of them, and also the admiral of Vienne strongly encouraged them, who valiantly upheld him and his people. Likewise Sir Renier de Grimaud in his galleys with his Genoese arbalestiers so thickly shot quarrels, to the point that those in the fort did not dare show themselves. So much did they strive continually to fight and attack that at length Ponthieu-de-Mer was taken by mines and the castle was scaled and taken by force and all those inside died. After Ponthieu-de-Mer, Sir Renier de Grimaud, who was a valiant sailor, spoke to the Admiral of France, saying, "Sire, you see from here to England is not much of a trip by sea, and there is an under-fortified town which is very large and which those who live there call Rye. The people around here say that those of Rye do not realize that they can now be attacked from here. For this reason, sire," said Sir Renier de Grimaud, "If it appears good to you, I will send a galley to Rouen, to pick up five large cogs refitted to carry two hundred horses, which are anchored there. I will also get other vessels to row over many of your footmen." The admiral thanked him very much for these words and asked them to do just that, and soon enough, Sir Renier left on his galley to obtain the navy which he hastily assembled. The admiral dismantled the castle of Ponthieu-de-Mer while waiting for him. It came to pass that Renier de Grimaud, just as he had promised the admiral, made a channel crossing with their army, to the number of four hundred horses and two thousand combatants, men-at-arms and projectile men, and arrived in England, where the English believed a battle line could defend the scarp. But it was to no avail, for the admiral and his company landed and chased them a league and more right up to Rye, and in that clash many Englishmen were killed. And in this way Rye was taken and overrun, and burned that day, and there was a great slaughter of people, and plenty were taken to the ships as prisoners, and a great many cloths and other valuables were taken. And a rich prior of England, the prior of Lewes, who sought to rally the defenders by withdrawing them to his monastery, which was nearby, sought to gather many people to roust the French, if he could. And for this, in the evening he came with a good five hundred combatants, the best that he had, but the admiral, who was wise and was wary of some such arrival, had set up a great ambush of three hundred of the best horses. So they saw them coming from a distance, and let the English approach, then sallied out of the trap, charged in their midst, routed them and took their chief, who was armed in a cuirass covered with vermilion velvet; and the Prior of Lewes became the admiral's prisoner, from whom the admiral, after holding him for a year, received seven thousand nobles[11] for his share of the plunder. From Rye in England the admiral and his fleet withdrew honorably without loss, and went to Paris to the king. And there was a great clamor about him and the Duke of Bourbon's men and the Constable, about the enterprise that he had accomplished in England, for never until now had the French done harm in England which anyone could remember.

11 A gold coin.

XXVI. How the Duke of Burgundy was chosen to cross into England, and why the army was not kept together.

Charles King of France rejoiced greatly seeing his enemies so abased, both in Guienne and in Normandy, subjugated by the efforts of the Duke of Bourbon, his Constable and others of his good servants; and to show his power he ordered in his council that Duke Philip of Burgundy, his brother, with the navy of Flanders and the royal galleys should go to England for conquest the following year, and the power of France; and that's what the army stationed at Rouen did. And the Duke of Burgundy, who had taken leave of his brother the king, went to Rouen, with a great number of good men, as many as three thousand men-at-arms, and the Duke of Bourbon went with him, who brought eight hundred. And the admiral of France Sir Jean de Vienne, and one of the Marshals named Bauldrain de la Heuse followed them with seven hundred and Sir Renier de Grimaud had eight hundred good Genoese arbalestiers to man his galleys and on top of this there was the master of the arbalesters who had a fine company from Picardy, and the Count of Flanders was obliged to come with seven to eight thousand Flemings from the other part of the sea. And there were parades of the lords at Pont-de-l'Arche, near Rouen, and there Bauldrain de la Heuse received them, and all the men-at-arms were paid for two months. And while the army of France anticipated crossing, news came to the King of France that the English army in great numbers had landed on Calais to head for Saint Omer and to Picardy and his captain was Jean Jouel, and this army was made to break up the army of the French lords. And this, indeed, the king ordered the lords and men-at-arms, that they should head to Calais to oppose the English and defend the country: so they did, and so the expedition to England, which cost a lot to mount, was broken off, and the lords rode to Saint Omer. So they found that the English were already between Lique and Ardres, and the lords of France were with all their people above Liques on a little mountain called Tournehen, and the English kept themselves down in the marshes because they were not strong enough to attack, so that they gladly kept themselves in a strong place. And the French and English remained facing each other for three weeks and there were fine skirmishes every day. And the Count of Flanders sent to the Duke of Burgundy, his son-in-law, a force of 10,000 commoners; and when the English became aware of so many men, they being close to the sea, and with the Count of Guines marching toward them, they chose to repair back to their country, whereupon the lords of France also withdrew.

XXVII. How the Duke of Bourbon learned news of the taking of Belleperche by the English, where his mother the duchess was taken.

The Englishman Robert Knowles, who many times had crossed the kingdom of France, was outside of Brest, which belongs to the Duke of Brittany, and thanked God that the French had not trapped him there having seen the lack of food where he was. So he crossed over to England and returned by sea to the Bourdelois and won back some places that the lords of France had taken in Guienne, which he found lacking guards. So he went in and took those places; he put captains and soldiers in them to guard them for the King of England. Especially he wished that the town of Niort in Guienne, which still had not surrendered to the French was domain and stronghold of the English who crossed the sea, and also some tributes. So Sir Robert Knowles had left Sir Thomas de Hanthonne as captain at Niort with a good company of men-at-arms and archers. During the time when the Duke of Bourbon was in the company of the Duke of Burgundy in France, where he made war on the English, two men-at-arms from Gascony, one named Ciquot de la Saigne, and the other Ortingo d'Ortenie, who had a good six score combatants and two hundred archers, seeing that now war had faded away in that part, requested from the captain of Niort Sir Thomas de Hanthonne that he should let them go with the company on their adventure and they did not hesitate, for they thought to do whatever pleased him and it would do honor to the King of England and gain profits for themselves. So he gave them permission willingly. Then Ciquot de la Saigne and his companion Ortingo d'Ortenie left Niort with their men equipped with good ladders; and they rode by night and day until they were in the Bourbonnois where through spies they scouted out the castle of Belleperche which belonged to the Duke of Bourbon and where his mother the duchess remained and kept her household. So, on coming to this place, they got their armed men through the door disguised as peasants, and held the lady prisoner, but made her suffer no indignities. But because the fort was well stocked with provisions for both people and horses, they made themselves masters, and held it. Soon enough, news of this came to Duke Louis of Bourbon, how the duchess his mother was taken by the English, together with Belleperche, and beyond that they had taken La Bruyère l'Aubespin. The Duke of Bourbon was angry and troubled about this, and concerning the capture of his mother, as much as this was a great marvel and the duke reached out day and night to the king in Paris whom he had given help, but he found little help, for the king was very anxious about his army, which had been broken up. The Duke of Bourbon saw that he had no help from the king, because he had much business at heart and had his men head towards his country to guard it until he came, namely Sir Guichard Daulphin, Sir Griffon de

Montagu, Sir Guillaume, and the men of Bourbon and Forez, up to four hundred, who headed as far as Saint-Pierre-le-Moustier, three leagues from Belleperche. That night the said captains and men-at-arms of Bourbonnois went to place an ambush near Belleperche, and there they found about two hundred Englishmen who had come from Bruyère to Belleperche. So they charged right into them putting them to flight, taking into captivity those whom they caught. The day before Sir Robert de Chaslus of the English had been taken, and the commander of the Marche with thirty men-at-arms, at Monteillis near Molins. So the men of the Bourbonnois remained nearly a month in the country, awaiting their lord, and during this the Count of Sancerre, the Marshal, came to the frontier, and had deliberations with the men of the Bourbonnois about what should be done. So it was agreed to go besiege La Bruyère in order that, when the duke their lord came, he would have to do only one siege. And by this way Bruyère was besieged: the commoners of the Bourbonnois came to the siege, a good two thousand of them, and ruptured its moats so that the water ran out, and these good people made so many fagots that these filled up the emptied moats; and they constructed a "siege cat" to undermine the foot of the wall, and afterwards they threw fire inside, and burned everything. By these methods were taken all the great captains of those inside, Sir Richard Mauverdin and Jacques Sadellier; and the remaining English inside were handed over to the commoners, who made some big roasts of them.

Mounted skirmish c. 1357
Yale Beinecke MS.227 Arthurian Romance f217r.

XXVIII. How the Duke of Bourbon besieged Belleperche, and how the Earl of Buckingham countersieged them.

In 1369, Duke Louis of Bourbon, who was much disturbed by the capture of the Duchess his lady mother, made haste to ride back to his lands to deal with these matters. But as he approached, it was made known to him how his people, whom he had sent ahead of him, whom with authority over the commoners, and the might of the Count of Sancerre, had taken la Bruyère and gained from the English the capture of their captains, and burned the town (and Englishmen too), about which the duke was somewhat amused, and he did not halt until he found himself in own his country. And promptly, with the people that he found and those which he had led there, he began to besiege Belleperche in winter, with eight hundred men-at-arms and two hundred arbalestiers because he knew that the captains Ciquot de la Saigne and Ortingo d'Ortenye were inside with a good six score combatants and more, and held the duchess in captivity. The Duke of Bourbon immediately made six siege engines which shot inside day and night. But the duchess, his lady mother, was terrified when they shot inside; so she ordered the duke her son not to shoot anymore. So he had pity, and did not batter the place with engines anymore. The duke's siege lasted three whole months through the coldest part of winter, when very often deeds were done by those of the host, sharp skirmishes, vigorous assaults, and also plain sallies by those inside. So had the Duke of Bourbon vowed that he would never move from the siege unless he had rescued his lady mother or taken the town by force. The Count of Sancerre, the Marshal Sir Louis, the knights, squires and men-at-arms of his countries of Bourbon, Forez and Beaujolais, with the chivalry of many places were there to deliver the lady, grandly enjoying themselves, seeing that the worst of the winter appeared to have passed, so the remaining time should be better and more cheerful for working. When they heard the duke say that, they were very satisfied. At this time the duke had a wooden palisade, with some ditching, built around himself, which enclosed his host. Therein, he put good guards at the entrances, so that those in Belleperche should not attack him, nor could anyone else enter against him, nor take him by surprise, so that he should not leave this siege shamefully. Ciquot de la Saigne, who everyday lost some of his men, seeing that he was besieged and that for whatever time it took, the Duke of Bourbon would not raise the siege. Nevertheless, Ciquot reinforced himself with men and supplies, and sent a message to Guienne to the English who were there saying that for God's sake they should come and help him, for the Duke of Bourbon had already sat before him a good three months. With hardly any delay the English forces in Guienne came to the Duke of Bourbon, namely the Earl of Buckingham, who had a good seven thousand combatants, and countersieged the Duke of Bourbon, whom he well believed to have damaged: for his fortification was only enclosed by small posts the size of an arm, and the height of a man, and a little ditch which men could jump over. At the arrival of the Earl of Buckingham, the knight who had led him back to France from England, Sir Mathieu de Gournay, came before the Duke of Bourbon, who wished to talk to him in confidence. The Duke of Bourbon was happy to oblige, since he loved him well. When the knight Gournay came to the duke, he made him good cheer, and the knight said to the Duke of Bourbon that, for God's sake he should extricate himself from danger he was now in. "For, my lord, you can well see that your position is hopeless, and is worth nothing." After the English knight had finished, the Duke of Bourbon responded, "Sir Mathieu, tell your master that I am in my country and my land and for the good of Madame my mother. Then tell him that I am ready and prepared to meet all his power and anything he is able to do, and I will live and die with this chivalry." There were a good two hundred knights around the duke; Sir Mathieu de Gournay, who saw the courage of the duke, left on this note and went to his master, to whom he reported the words of the Duke of Bourbon just as they had been said to him.

XXIX. How Duke Louis of Bourbon recovered Belleperche, and how the Earl of Buckingham left and then returned; and how Big David was killed.

The Earl of Buckingham,[12] an Englishman who with the large number of men countersieged the Duke of Bourbon before Belleperche, knew how the duke sat there in hopes of taking the castle and delivering the duchess, his mother, who was inside. The earl restored his power so that he might remove the duke from the siege and rescue his men who held the fortress. When the earl heard his knight, Sir Mathieu de Gournay, report the words of the Duke of Bourbon that "for nothing would he leave" immediately the Earl of Buckingham, that evening, ordered his Englishmen to make fagots and a great stock of beams for an attack on the next day, and the Duke of Bourbon great ordinance to defend himself well. And before the Earl of Buckingham had come, the Duke of Bourbon had dismissed most of the useless people and commoners and had retained no more than a chosen number of men, and for them, when he saw himself countersieged, had ordered that each man at arms be properly armored to guard the palisade, where there were but eight hundred armored, and for every two men-at-arms one Genoese arbalestier; and in this way the Duke of Bourbon wanted his men to be able to defend themselves from their enemies, commanding them, that no one for any reason should abandon his defensive position. And further the Duke of Bourbon had the great arbalests[13] of Chantelle put in front of the English in battle formation, these being very fine, and they did many good things, as you will hear. And still later, the Duke of Bourbon had scattered around his palisade four bushels of caltrops, from about two lance-lengths around his enclosure. And on the morrow, at Matins, the Earl of Buckingham came from his tents with his Englishmen deployed in battle formation on a large field before the fortress of the Duke of Bourbon. And once they were in the battle, Thomas the Genoese and Dommiges had the big arbaleste of Chantelle shot right into the earl's cohort, which killed two men and dismayed the English, who had never seen so great a shot. And afterwards, six arbalestiers let fly simultaneously from the fortress, which made so much damage in the battle it was marvelous, and likewise the cannons. And this time the attackers pulled back two stones' throw for a time and after a space, the Earl of Buckingham had it cried out that all the men should go to the assault, and that they should strive to gain and take this miserable enclosure, and that each one should carry a fagot, and so they

12 The youngest son of Edward III; Earl of Buckingham (1377); Duke of Gloucester (1385).

13 A heavy crossbow, often used in siege/countersiege because of their great power, but slow speed to reload.

did; but they were not able to approach the palisade to the distance of three lances, beyond which they could not go, lest they plunge into the caltrops, where they would fall like rain; and on the other part, the shooting by the Genoese who were at the palisade was so great and so dense that no men were better made use of; nor were so many men wounded, as were these Englishman who retreated shamefully. And at their retreat, the Duke of Bourbon had the standard of the golden escutcheon sally from his fort with fifty men-at-arms and fifty arbalestiers and pounced upon the last stragglers, found in a turnip field, where a good thirty-two of the English died. The Earl of Buckingham, who was in lurking in his forest hideaway, sent a herald to the Duke of Bourbon telling him that he should abandon the place or he would make off with his mother and would ruthlessly raze his castle in front of him and his palisade. Then the Duke of Bourbon by the same herald sent back that though Buckingham made off with his mother, who was the duke's pride of lineage, and razed the castle, as far as the fortress was concerned, he would certainly never have it, save by the sword, "as far as this, earl, that you ordered me to come tomorrow, to have it by force; come when you like and you will find who will be there to receive you."[14] And that very night the Earl of Buckingham decamped at midnight and sent to seek the duchess mother of the Duke of Bourbon, at the castle, to lead her to his lodging and then set the castle on fire. When the Duke of Bourbon and his men saw the fire taking the castle, they were sure that the English had decamped; at that hour the duke took twenty-six valets and thirteen ladders and had them go in the direction of the garden, to enter the castle if they could, and that the first who got in would have one hundred francs. So the valets rushed to win that, and they found that the English had left; and entered by the ladders which was a shrewd enterprise, and the valets closed the postern of the castle out of which the English had sallied; also, they extinguished the fire, which had not done great damage, and came out to cry that more people should be sent in, since they had secured everything and about which there was great joy among the duke and those of the fort. Immediately the Duke of Bourbon sent fifty men-at-arms to the castle, and one of the standards. The next day at dawn the English who had decamped saw the standard of the Duke of Bourbon on the castle tower of Belleperche, and the crenellations full of bascinets, which enraged them, and said that they were the most dishonored men in the world. But those who said this took the road to Guienne and lodged six leagues from there in Limoise and Pouzy and there was a great debate among them, for they said to the Earl of Buckingham that he was the most dishonored knight that they knew of, and all those with him: for the Duke of Bourbon had recovered his castle and done them great damage, and they had done nothing to him, for which the Earl of Buckingham should hold himself dishonored. Therefore he and his people should turn back to

14 A stock phrase.

Belleperche; and then coming they should load up with doors and gates of barns and not let any who did not carry to attack, and they should make out of them a great pile before the fort, for they all held themselves to be shamed, because the Bourbonnois were so few in their palisade, and they said, "By St. George, my lord Buckingham, it is astonishing to us and great shame is ours, that we have sat before this sad fort for so many days, and have accomplished nothing by it. Not one post from their palisade has been a little uprooted by force: rather they have killed and wounded plenty of our men by their strong shooting. But since he came," said the English to their master the earl, "and we are returned to this place, let's do it in such a way so it looks like we have a little dignity." The Earl of Buckingham, who listened to these people, wished them good luck and ordered up all the equipment for a fierce attack the next day. And Duke Louis of Bourbon, who had not as yet moved from his place to retake the castle, when he saw the English return, went all around his palisade among its defenses, which were as he had ordered them, and admonished each one to defend himself well, and hold firmly in his place, and so the duke said to them, calling them by name, "My friends, make sure that this work will not be in vain: at this point it's make-or-break. The English are very resentful of our retaking the castle from them, and even more that they have not—God be thanked—harmed us much. Let's do this in a way we won't regret. I, for one, have faith that through God and you, my lady mother will be taken from their hands. Although they hold her now, in time they will release her. I know very well that in defending yourselves you will do your duty." Then each of the knights said to the duke that there would be no chance of his dying, since they would assiduously maintain their defenses, and were prepared to deal with any who attacked them. And while the English had intended to attack the French on the morrow, and to drive them by force from their fortress, that night it happened that a terrible snow fell that was two feet deep and more; whereupon the English had decamped at daybreak and went a good ten leagues in the direction of Montluçon to take up lodgings. And then it was ordered that the gentlemen of Bourbonnois and Forez should mount their horses with the Marshal of Sancerre, and go after the English, and the duke should withdraw to Molins, and so he did; and because of this deep snow which now had fallen, the English were found dispersed over the country, and were killed whenever they were found. And the English headed to Montluçon, so they could be close to Guienne: and in a town near Montluçon was lodged one of their captains named Big David Olegrève, who was one of the hugest men that one could ever see, and one of the most arrogant, and he carried two swords, one belted on and the other at the back of his saddle. So the Marshal of Sancerre and the men of the Duke of Bourbon went at dawn, to attack his lodgings, and the lodging was destroyed with as many dead as there were English, a good three hundred men-at-arms; and at the same place Big David was killed by the hand of the Marshal of Sancerre, and there was one of the best plunderings that one had ever heard of at this time, and more damaging to the country of Guienne. Of the seven thousand English combatants which were with the Earl of Buckingham, they lost a good three thousand of them coming to Belleperche, according to what Poqueron and the Borgne Foucault reported, who were English then and since have been French. Then there was a great clamor, through the realm of France, in Paris and other parts and by the duchy of Guienne, bigger than one had heard for long time past, that Duke Louis of Bourbon had expected seven thousand combatants but had not had but eight hundred, and the duke was countersieged and had siege upon siege before Belleperche, which had never been seen in this realm, and the Duke of Bourbon recovered his castle where the English were and there were killed in the country of the Duke of Bourbon, a good seven hundred men-at-arms, both before Belleperche and in the defeat of Big David.

The renowned Bertrand du Guesclin was a recurring figure in the Good Duke's military life, hardly surprising given Guesclin's role as Constable of France. The image is of his tomb effigy in St. Denys cathedral where his body lies buried next to the king he faithfully served, according to that king's order. Guesclin's heart, however, was transported back to Dinan in his beloved Brittany to be enshrined in the basilica of Saint-Sauveur there.
Robert Charrette photographer, used by permission.

In this 15th century siege illustration from La Chanon de Bertrand du Guesclin, *Guesclin (left side, empty hand raised) appears in a garment and armor remarkably like the harness he wears in his tomb effigy, along with the battlefield addition of bascinet and gauntlets. The three basic elements of a siege are shown: investment, escalade ("storming"), and undermining.*
British Library, Yates Thompson 35, public domain.

XXX. How the king put the Duke of Bourbon in charge of the conquest of Poitou; and how the lord of Clisson was rescued; and how Montcontour was taken.

After a short while when the Duke of Bourbon had remained at his hostel and visited his countries, in no time at all the King of France sent to seek him praying, and requesting that of all the pleasures he might have, he would have the duke come to speak to him. The duke did not go at all at this time, and so it was ordered three or four times before he was finally willing to go, which made the king unhappy; but the king very much desired him because of the great renown which he saw in him. In the end, the chivalry of the Duke of Bourbon, of whom he had some fine ones, advised him on how things were, whom he should seek out, and that which he should not refuse, notwithstanding the little help that the king had given him. So the duke went there, and when he was in the presence of the king, the king spoke fine words to him, and greatly praised the things he had done, and the king apologized that he had helped him so little, because of the great affairs which busied him every day. To which Duke of Bourbon answered humbly, "My very redoubtable lord," said the duke, "you have done plenty for me, and I am content with you, and I should be; but there are quite a few in your service with whom I am not pleased, and God bring me to account if I malign anyone. By my faith, I am dedicated to your service." The King understood well enough what the duke was hinting at, and said to him, "Good cousin, I pray you that you have no displeasure in anything, for by my faith, I have confidence in your good service, as indeed I should; and I have a request to make of you, that I pray you indulge me in among the other good deeds you have done for me, namely that you agree to be in charge of a mission to Poitiers, together with the Constable, your company and some officers." To which the Duke of Bourbon answered the king, "Sire, I wish to obey you always, but this puts me in a rather awkward position, since I and the poor gentlemen of my country, who have served me in my great need, are not in good shape to serve you well, for they have used up their substance in my service and also my own resources have had no relief." "Ha ha ha, good brother of Bourbon," said the king, "I pray you, don't fuss about this at all. For I will assure you that I will refresh them, both you and them, and that you shall lack nothing." Concerning this offer the Duke of Bourbon thanked him humbly, and said to him, "Sire, I thank you, for I swear that I would have reached a desperate condition before I failed to obey you." "I know it well, good brother," said the king, "and you have proven it to me." Thus was undertaken the journey to Poitiers, and immediately in March the Duke of Bourbon and the Constable rode into Poitou with three thousand men-at-arms and eight hundred bowmen. They stood before Poitiers where they shot at the town who were well toughened, news came to the Duke of Bourbon and the Constable in the middle of the night by a gentleman and a herald that the lord of Clisson ordered in great haste that they should ride from Montcontour nearby to him, or else he was lost. For Sir Walter Spurton, an Englishman, had left Niort, and come before him with more men by half than he had; and the lord of Clisson was not able to get any victuals because the English kept him very short. So the Duke of Bourbon and the Constable left in the middle of the night to head in that direction and they went to Lodun to feed, and the lords did not stop at all on account of the fear they had about Clisson, and they were that same day near Montcontour between Vespers and sundown, and Clisson was overjoyed that the lords had come to rescue him. That night Sir Walter Spurton, who saw the lords' army approaching, decamped and went to Niort in great haste, and the next day assailed Montcontour, which was one of the best assaults which one could see after Saint-Sévère. For the Duke of Bourbon and the Constable encouraged their people and soldiers to do well, concerning which point there is no exaggeration, and more so had them trained to climb the walls with iron hooks, and to mine, to climb ladders, to shoot and throw spears, to dig ditches and do all the work which is related in such a case, and permitted in war. So much they did that they took the lower court around the church of Notre Dame de Montcontour, and the next day the castle was strongly attacked on ladders in two or three places: and the first who got in was Sir Chatard de Cleaux, who was of the house of the Duke of Bourbon and a squire named Marrago who served Sir Jean de Digoine. The castle of Montcontour was taken, and during the assault the captain inside, who was English, had called the Constable of France a perjurer and said that he had broken his faith as a prisoner at Najera in Spain, and his name was Jehannequin Louet. When the castle was taken, the Constable had the same Jehannequin Louet hanged, armed in all pieces and with bascinet on his head, from the crenellations of the castle.

XXXI. How Poitiers surrendered to the Duke of Bourbon in the name of the king, and other places like La Rochelle; and how at Benon all were killed by the Constable; also how the duchess, the duke's mother, was delivered, and how the Captal de Buch was taken.

As soon as Montcontour was taken, the Duke of Bourbon and the Constable of France with all their people returned towards Poitiers to camp in the very place from which they had left, to treat with those of the town, who were much more amiable than they were before, because of the capture of Montcontour, and also of Sir Walter Spurton, who was their protection and who had very badly pulled out. The people of Poitiers made their agreement with the Duke of Bourbon, and rendered obeisance to him in the name of the king, as long as the Duke of Bourbon promised and swore that before his people should leave the town, they should take the castle, or otherwise the English who held it would destroy them. Also the duke promised them that he would never budge from the town if the castle was not in the hands of the king. They opened the gates and the lords entered on a Monday. And the following Sunday they attacked the castle by means of a great plan they had devised in the town, and there were in the castle not eighteen Englishman; at the taking of the castle the first to enter was Sir Guichard de Châteaumorand where he gained some fair English chambers and the seals of the duchy of Guienne, which he gave to his lord, the Duke of Bourbon. And thus the town of Poitiers was overjoyed when they saw that which the Duke of Bourbon had promised; so they asked for more, that he would deliver them from a place nearby called the tower of Citri, which had made strong war against them. To which the Duke of Bourbon said that he would do his duty concerning the taking and there he sent immediately some people from his household, who remained there seven days and then they took it, and the people of Poitiers were ever so happy; and they gave the Duke of Bourbon two hundred marks of silver for the good services which he had done them. The lords decamped from Poitiers, and they went to Pont-l'Abbe which town they did not dare to hold; but the castle was very strong and Sir Bertrand de Caselis held it.

And the castle was attacked so violently that in the space of eight hours it was taken; and Sir Bertrand de Caselis hid in a tower in the marshes where he had nothing to eat: so he surrendered to the lords and was made prisoner. And from there the lords went to Surgières, where there was a very fine castle, and they took it by attack in full force; then they went to Benon and three leagues from La Rochelle, and there the Constable lost four of his gentlemen who directed all of his affairs, who were in their lodgings, where they slept in their bed. So their valets had by chance left the door open, while they played at dice, and the gentlemen were killed by those of the garrison of Benon, which was the greatest heartbreak that the Constable had in France; and for this outrage, Benon, which had three hundred inhabitants, was attacked the next day. The assault lasted nearly the whole day, but in the end it was taken, and the Constable had all of them killed, sparing no one, because of the anger of his people. From Benon the lords rode to La Rochelle, where those of the town entertained the lords for three days. And in the course of these revels the townsmen knocked down the castle so that nevermore could there be a master of their town. And they presented themselves to the lords, who reproached them for what they had done, and they from then on were good and loyal to the king, and did great harm to the King of England, for this was the port that secured a hold on all Guyenne. La Rochelle having been returned the lords went to Saint Jean d'Angelis, who without delay opened up and made obeisance to the king in the hand of the Duke of Bourbon. They went to Xainctes which submitted like Saint Jean d'Angelis. When these things were done and the country was returned to the King of France, the Duke of Bourbon asked the Constable to make a company to go to the tower of Brou where the duchess his mother was prisoner, which was no more than seven leagues away. In this tower the Earl of Buckingham had left her on his return from Belleperche, under guard and put into the tender care of Ciquot de la Saigne, his squire, seeing that he had been captain of men-at-arms who had taken Belleperche and the lady, and now held this tower. The Constable was very happy and said, "As God wills, my lord, and by the eyes of God, this request is a good thing. But quickly, let's go rescue the good lady!" And, soon enough they mounted up and went there and besieged the tower. And there, Ciquot de la Saigne, who saw himself badly fortified, and that he was far from help, surrendered to the Duke of Bourbon the tower of Brou and his mother the duchess, who highly praised Ciquot to the duke her son. For this the duke sent to him and set all his men free, and let him keep his valuables. When the tower of Brou was returned, the Duke of Bourbon's people went out hunting near Sebise. And the Captal de Buch had put an ambush of his people, right where they were, between Sebise and the tower of Brou.

The people of Bourbon and the Captal came upon each other, and they rushed upon each other, and it turned out worse for the Captal, who was captured and turned over to the Duke of Bourbon, who then led him to Paris, and gave him to the king. The Duke of Bourbon, who now had his mother back, was overjoyed after they, he and the Constable, left Poitou, travelling a full-day's ride to Paris to the king, who received them happily, and celebrated the fine deeds which they had done in delivering a great part of the Duchy of Guienne from his enemies and putting it in his obedience.

XXXII. How the Duke of Bourbon was charged by the king and the Duke of Berry to go make war in Auvergne; and what places he took, and how he had chalices returned to the churches.

While the Duke of Bourbon and the Constable abiding at Paris with the king, in 1375, the Duke of Berry asked his brother the king if it would please him to give him the Duke of Bourbon, who wanted to ride into Auvergne, where there were seven or eight fortresses that much destroyed the country, and especially there was one of them where there was an English captain who had a good three hundred men-at-arms in one place above Clermont and at a distance of two leagues from there, called La Roche Senadoire, and the English captain Sir Robert Channel. There were other places and other captains; La Roche over Aiguesperse; Ambur; Tracros, in Gourdinot's custody; Saint-Angel; Charlieu-le-Paillhoux and Charlieu-Champmagois. The king and the Duke of Berry asked Duke Louis of Bourbon to take on the task of going into Auvergne, to make war against the English. So the duke departed with his people and went into Bourbonnois, passed into Auvergne, and went before La Roche over Aiguesperse, and the duke stayed there but one night, and by morning it was taken by full assault, as were all who were within. Then the duke went before Ambur, a very fine place, where there were a good eighty combatants, and on arrival there was a big skirmish, for those inside came out, and there was a fine skirmish with lances and swords between the two sides; and there Sir Girart de Grantvau, a good man of his body, was wounded and Jean the bastard of Châteaumorand was killed. But in this skirmish there were taken eight men-at-arms from those of the fort who had more authority, and four killed; and the Duke of Bourbon on the morrow had those eight led before him to have their heads cut off, if they did not surrender the place, and they could well do it, since they had been apprised of which among them preferred living rather than dying in such a way. So they surrendered Ambur to the Duke of Bourbon, both their bodies and the place. And later on, within an hour, the Duke of Bourbon and his men made to leave and go to Tracros; and those men who he sent to scout ahead encountered the English of Tracros, those swaggering adventurers who set upon them, but were knocked down on the spot by the duke's men, who arrived in a hurry, albeit a bit late. That night the Duke of Bourbon, who had come there, selected some men from his household guard and said to Jean de Châteaumorand: "Take my pennon, and go all around the place so that no one sallies out." He carried out his order, and that night there was much discussion among the duke's men as to whether those in the fort would surrender, or if when they were captured they should be hanged by the neck because they were men of evil renown. So was the talk until Gourdinot, warden of the place, surrendered to Jean de Châteaumorand, the squire who carried the pennon of the Duke of Bourbon; and at this hour, which was not yet mid-day, the duke enacted the treaty that his household had drawn up, to his delight; and he answered that it pleased him well, because he still had great deeds to do. The one who spoke about this to the duke was Châteaumorand, who asked him to be willing to give the movable goods in the fortress to the people of his household, which the duke did freely, while Gourdinot, who had surrendered to him, should remain his prisoner and this he granted to him. On the morrow Gourdinot and his men of Tracros, who were not but sixteen men-at-arms, were all prisoners. Inside were two hundred marks of silver, of which one hundred marks were in chalices from churches which they had thoroughly robbed. So the duke said that he wished to have the chalices, and he would generously recompense the companions. The Duke of Bourbon moved by pity sent the chalices to the city of Clermont and had it announced to all the churches which had lost their chalices, that someone should come to Clermont, and they would be given back, and it was done.

XXXIII. How the Duke of Bourbon convinced the lords of Auvergne to besiege La Roche Senadoire which he was besieging.

Duke Louis of Bourbon, who had delivered Tracros, left with all his host and went to Clermont just two leagues from La Roche Senadoire, and the duke summoned the lords of Auvergne, the Count Dauphin, the lord de la Tour, the lord of Montravel, and the other great lords and one called the lord of Laqueulhe, one of the valiant men of Auvergne. The Duke of Bourbon said to them: "My lords, I have delivered three places, and near here is one which has ruined the whole country, for there are four captains and three hundred men-at-arms, and the place is not vulnerable, without the grace of God." Now the lords of Auvergne answered and they said to the duke: "My lord, you are asking from us that which we ought to beg from you with joined hands. For this place destroys all of Auvergne and they raid all the time before this town." The Duke of Bourbon then said that the people of Auvergne should go on one side and he and his people on the other, to besiege La Roche Senadoire, and he commanded that the peasants should bring some victuals to the siege, and all the equipment that they could find for attacking. So it was said and done; and on the morrow the Duke of Bourbon decamped and went with his men to his strongest place, where he had his tents and pavilions set up. That night as the duke camped, those of La Roche Senadoire made an attempt to ride out on horseback, and threw away a good sixty of theirs in this foolhardy action. But the Duke of Bourbon who always did things in an organized fashion had trained his guard so well that these sixty horses were captured where there were only five men-at-arms, the rest being merely pages… and what a bouquet of horses! The English who saw their place at La Roche Senadoire besieged on two sides, on one by the Duke of Bourbon, on the other by the lords of Auvergne and a great multitude of the commons, strongly feared that they should ascend by force between the two places and for this made a low palisade between the two mountains, which was six hundred feet long; and it was made so high on their mountain that scarcely an arbalest there could hope to shoot over it. And each night the English set a guard with a hundred men-at-arms inside this palisade, so that none might be able to get up to them on the mountain.

XXXIV. How, with the Duke of Bourbon present in his host, the bastard of Glarains fought for the quarrel of the lord of Montravel, a Gascon Englishman.

While the Duke of Bourbon considered and examined how one could take the place, it happened that one Vespers, on the night watch, an English Gascon and one of the men of the Duke of Bourbon had words together; that Gascon was Perrot de Lignaige, and Bourbon's man was called the bastard of Glarains. For Lignaige had said that the lord of Montravel, who was his prisoner, had broken his faith to him. And if he wanted to say the contrary, he should come forward, and he would fight him, or if there was anyone else there willing to dare it, he would fight him likewise. To this the bastard of Glarains responded: "I am neither friend nor relative of the lord of Montravel but if you have as great a talent for fighting as you appear to, tomorrow I will fight you before my lord the Duke of Bourbon. If the outcome is such that I defeat you, you will be my prisoner, and if you defeat me, I will be yours; and this you ought by no means refuse, if you have the desire to fight, for this is the life of arms." Concerning this the Englishman said that he would speak to Sir Robert Chennel, his captain, and that he would make his response. And the bastard of Glarains answered that he had great confidence in his most redoubtable lord, the Duke of Bourbon, that he was much to his liking, for the duke refused nothing to him which touched the bastard's honor. And so, for this time, the two separated. And this Perrot de Lignaige was to make a response to the bastard of Glarains, between noon and Vespers, which he did; and he had permission from his captain to fight on the third day provided that the bastard of Glarains vouchsafed him, and sent him surety and safe conduct from the Duke of Bourbon for him and fourteen companions. And this having been arranged, the Duke of Bourbon had the lists made and on the third day the Englishman Perrot de Lignaige came and the Duke of Bourbon receive him grandly and honorably because the thing was to be done before him. Lignaige found his beautiful tent pitched in the lists, for him to take off his armor, and to receive his companions who would come with him, and the bastard likewise, and each had his chair of honor. And when they were in their chairs they were asked if they had anything more to say, and they said no. Whereupon the heralds cried "Do your duty!" So they joined battle and they did some fine fighting striking some blows on each other with their swords, after the throwing of lances; but the bastard of Glarains drove back his adversary Perot de Lignaige a good six paces in fighting with the sword and in the end the bastard threw his sword down and laid hands on Lignaige the Englishman. Holding him tight he threw him to the ground, and threw himself on him, and lifted Lignaige's visor, and gave him three blows of the gauntlet on the face, and then the Englishman who felt himself injured and ill-used surrendered, shouting so loud that one could hear him clearly. But nevertheless the bastard snatched away the Englishman's sword and was ready to kill him with it, when the Duke of Bourbon said that was enough and enough had been done. And with this, he had them removed from the place, for he did not want the Englishman to die, for the reason that all that was needful had been done in his view. Subsequently, this good deed reflected great honor on the Duke of Bourbon.

During this judicial combat, one of the captains inside named Nolimbarbe, who guarded one of the towers, requested that he and his companions and he himself might leave, along with their horses. There were many of the lords of Auvergne and others who desired to be rid of them who counselled the duke to release the English; but he did not wish to do it at all, so he vowed that none of them would ever leave, if the place was under his command, and the English in his power; and so did it transpire, as you will hear.

XXXV. How the Duke of Bourbon honorably took La Roche Senadoire, and other places, which he turned over to the Duke of Berry.

When the quarrel of the two soldiers was finished, and the bastard of Glarains had vanquished his adversary, the good Duke Louis of Bourbon had reflected on this palisade, which was so high, for he had already kept his siege before La Roche Senadoire for three weeks; and so as to dispose of this sooner, he reinforced his guard for the space of three days, by fifty men-at-arms per day, and at the end of three days, towards late evening, the Duke of Bourbon commanded the lords of Auvergne that they should all be armed at dawn, with their men, and ready to climb the mountain on their side, for it was his intention to have the palisade attacked at once with all his might; and that they should make the action so secret that no one should notice them, for which purpose he wished to make his men sleep fully armed, and then to join with his household guard, according to his plan. The night passed, and in the morning at Matins, each one sallied from the tents and pavilions to join with the household guard, and with their palisade guard, whereupon there would come to pass many fine deeds of arms: for the English guard was a good hundred combatants strong, who roughly and fiercely defended themselves.

However the palisade was not very well fixed in the ground because it was rock and there had great and fearsome pushing of lances on one part and the other, and the affair was so rough that our men by force took the palisade by shooting at them, until the men-at-arms in it toppled to the ground a good ten fathoms. The English captains who defended the palisade saw their numbers diminish, so grievous and harsh were the attacks, exposing them to yet more danger. What frustrated them the most was that they never had a chance to meet the Bourbonnois in hand-to-hand combat, since the duke had exhorted that they should take pains to attack very roughly, and take the castle without delay. Within a few hours of this being said, the palisade was taken, and the high ground was won, and those inside were completely overwhelmed. The Duke of Bourbon was overjoyed by seeing his knights and the squires of his household and country, and all the men-at-arms who were ready to undertake any risk, destroying the palisade and garrison and proceeding in force triumphantly. During this melée, the pennon of the Duke of Bourbon continually carried by Jean de Châteaumorand passed through the breach in the palisade, with those who followed him. Then the English who saw this did not know what to do, outside of retreating into the fort and while they retreated the pennon rushed forward with the valiant men; and in this retreat of the English, who ran away, there were killed and taken a good fourscore of the better men-at-arms from inside, excluding the captains; so that on the one hand, Nolimbarbe retreated towards the right, while to the left, on the other hand, which was the strongest defensive position, was the destination of Sir Robert Chennel, Jacques Bardenay, the son of Jean Jouel, Thomelin Maulevrier, Sir Richard Credo, son of the mayor of London. While they retreated from certain lodgings which were high up, to go to their fort, the pennon of the Duke of Bourbon and the people of his household charged them so close that as they entered the tower, the pennon of the Duke of Bourbon rushed among them very well accompanied, so that those Englishmen were not able to close the door of the tower, and so they surrendered to the one who carried the pennon of the Duke of Bourbon. The prisoners who surrendered to him were Sir Robert Chennel, captain, the son of Sir Jean Jouel, Sir Richard Credo son of the mayor of London, and Thomelin Maulevrier, and so that very strong place was delivered. In this way the pennon of the Duke of Bourbon with his companions, namely Sir le Barrois, Bonnebault, Sir Gaulchier de Passac, the lord of Cordebeuf, the Borgne de Veaulce, Sir Odin de Rollat, Sir Phelippe Choppart, the lord of Billy, Jehan lord of Chaugy, Phelippe Berault, Michaille, the bastard of Glarains and five or six others of the household of the Duke of Bourbon, with his pennon, headed over to one of the other towers where they found already before it a great party of people of Auvergne who were climbing up there, and the lord of Montmorin who was a valiant knight, and who had a fine company, and Geraud, lord of Laqueuilhe, accompanied by good people and that valiant man, the lord de Lafayette and others who were advanced by the advice of the lords who had held very close to the English when they had arrived there so that the English could not flee. But when the English saw the pennon of the Duke of Bourbon approach them, the captain Nolimbarbe surrendered with all of his companions to the Duke of Bourbon. So was La Roche Senadoire taken without a word of a lie. Leaving there, the Duke of Bourbon sent to Clermont six English captains to be held as prisoners in the tower of Monnoye, about which the people of Clermont were very happy and joyful and the duke and his people and those of Auvergne rode to Saint Angel, a place which had done much evil. They remained there a day, thinking to treat with them, but those in the castle did not want to listen. Then it was noticed that the abbey was covered by wooden shingles, thereupon they fired several incendiaries, so that it spread throughout its buildings, and all the English horses were burned up as well as some of their valets. The men-at-arms retreated into a tower that was there, where they had nothing to eat. It was impossible to take it by force, for it was very well built; in which attempt a young knight, whom the Duke of Bourbon loved well, was killed: Sir Jean de Digoine, who hailed from Clermont. In the end, those in the tower surrendered to the Duke of Bourbon on the condition of keeping their lives. So the duke vouchsafed them, sending Châteaumorand with his pennon to the tower, and each of the English came out with their weapons in their hands; and the duke went to Charlieu-le-Paillhoux where the lords of Auvergne had remained four months, and they had not taken it, and holding the place was Jean D'Ussel, and the commander of Belle Chassaigne. So the duke camped; he had very many men on one side and the people of Auvergne who had plenty of men on the other. The first day the Duke of Bourbon had put equipment on carts, and those of Auvergne likewise, to whom the duke had shown the method; and the second day there was a great and strong assault, three times a day, in the way that one takes a place by full assault. The nephew of Jean D'Ussel was taken inside, the worst man that one could find, and who had done more evil deeds in the county of Auvergne, and who the Duke of Berry most desired to have, and for this the Duke of Bourbon made a present of him, so he was put in the tower of Riom. After this capture the Duke of Bourbon headed to Charlieu Champmaigois, which Berengon de Chirat held, and who freely surrendered to the Duke of Bourbon, and went to his own country. So the Duke of Bourbon delivered the whole country of Auvergne from the English, and gave it freely to the Duke of Berry who recognized great nobility in him and knew him for having a very great good will.

XXXVI. How the Duke of Bourbon prepared himself to go to Spain and for the first time to attempt a voyage to Granada.

At the beginning of the year of grace 1375, the Duke of Bourbon had delivered Auvergne from the enemies of the realm, concerning which he was accustomed in all of his deeds to praise God and he was very devoted to the Virgin Mary; and because of this after the taking of these places he went on a pilgrimage to Notre Dame d'Orcival, and there offered his pennon, which is there to this day, that which he had vowed to do when he first saw it planted on La Roche-Senadoire, because it was the closest place dedicated to the veneration of Our Lady, and there the duke founded a perpetual mass. Having made his offering he left and went to Ardes, towards the Count Dauphin who celebrated him very grandly and from Ardes went to Puy-Notre-Dame, where he had made a vow. He stayed at Puy on his pilgrimage, and already had remained two days for his devotions when there came to him an honorable herald on behalf of King Henri of Spain [=Castile][15] who carried letters for the Duke of Bourbon, the most beautiful which was ever able to be seen, whereas the said King Henri prayed and requested the duke that he should be pleased to come to Spain and that the duke should find good things there when he came. For the seigneurie of Bourbon had strongly aided him to conquer his realm, namely the Count de la Marche, who was of the blood and the arms of Bourbon: "And for the great renown, good chivalry, probity and wisdom which I have indeed heard of you, I send you my special herald Moniquot who will attest by my letters patent what my intention and my enterprise is, by the aid of God, to enter into Granada in the new season with all the strength of Spain, and I above all desire your company. Concerning this thing I pray you not to fail me; and if you please lead two or three hundred knights and squires, and I will promise that I will leave some of my goods all of which you may wish to take of them."

Duke Louis of Bourbon was very happy and joyous over this and it appeared to him that God had sent it when he saw something honorable to employ himself with in the new season. On this the Duke of Bourbon freed the herald of the king named Moniquot, gave him an escutcheon of his arms, and some rich robes of cloth of gold, and his device, and sent him on his way; and the duke wrote honorable letters by way of the said herald to the King of Spain: that by God's will, he would be in his presence by the end of May; and on this the duke returned to his country of the Bourbonnois and to put in order to make ready for his voyage. When the duke was in his country the King of France was most upset, and all his friends, concerning the voyage which he had planned, and the king ordered him and required strongly that he should not go at all. Concerning this the Duke of

---

15 Cabaret consistently refers to the kingdom of Castile in the Iberian peninsula as "Spain."

Bourbon responded to the king that he had written to the King of Spain by his herald that he would go there, that he had vowed to, and it was in the service of God, for through these letters he had seen the King of Spain hoped to make his way by conquest to the Saracen realm of Granada, and that he did not wish to lose this voyage. Then the Duke of Bourbon assembled his people go there in good order. When the season came and it was time to leave on the voyage, there came to him all those who had been levied in the town of Brioude, so that they should continue directly to Avignon. The Duke of Bourbon led a hundred knights and squires of his house and there were of those one hundred gentleman seven bannerets,[16] who were Sir Guichard Dauphin, Sir Griffon de Montagu, the lord of Châteaumorand, the lord of Rochefort, bastard de Bourbon, and Sir Lionnet d'Araines, de Beauvoisin, standing in the company which Duke Louis of Bourbon led with him.

16 A knight banneret, sometimes known simply as banneret, was a knight who led a company of troops during time of war under his own banner and heraldry.

XXXVII. How the Duke of Bourbon came to Avignon, visited the Pope, and continuing on his road was entertained by the King of Aragon; how King Henri of Spain made great cheer for him and how he returned because the voyage to Granada didn't take place.

Duke Louis of Bourbon contemplated the noble company of knights and squires who came to serve him and accompany him to Granada as his grace desired, and much rejoiced, and told them: "My lords, brothers and friends, please God, you with me, and me with you, going in his sacred service against the miscreants, which we all ought to enjoy. For we cannot have a better master: everything which we are doing should be done in his honor." Then the company replied: "Well said, my lord." Then they left from Brioude, the Duke of Bourbon and his company, to go to Avignon, and to be there on a certain day because Pope Gregory XI from the household of Beaufort wished to leave Avignon and go to Rome. So the duke rode out, and had two days before the Pope left. The Pope made great cheer to the Duke of Bourbon, and blessed him, gave him absolution from punishment and guilt for the voyage against the miscreants which he was making. The Duke of Bourbon led the Pope by his right hand on the bridle of the white destrier, from the palace just outside of Avignon along with the prefect of Rome, who was there in court. Outside of the gates, just as the Pope had told the duke to mount on the horse, which he did, and escorted him outside of Avignon, one league, where they spoke of many things together and having given leave the Pope gave his blessing to the duke who returned that same evening to sleep at Avignon. The next day the Duke of Bourbon with his people went by daily stages to Aragon where he found the king Don Jean, who much loved the minstrels, who received the duke so grandly in his city of Barcelona that it was marvelous, and that king prayed to the Duke of Bourbon that he would be pleased to be at the betrothal of his son, the Count Don Martin, and of the Countess de Luna, which was to be held on his road to Spain, at a castle named Mousson-des-hospitalars, halfway from Barcelona to Zaragoza. The duke agreed willingly and he went there and led the spouse; and the nuptials lasted three days, and on leaving the celebration, the Duke of Bourbon went to Notre Dame de Montserrat, which is a very devout and beautiful pilgrimage, then to Lerida, and the abbey of Popellet outside it, in which the kings of Aragon rested; and then to the royal city of Saragossa; leaving there Duke Louis passed Saragossa on the left hand and entered Spain and was encamped at San Domingo de la Caussade. The duke did not want to enter, because of the dissension which existed between the King of France and the King of Navarre. From San Domingo the duke went to the hospital of the queen, where everyone who passed as a pilgrim could have board for three days, and some money when they left. This is four leagues from Burgos. Then King Henri of Spain sent before him a good five hundred knights, and with this the man whom he loved best and who governed his business, named Peter Mace, together with a grand seigneur of Spain named Sir Peter Farrandon de Valasque, lord of Bruesque, who led the Duke of Bourbon to Burgos to King Henri, who summoned him before his closest friends and the grandees of his country, and received him, reveling greatly with those who were most happy in his vicinity. And Duke Louis of Bourbon remained at Burgos with King Henri for the space of ten days, and during this period the marriage of the sister of King Henri of Spain with the young King Charles of Navarre took place, and also there were the nuptials of the youthful heir of Spain, son of King Henri, to the daughter of the King of Aragon where there were great celebrations, according to the custom of that country, and four days having passed, the King of Spain prayed to the Duke of Bourbon that he should come to his castle of Segovia where he would see things which would please him, as well as the fine delight of the hunt.

And when King Henri and Duke Louis of Bourbon were at the castle of Segovia, the king led the duke to show off the young heirs [=*infantes*] of King Dom Pietro, whom he held in an iron cage, and there they had been put in the cage at the age of eight and at this time they already had been there twenty-eight years. Henri said to the Duke of Bourbon, "See there the children of the one who had your sister killed, and if you want to have them killed I will hand them over to you." To these words the Duke of Bourbon responded very shortly, "I would not willingly consent to their death for the willful evil of their father, since they were not able to do anything about it." And these words were heard by many knights and squires both Spaniards and French, who held it for great valiance. The next day King Henri hunted a bear in the vicinity of the castle of Segovia where he had great enjoyment in the hunt and great pleasure. Leaving the castle of Segovia the Duke of Bourbon asked, as a benefit from King Henri, for the freedom of a knight of Touraine, Guichard d'Angle, one of the best knights of the world, who for a long time had been there as a prisoner; and likewise for a squire, named Jacques Sadellier, which he was given out of Henri's good heart. When the King of Spain was at Burgos, it was announced to him that the King of Portugal had defied him, and was provoking him, for which it was convenient that his army withdraw from Granada, which caused great damage to him and to Christianity and great anger among the whole company. And seeing that the voyage would not take place, the Duke of Bourbon asked the King of Spain for leave to go. The king did not wish to grant it, and instead asked that he should seek out volunteers. So the duke responded to him that: "The enterprise of Granada is not taking place, the King of France has ascertained." For this reason, he had been ordered to leave at once, so that he might bring news with him within ten or twelve days. King Henri of Spain, seeing that the Duke of Bourbon could not bear to remain, gave him leave with great sorrow, pleading with him that he should work, out of love for him, to conciliate the young King of Navarre (who had his sister as his wife) with the King of France. So the duke told him that he would do what was in his power, and on his departure King Henri presented the Duke of Bourbon gold, silver and housewares, but of all this he wished to take nothing, other than some dogs known as Allans, figured leathers, and flocked carpets, and six beautiful horses—genets—indeed to each of the bannerets he gave a genet, and his order of the band. Thus, Duke Louis of Bourbon left King Henri of Spain, who prayed, that were he needed and were to be asked, he would return to him. So the duke rendered his salutations, and they parted good comrades, and went to visit the church of St. James in Compostella for a pilgrimage, then he returned to his country, and dismissed his people, thanking them profusely. And with the people of his house turned towards France where he found some tidbits of news; for the lord of Rivière had put dissension between the king and the good Constable, spreading rumors to the king that the Constable, Sir Bertrand de Claiquin, was in league with the Duke of Brittany; and all this Rivière did to make the lord of Clisson Constable.

XXXVIII. How the dukes of Anjou and Bourbon were not able to keep Constable Claiquin in the service of the king any longer.

This valiant knight, Sir Bertrand de Claiquin, whose chivalries and deeds were such that for his prowess he was Constable of France, was very unhappy about the words which people reported to him, and he had great sorrow because of it, for he was a knight of great heart and said: "Since the king holds me for suspicious who has served him loyally, I will not remain here in his realm, but I will go to Spain, where I have a very honorable life, for I am duke there, and I will return my sword to him." Because of this, there was a great clamor in the realm, which was a marvelous boon for the lord of Rivière; and so much did people come to hate this valiant knight, Sir Bertrand de Claiquin, and many grand seigneurs remonstrated to have him dismissed who had served him so well, as if he were a bad example for others! Charles[V], the King of France, learned of this, and, wishing to make amends, sent the dukes of Anjou and Bourbon to Brittany, to appease the constable's anger; and they went to Pont-Orson, and there summoned the constable, who came to them willingly. Having come there the Duke of Anjou said "Constable," he said, "My lord the king has sent us to you, me and my good cousin of Bourbon, because you have been disheartened by certain words attributed to you, namely that you have taken the part of the Duke of Brittany, but you should rejoice in the fact that, for his part, the king believes none of this. See there the sword of honor of your office: take it back up, the king wants it, and you can come with us." After this speech by the Duke of Anjou the good Constable answered: "My very respected lord, I thank you humbly for the words which you have given me and some words which you have also said, that the king does not believe at all, of which I thank the king despite the great fuss that has transpired. And I wish well, my lord, that the king should believe that I have served him well and loyally, as an honorable man, and with no treachery; for if I had served the Duke of Brittany who is against him, I would have been the traitor to him, who is the greatest king who now lives, and this little bit of honor which I have acquired in this world I would not like to lose for anything which lives. And say to the king that I love my own honor more than all of the lordships and goods which he is able to give me, and I assure him of that. So thank you for the sword which you have brought me. I can't take it back up again, give it to another who pleases him. For to remove his suspicion and everyone else's, I'm going to Spain and I swear to you by my faith that never again will I ever remain in this realm." This very much upset the Duke of Anjou, and he said to the constable: "Ha! ha! Good cousin, don't do that, and don't even think of it." And then the Duke of Bourbon spoke to him: "Good cousin constable, I pray you that you should not do what you have said. For my lord the king wishes you great good, and you have well deserved it, and you do him wrong to abandon him in this manner." And then the good Constable responded: "Ha! ha! My lord of Bourbon, I have been at your side throughout the great affairs of the kingdom, and you and I have chased said Duke of Brittany out of his country, so that he no longer has so much as a single castle; it is inconceivable that I would have allied to him. And to the fact that you ask me to stay, let me say that you are one of the lords of the kingdom who has most pleased me, and whom I would most willingly believe, and to whom I am most beholden after the king. But I swear to you and promise by my faith, that concerning that which I have said, you will not change my mind. I beg of you that you never forget the love you have always had for me, for wherever I shall be, I will serve you with might and main, and will never forget the joys you have brought me. And I pray that you remember the one who has conspired against me, for you know the deceptions he has done you, and continues to do. And I will tarry more than two months which I will spend in good company in your country, and you will see that I will not be leaving by myself." And then the Dukes of Anjou and Bourbon went to report to the king the words of his constable, who for no reason whatever could be persuaded to remain, so that the king was very upset and distressed. And, after the Duke of Anjou had spoken, the good Duke Louis of Bourbon said to the king, in the presence of all: "My lord, you have undergone today one of the greatest losses which has befallen you in a long time, for you have lost the most valiant knight and the greatest gentleman that I believe any have seen among his peers, and those who have brought this about have done a great wrong." At this, the speaker went quiet, and ceased to talk about the constable.

XXXIX. How the Constable Sir Bertrand left from Brittany in hopes of going to Spain, passed through the Bourbonnais, where the duke entertained him, and went past Chateauneuf de Randon, where he died, and kept the castle.

It came to pass in the year of grace 1389, that the good Constable Bertrand moved from the country of Brittany to leave the country and realm of France as he had told the dukes of Anjou and Bourbon; and for his good praise there appeared to serve and accompany him many barons and lords of many parties whom he thanked for this offer although he did not wish to lead them with him to carry out his march, outside of three hundred men-at-arms. His affair was well arranged, and he took to the road which would take him to Spain, and he and his company came to pass through Bourbonnois, where Duke Louis was, who entertained him grandly, and then imagined to convert him and keep him as he had great regret for his leaving; but the duke was not able to provide any remedy, and at his departure gave him a beautiful chalice of gold enameled with his arms and asked him of he would be willing to drink always from it for the love of him and he also gave him a beautiful belt of war, very rich, of his order of Hope which he put on his neck for which the constable thanked him and was very joyous. They took leave one from the other and the Duke of Bourbon gave him ten gentlemen of his household to conduct him for four days; of whom there were Jean de Châteaumorand (who carried the banner of the Duke of Bourbon) Gauvain, Michaille, Perrin d'Ussel, Sir Odin de Rollat, Champropin, the bastard of Glarains, the Borgne de Veaulce, and others. And these were the people that the constable loved the most of whom he knew; and they conveyed him to Puy-Notre-Dame, where the citizens asked him that for God's sake would he be willing to go before Chateauneuf-de-Randon, which was destroying the countryside, and that before he left the realm he should deliver it from the English; and that would be a praiseworthy memory of the good things which he had done. And after he had visited the church of Notre Dame and made his pilgrimage he spoke to the companions who were conducting him there: "My dear companions, brothers and friends, since we are not far from there, I pray you, accompany me there, and you will see what we will do. For, with God's blessing, we will have at them, lads, and if the sun can get in, so can we." At these words the companions laughed and said that they would accompany him with a good heart. They left from Puy, the constable with his company, and rode before Chateauneuf-de-Randon, where he placed a siege; but before it he had said to those of Puy: "My friends, this is the last English place which I know on the route I am following. Yet I vow to God, I will have it." When the constable had visited the place he put his siege in good order, and commanded those of Puy how they should supply the siege army with provisions, with artillery, and also with mangonels and other engines to throw inside: so they did it. There the constable sat for three weeks. There were some beautiful deeds of arms done at that siege, there were many of the seigneurs of Auvergne and of Velai, who willingly strove to deliver this place, and as assaults were made by those of the attacking army upon those of the castle for several days, seeing that they were not able to hold out any longer it happened that on the fifteenth day that the constable had besieged the castle he caught a malady from which he died; and the English, who were inside, seeing that there was no hope in their situation, but rather that in the long run they would be taken by force, surrendered themselves to the good constable. At that point they did not know that he was dead, and they went where it seemed to be good to them. So it was a great grace of God to the good constable that he never besieged a place but it surrendered itself to him, alive or dead. After Chateauneuf-de-Randon was surrendered, the death of the valiant and sturdy constable was known to the king, about whom (the constable) tears, cries, and lamentations came from his people and throughout the country. So the noble men of the Duke of Bourbon prepared and embalmed him. And they led him through Forez to Molins-en-Bourbonnais, where Duke Louis made for him a very solemn funeral in the church of Notre Dame, where at the first the duke had founded a college of canons perpetual. And before the duke had sent to King Charles news of the death of his good constable about which he was sorry. Because the king remembered some of the agreeable services which the Constable Sir Bertrand had done for him in his life he wished to recognize him after his death. For the king had ordained that after his decease the same constable should be buried honorably at his feet in St. Denis where the kings of France lie. Likewise, the good Marshal of Sancerre, who had served him loyally; it was so done, and they now lie together. And they did not stay long after that, the year following King Charles of France, fifth of his name, passed out of this world, who so valiantly and wisely had governed his realm; thus ended the year of grace of Our Lord 1380, and for this he was buried so highly in the royal tomb at St. Denis as belonged to such a prince; and the funeral lasted for fifteen days.

XL. How the princes and dukes of France of the royal blood led the young King Charles to be crowned at Reims, and concerning those who were sent to Nantes to guard it from the English.

In the year of grace 1381 the princes of the blood royal, the Duke of Berry, the Duke of Burgundy, and the Duke of Bourbon led the young King Charles, son of the deceased, to be crowned at Rheims and they hastened the ceremony because the English who had passed before Paris were going to Brittany, and for this reason they led the young king to Rheims where he had great chivalry and very fine feasts. And after the anointing was done the king sat at his high table of honor and directed the Duke of Bourbon who was peer and chamberlain of France, three of his knights, of whom one was to his right, another to his left, and a third behind his back, and also a squire at his feet; when the king was seated he held his feet in the lap of the squire. The three knights were Sir Guichart Daulphin, Sir Gui le Baveulx, and Sir Jean de l'Aye, and the squire who was under the table where the king held his feet was Jean de Châteaumorand; and such was their proper placement around the king. And in the evening, when the sun set, three riders came one after the other announcing to the king and his lords, that the power of the English which was a good seven thousand combatants had come before Nantes, where the Duke of Brittany should have stopped them. So there was great counsel between the lords and they ordered that Jean de Châteaumorand and Le Barrois, who had four hundred men-at-arms at the frontier of Pouencé, near Angiers, should lead their people before Nantes, and that they should hasten before the English came there and that they should ride night and day. So they did, and they were at Nantes first before the English by some three hours and Châteaumorand and Le Barrois went with their people to the new tower, of which the captain was Guillaume Leet, who let them in most willingly, and warned them to be careful. Just as the French entered in, they put at each of the four gates of the city twenty-five men-at-arms, and remained in the place in the middle of the city in good order, and they demanded from the said captains the keys of the gates, but they were unable to find a man who knew for a fact who held them. Then Guillaume Leet came to Châteaumorand, and said to him secretly in his ear: "Go into the church cathedral and take a grand villain, a rich and sleek old canon who is there, and I am sure that you will find on him the keys under his surplice. If you don't find them on him take him and put him outside." Châteaumorand and Le Barrois entered the church where they saw the old canon whom Guillaume Leet had told them about. They took him by the neck. The canon began to say "Ha, my seigneurs! Watch what you do, you will be excommunicated!" and they replied "Priest, give up the keys!" He in turn said that he didn't have them. Then they searched him and found on him the keys of the city, under his robe in a hunting purse. So they took the canon and led him to the companions who were in the place and said to them: "My seigneurs, be happy, for see here the traitor who had sold the city to the English, and concealed the keys." So he was regarded as an infamous one by the city; and then he was tied to a tree in his pourpoint (undershirt) without chaperon so that everyone could see him. Yet there was a great force of the English coming before Nantes, where they encamped all around in three places that is in Richebourg, in Saulsaye, and in the Fosse where one stored the salt. These are the three places on the land side, for they were not yet able to besiege the bridges, and there were many amazed that they had failed in their enterprise. So those who were in Nantes saw good order in them; that is to say two hundred men-at-arms of the guard in the place which is in the middle of the town and forty bowmen and twenty-five men on horse to watch all around the city, and twenty-five arbalestiers; and, by day, there were in the place a hundred men-at-arms, and fifty bowmen and the gates well supplied. When this was done, Châteaumorand and Le Barrois sent back a messenger to tell the king how they had recovered the city of Nantes and the arrangements which they had made there.

With the passing of Charles V, Charles VI the Well beloved, also known as the Mad, came to the throne of France. Maunscript painting attributed to the Mazarine Master. Wikimedia Commons, public domain.

A 17th century depiction of Louis II of Bourbon. The duke wears correct, if poorly depicted, armor for the 1380s. Wikimedia Commons, public domain.

XLI. How Sir Pierre de Bueil d'Anjou came to Nantes and joined the Duke of Bourbon's men.

The uncles of the newly crowned young King of France, when they heard that Nantes was well garrisoned by their people, were very happy and for that they saw the requests of those who held it to be reasonable, so they approached the king and told him that there was good need that those holding Nantes should have help and aid for they were besieged by a great army. To which answered the king replied: "My good uncles, you know better than I what this amounts to. Make whatever arrangements about it which please you." Then the lords advised that it was best to send the lord of Clisson, who at the sanctification of the king had been made Constable of France, to whom they said how Châteaumorand and Le Barrois ascertained that the English were encamped in three siege-camps so that the one was not able easily to succor the other, and if he arrived there with a sufficient force, great things could be done. For this the lords said to the Constable of Clisson that he should promptly disburse funds to enlist men. Finally, Le Barrois and Châteaumorand had petitioned the Duke of Bourbon, their lord (for they were of his country and his house), for similar arrangements, requesting that he should send them their companions, those of his house, for there could be none more honorable. So the Duke of Bourbon complied with their request, and quickly had his men leave his house for their destination, to the number of sixty men-at-arms, and he retained but two squires for his service. As long as the lord of Clisson "mulled this over," as they say, a knight of Anjou and a very valiant man, named Sir Pierre de Bueilh, found people everywhere willing to go to Nantes in aid of the French who were besieging it, and were already at Angiers with two hundred men-at-arms. So they sent to him to seek out Châteaumorand and Le Barrois, to come soon, and that they should put him surely and his people among the bridges in front of the city of Nantes. They came as they had ordered him, and to this knight, named Sir Pierre de Bueilh, when he was in the city and his people lodged, and his horses sent off, they consulted together, Châteaumorand and Le Barrois and him, as it appeared to them to be a good thing to do, for Bueilh had scrutinized the castle, as the lord of Cusenton, Englishman, who was lodged in front of the castle had the arrangement of the watch. In their lodges he did not have a good arrangement and he sallied out against them and struck them with great damage. The lord of Bueilh wished that he could strike them back just as much: but the others were not willing to, for they awaited their companions from their lord's household, the Duke of Bourbon's, saying that when they had come they should try to inflict harm to the English. So the companions came from there in two days and meanwhile they watched for where they could attack them.

XLII. How the people occupying Nantes for the King of France fought against the English.

Day and night, the men-at-arms sent to Nantes for the King of France, together with the Duke of Bourbon and Sir Pierre de Bueilh, and they did not cease to think how they could harm the English who besieged them. So it happened one day, that all of the company of the Duke of Bourbon and the lord of Bueilh then residing at the castle went out and they went to attack the English guard of Sir Estienne de Cusanton, who was in lodgings at Saulsaye, around Matins, during the changing of the guard. The French charged into them, there being a good hundred and fifty English men-at-arms, and as many French, and of those who were encountered, one party of the English was taken and the other fled. They held captive the captain Sir Estienne de Cusanton, one of the most valiant knights of England, and thirty-six men-at-arms of his; and there were a good sixty killed. They were deployed throughout the buildings well in advance. The English put themselves in battle order before, which profited them little, for the companions pushed them inside and freely led away from Nantes their prisoners, and sixty horses of carriage; and they gained there some good equipment and this was the first sally they made from Nantes. Before the camp of the Hainaulters who were at the other gate, they had valiant men; that is to say the lord of Vertains, the canon of Robessart, Thierry de Semain, the bastard of Vertains, and Maubeuge's children, a good three hundred combatants [in all], placed behind ditches and within strong bourgeois houses. They started a mine, because the Hainaulters are by custom good miners, and they mined well for the space of ten days, so the French counter-mined in the opposite direction. These mines came so close that one was able to converse with the other. As the mining continued, it happened that the day was Christmas Eve and some of those from Nantes had taken a man, a Gascon, who told the French captains how the Hainaulters did not intend to do anything that night except play dice in the house of the lord of Vertains. They were instructed to open the gate that was near them, so that they could go in and fight, and so it was done. And on this Christmas Eve at midnight the companions from Nantes, who were a good seven hundred combatants, struck heartily at the camp of the Hainaulters, who were enjoying themselves at dice and they defeated them and spoiled them and there were killed Thierry de Semain, and one of the younger sons of Maubeuge, and the bastard of Vertains and a good sixty men-at-arms, and they took twenty-six good prisoners. Among those who were killed of the insiders was Macé des Ymaiges, and there Sir Tristan de Jaille and Pierre de Sury of the house of the Duke of Bourbon, and Robert Guy were taken; and the Hainaulters retreated into a high house for safety and their camp was overrun and there were many of the Duke of Bourbon's men wounded but all was gained and thus went the day. So the companions retreated inside Nantes: for this time, they didn't go any further and the next day they recovered their prisoners for others, and their mine was broken about which they did not do any more on this side. After four days the Marshal of Savoy Sir Boniface de Chalant wrote some letters to Châteaumorand and Le Barrois, who received him in their company, for he had thirty men-at-arms, gentlemen, and because they knew him to be a good knight they sent to inquire and there was a good company inside the town. Sir Boniface having come, they resolved to inform the lord of Bueilh, Châteaumorand, Sir Le Barrois and the others who had led, how they had been able to do damage to the camp of the Earl of Buckingham, chief and principal captain of those people who were lodged before the gate in Richebourg, and he had made his barrier out of two wagons because when the English saw them open the gate they pulled back just to their barrier and when they did not open it they stationed themselves in their house to shoot. So they advised one day that those inside should make a mine under the gate so that the English could not see them lower the bridge and that they and their people would be able to hide in the ditches without being seen by the others. So it was done, and one day after dinner, four hundred men-at-arms and three hundred good arbalestiers of the garrison of Nantes were pushed into their pits and trenches, by means of an ambush and they lowered the bridge and made to sally out a hundred men-at-arms feigning an intended skirmish at the barrier, as would be customarily expected. Just as the English came to their barrier and to their wagons to chase those men-at-arms inside the gate, and the French sallied out in an ambush from the ditches against the English, who were four hundred men-at-arms and the hundred arbalestiers who they drove back outside of their barrier and well ahead in the road, where six bannerets of the English were killed and many others; and the English bannerets were Sir Hue Suverin, Sir Guillaume Clinton, Sir Jehan Burley, Sir Fitz Watier, Sir Jehan Franc, and Sir Thomas Trivet. There were many well wounded among the garrison, but none of them died and none but Robert Gui de Riom was taken; and when he had been disarmed the English who were unhappy about their loss did not take themselves to guard him; so Robert Gui left them and took himself to the ditches and went in there with his companions, who began to laugh. Then the English were much discomfited by the deaths of their barons and their people who they had lost in the skirmishes which they did not know what to do about. A malady of diarrhea arose and went from bad to worse in their army, which much disemboweled them: for great numbers of their people died of this disease; and they had held the siege before Nantes from vintage time up until Christmas which had lasted three months and twenty days.

XLIII. How the Earl of Buckingham removed himself from Nantes, and how the fifteen English did not perform their arms with fifteen of the French.

Charles, King of France, in honor of his coronation, made many knights, many of whom he had in Nantes, and they and their companions greatly held up against the English. The Earl of Buckingham who saw the infirmity of his people and that he had no profit anymore from holding his siege before Nantes, had planned to leave for this reason; but he delayed some, because fifteen men-at-arms of the house of the Duke of Bourbon had proposed a battle on an island near Nantes against fifteen other English men-at-arms, from the house of the Earl of Buckingham, to fight to the end, and that there should be no judges but only two heralds, one from France and one from England. This thing was promised and sworn but the English defaulted as you will hear. This enterprise cost the Duke of Bourbon three thousand francs in harness and equipment which he ordered for his people, every day, for the space of three weeks; and the fifteen who were of the house of the Duke of Bourbon did not fail to require the English to hold this battle, but the English sent them some well-chosen words and said: "Wait, wait, we will tell you in good time." About this the Earl of Buckingham seeing that he was losing many of his Englishman to diarrhea, and one evening broke camp with all of his people, and in the next day in the evening the fifteen Englishmen sent by a herald to the fifteen French of the house of the Duke of Bourbon that they were not at all able to hold that battle then, but they wished to go to Vannes, where their master the earl had gone and accomplish then their arms. The Duke of Bourbon's fifteen gave no other response but to say to the herald that if the Duke of Brittany wished to give them good security that they should do and accomplish them there. They left the siege of Nantes without gaining any profit, the Earl of Buckingham and his Englishman rode to Vannes. After them the French captains sallied forth, Sir Jean de Châteaumorand, Sir Le Barrois, Sir Pierre de Bueilh, and the Marshal of Savoy, who were eight hundred men-at-arms, who skirmished and kept close to the English, and gained much from their carriage before they got to Vannes. The French withdrew to castle Joslyn, where the lord of Clisson the new Constable of France had come, and those of the garrison of Nantes demanded leave to go so they could return to their masters. The constable refused, and asked them that they should wait for the English to embark and at that time the fifteen of the house of the Duke of Bourbon who were returned to Nantes in their station with the others sent to the fifteen English that they were prepared to accomplish their promise and that they should send to them good assurance from the Earl of Buckingham their master and from the Duke of Brittany and then they would come willingly. So a herald carried the safe conducts to Sir Jean de Châteaumorand, to Sir Le Barrois, and to their companions, and that with them they were able to leave forty gentlemen to accompany them, and they willingly received the safe conducts believing that the fifteen Frenchmen would certainly not come; but notwithstanding the safe conducts the fifteen sent Cordellier de Gironne, a squire of the personal squires of the King of France, for the assurance of the Earl of Buckingham and the Duke of Brittany who brought it and the fifteen companions went with Cordellier to Vannes to the Duke of Brittany and to the Earl of Buckingham who was there and notified them that those who had made a promise were come all ready to accomplish it the next day after mass.

XLIV. How five noble Frenchmen performed arms at Vannes, against five noble Englishmen and what happened.

The Earl of Buckingham, seeing that this was in earnest had great counsel with the Duke of Brittany about what should be done. The response which the Earl of Buckingham made was that his people were not up to the mark, and it had been a year since he left England and also that he and his people had been at siege before Nantes for three months, for which reason their harness was very deteriorated. For this reason he was not in favor of performing arms especially to extremities but he had thought to give his advice to some of his servants that if there was any from the household of the Duke of Bourbon who wished to perform specified arms, to this he agreed willingly. So the companions of the agreement were much amazed and infuriated thinking that they would not fight at all. So they decided that they should not hold the agreed-on combats but it would be good to do something of the sort for which they had come and they should take what the English were offering. The arms which the English wished to do were five blows of the lance, five of the sword, five of the axe, five of the dagger, all on foot; but the next day early in the morning there were only five Englishmen who wished to perform arms and from the Duke of Bourbon's men another five: namely Jean de Châteaumorand, Sir le Barrois, the bastard of Glarains, the Viscount of Aunay, Sir Tristan de la Jaille; and the five English were Sir Walter Cloppeton, Edward de Beauchamp, Sir Thomas de Hennefort, Brisselai, and Sir Jehan de Traro. All the companions standing on the field where the Duke of Brittany and the Earl of Buckingham were accompanied by their people, the first to perform arms from the French was Jean de Châteaumorand against Walter Cloppeton, an Englishman, of which they were not able to do more than three blows of the lance on foot, for Sir Walter Cloppeton was wounded right through by the lance between the lames and the piece, and it passed through as he fell to the earth and of those two there were only these three blows, for Cloppeton was carried off. Sir Le Barrois, who was armed, entered the field to perform arms against his companion, Thomas de Hennefort, who entered the field likewise and they did their five blows with the lance very chivalrously; and when it came to swords, when they attacked at the first blow of the sword Le Barrois wounded the Englishman between the piece and the gardebras and damaged the mail and pierced the shoulder completely so that it was necessary to lead off the Englishman without doing more arms. Then came the bastard of Glarains and Edward Beauchamp and when it came to combat with lances Edward Beauchamp turned his shoulder a little and in such a way that the bastard of Glarains twice knocked him to the ground with two blows of the lance, notwithstanding that he was large of body and a good gentleman; and then the Englishmen said that Beauchamp was *dronch*, that is to say, drunk. They picked him up and led him away. Then Sir Tristan de la Jaille approached his English companion and they accomplished all of their arms up to the axes; and when it came time to attack Sir Tristan knocked down his Englishman with the second axe blow, and badly wounded him and that was that. The Viscount d'Aunay came into the field to his companion who performed his arms beautifully, but the viscount wounded the Englishmen with last blow of the lance, between the avant-bras and the gardebras, and pierced the arm right through, so that he did no more. So were the arms accomplished that day in which the five noble men, the French companions, had the better of it, and the five noble Englishmen the worse as you have seen above.

XLV. How when the arms had been accomplished Sir Guillaume Farrington, an Englishman and Jean de Châteaumorand fought and what happened; and how the knight was put in prison and how Châteaumorand said some fine words.

The Duke of Brittany and the Earl of Buckingham, who had seen these arms, retired to their houses, and the French disarmed themselves; and because it was almost night the Duke of Brittany sent one of his knights, the maître d'hôtel, to summon them to supper with him. They conceded the point to him as they had been in his city and all those who had performed arms came to supper and the Duke of Brittany highly honored them, making them all sit at his table and serving them very grandly. On the removal of the table came a knight, fair and grand, named Guillaume Farrington, who urged Châteaumorand to perform arms that Sir Walter Cloppeton, his cousin germain, had hardly been able to accomplish. So Châteaumorand agreed with him if it pleased the Duke of Brittany, but the duke did not wish to allow it and it infuriated him most feloniously against his English knight, who had come to make demands at his table. But Châteaumorand begged so much to the Duke of Brittany that the next day at sunrise he was armed in the field against the one who had demanded it, to accomplish this, and more which he had not demanded, because it was necessary for his companions to mount up the next day. When they were together in the field the English knight had no armor at all on his legs for he had a disease in one knee, on account of which he was not able to arm himself there, and they sent via Cordellier de Gironne to urge Châteaumorand that they should not have more armor on the legs and they should guarantee not to strike at uncovered areas. This having been done the two knights in the field struck lances and with that stroke did their duty well; at the second blow they came strongly together, and the Englishman, Sir Guillaume, struck Sir Jean de Châteaumorand on the arms and Châteaumorand struck the Englishman under the cincture and so much so that Sir Guillaume Farrington fell to one knee, and put a hand to the ground; and with the third blow of the lances they came in contact strongly against each other but when it came to the clash Sir Guillaume lowered his lance and crouched a little from which he pierced Sir Jean de Châteaumorand right through the thigh, and it was advisable to carry him to his lodging; on account of this blow there was a great cry from the company present seeing that the English knight had promised not to make an attempt by arms on uncovered areas, especially in the legs. Then the Duke of Brittany and the Earl of Buckingham, who had seen this impropriety, had the Englishman Sir Guillaume taken, and disarmed to his little pourpoint and went to have him hurled in prison. And they said to le Barrois cousin germain of Châteaumorand: "Go to

Châteaumorand and tell him that we are very unhappy and indeed infuriated that this knight has failed to do what he had promised and we are delivering him to Châteaumorand to be his prisoner, to put him to such ransom as pleases him and if Châteaumorand dies you together with his friends can do what you like to that knight." This was considered very just on the part of the lords to maintain their sureties and safe conducts. So Châteaumorand heard the response from Le Barrois and Cordellier de Gironne, to which Châteaumorand answered that he thanked heartily the Earl of Buckingham and the Duke of Brittany for the good reason and justice which he found in their lordships and that he would prefer that Farrington had damaged his honor over him than that he, Châteaumorand, should have damaged his over Farrington. "When you inform me that he ought to be my prisoner I thank you humbly. Please know that when we came from our side before you to perform arms with your surety and safe conduct neither my companions nor I came motivated by avarice nor covetousness and it would turn to my dishonor to wish take ransom from your knight; for that reason I beg you to let him out of prison and do what you please, for the deed of arms involves risk. You well know that Sir the Duke of Bourbon to whom we belong gives us what we need and he, who sends us out in the world to acquire honor, would be discontented with this covetousness." The Englishmen and the Bretons found these words to be very honorable and the Earl of Buckingham sent to Châteaumorand a golden goblet and 150 nobles; but Châteaumorand returned the gold coins to him, letting him know that he had enough money for his affairs. He kept the goblet to drink from for the sake of his honor. At that time Châteaumorand told his companions that they should not delay riding back on his account, for he did not think himself in such bad shape that he could not follow their trot. Then the French left from Vannes, and they went to castle Joslyn, and the English departed and went to the castle of Ermine to embark on their voyage. For the six thousand combatants who were to disembark and come before Nantes they could not find more than three thousand at the castle of l'Ermine to embark. The Duke of Bourbon's men at castle Joslyn took their leave from the Constable Clisson so they could go to their lord, but he still did not wish to give them leave, for he much feared a big dispute which was simmering between the Duke of Brittany and the Count of Penthièvre: for the Count of Penthièvre had espoused the daughter of the lord of Clisson so the Duke of Bourbon's men said to the constable that nothing would suffice but that they should go to their master. When the constable saw this he prayed much to the captains that they should leave their people with him and go to the Duke of Bourbon their lord themselves. So they did it, and the captains went to Paris to the Duke of Bourbon their master who saw them most gladly and feasted them as one ought to do to such men who are accustomed to do good things.

XLVI. How the Duke of Bourbon took on the responsibility for the king and the Duke of Berry for the second time to go and fight in Poitou and how he had Taillebourg.

When the Duke of Bourbon's men were with him they found that at this hour some Poitevins had come to the king and the Duke of Berry, that is to say the lord of Partenay, the lord of Poulsauges, the lord of Torsay, and the lord of Couhe to request from the king and Duke of Berry that they should be willing to give aid and succor, for all of Poitou was destroyed by five or six places which the English had: primarily Taillebourg, a beautiful castle and seaport, Bourg-Charente, Le Faon, Monleun, and Vertueil. So the Duke of Berry who was Count of Poitou asked the Duke of Bourbon, because of his blood-tie, that he would be pleased to take this commission. So he, the Duke of Bourbon, was not willing to undertake that, saying to the Duke of Berry that it was too great a thing for him, that he lacked the money and that the castles were very strong for he knew it well. To which the Duke of Berry responded to him: "Good cousin, don't you worry about finance, for you see here these barons of Poitou who asked for you so strongly from the king and from me; and at your coming they will establish a tax which will amount to sixty thousand francs." To this responded a good man, a clerk who managed the affairs of the Duke of Berry, and then was bishop of Clermont, who said to the Duke of Bourbon: "My lord, take heartily this commission and you will not lack silver, for when you assemble your troops, give me two men of your household, a knight and a man of finance and you will find the money that is reckoned due you, that is to say the sum of sixty thousand francs." The Duke of Bourbon said to the Duke of Berry that he was willing to do his pleasure, but he was not able to do this without the knowledge of the king, and permission to leave. So the Duke of Berry immediately went to the king and asked him that he should be pleased to give license to the Duke of Bourbon to go into Poitou. So the king was content with this and the Duke of Bourbon then ordered Châteaumorand as the knight, and Seguin, his treasurer, to go to Poitou, to raise that tax, and the Poitevins were very happy when they knew that the Duke of Bourbon was coming to Poitou. So they raised their hearth tax, which was done in three weeks, and the Duke of Bourbon whose men were battle-ready took to the road to Poitou, where they formed, together with those in Poitou, what was a fine chivalry of six hundred men-at-arms. Having done the muster of his people and the Poitevins he went before Taillebourg, the best castle of Poitou, and he lodged the Poitevins beside the river, and the duke lodged himself up high with his engines, and the equipment which those of Poitou had made, which shot day and night against the castle; but those within the castle, a great number of men, often launched skirmishes against the Poitevins, especially at the times they needed to get water for themselves and their horses, of which they would have none if they could not take it from the river.

Seeing the way that those of the castle held on, the Duke of Bourbon ordered one day that three hundred men-at-arms led by Blain Loup, who was Marshal of Bourbonnais and a valiant knight, should go lodge with the Poitevins in their tents and pavilions, they in turn would pounce upon them from the tents and give them chase as far the bailey, depriving them of the water. And so they did. The morning following the night in which this ambush was set up, the skirmish began. Those in the castle charged out strongly against the Poitevins, but the men that the Duke of Bourbon had positioned there emerged from the tents in full attack, under orders to break said skirmish, to enter the bailey, block the door, and deny them passage, thus depriving them of water. So they did. Each one of the Bourbonnois willingly followed the pennon which Châteaumorand carried, and they did their duty well. And the lord of Beauvoir, Sir Blain Loup the marshal, Bliomberis his brother, Sir Robert de Vendat, Sir Ouldray de la Forest, Tachon de Glene, Guichart le Brun all behaved so joyfully and they did things so well, that some beautiful arms were performed there. So the English were broken and from those in the castle there died seventeen English, and of the Poitevins two men and the constable was taken from within by Sir Blain Loup, whom one called Bertrannet de Lirisson, and they gained the low court and the tower of the bridge, because of which they were not able anymore to have water, about which there was great joy in the army. For one saw well that without water they would not be able to hold out at all. But nevertheless those of the castle held out for three days, and at the end of the three days they made their treaty by which they were all allowed to go free with their horses and their harness, and they surrendered the castle. The Duke of Bourbon did not want to agree to this at all, without the agreement of the seigneurs of Poitou, of which he sent to inquire and had counsel with them and he asked them "Good seigneurs, how does this matter of the treaty appear to you?" They responded to the duke, "By God my lord, we ask you by no means not to refuse it, for this castle is the key of Poitou, and a seaport, a place from which more bad things can come, for the English are able to enter from the sea without danger to their people." At that time the Duke of Bourbon ordered Sir Guillaume de Neullac, and Sir Jehan de l'Aye, and Sir Blain Loup, his marshals, to have them evacuated according to the treaty, and the duke gave the castle of Taillebourg to Sir Guillaume de Neullac to guard, in the name of the king and the Duke of Berry.

XLVII. How the Duke of Bourbon had the Bourg-Charente, le Faon where le Cordelier was hanged, and Montleun where they had a very bad time.

After Taillebourg surrendered, the Duke of Bourbon decamped with his people and the Poitevins, in great joy and happiness, and they said "Praise be to God, see this good beginning"; and they went before Bourg-Charente, a very good castle, which belonged to the lord of Roche-Foucault. So the castle was besieged on all sides; they remained there before it besieging it for eleven days and during the said eleven days some ingenious strategy was used. For there were some in the garrison who were from the country and they sometimes came out to the army to speak to their friends and there was one who had his cousin germain there. So the Duke of Bourbon said to those who had friends in the castle that he would pardon them of all wrongdoing, and in addition give all four of them a hundred francs each, if they would enter through a tunnel by night, and meet with those within who would combine with them, and assure them that they might leave by the tunnel without fear, and that this was to be told in good faith, after which they would be led out without fear of harm. All these things were promised them. So the four returned to the castle, and at that convenient hour, they filled the well with dogs which they killed that night and with earth, ordure and other putrid things, so that those inside had no water, and the English in the castle were most embarrassed as those who have been betrayed, and they wished to make a treaty with Sir Guillaume de Neullac, with whom they were well acquainted, that, by God, should withdraw securely, and that the place should be surrendered to the lord of Roche-Foucault. So Sir Guillaume de Neullac did that, as he was kinsmen of the lord of La Roche, who supplicated the Duke of Bourbon concerning it: so Bourg-Charente was taken. The Duke of Bourbon and the Poitevins left there, and they went before a place called le Faon, which did not have any enclosed ditches, to supply water. So the place was strongly assailed, and it was not taken that day, excepting only the low court, where there were many good men wounded; for there was a Franciscan who performed marvels of shooting from a rock thrower, to the point that he killed four gentlemen, and people said that he was the strongest arbalestier in Poitou, and he was armed. The next morning the Poitevins and Bourbonnois assailed the dungeon, and there was a fierce assault and strong one, and those of the fort defended themselves, and the Franciscan was shooting, but the French took it in the way in which one is able to do by a good assault and so many of the men inside were killed with the exception of the Franciscan arbalestier who had taken his habit and had fled to his monastery. Then the whole army demanded to know where the Franciscan was; so he was revealed to be in the church on his knees before the altar. Then Sir Jean Roye ran to that place, because the Franciscan had killed one of his squires with his shooting, and he took the Franciscan in his habit and went to hang him from a tree, concealing himself so that the Duke of Bourbon did not know about it. The Duke of Bourbon left Le Faon and went before a fine town and strong castle named Montleun, where the duke established his siege, him and all his people, in a manner which no one was able to attack. The duke remained there three days before the city, to make some good preparations to attack it, and three days having passed it was assailed on all sides, and he took this town by assault. The duke had all of his army lodge inside, and put a great guard all around the castle which was strong and sat upon a rock. The Duke of Bourbon ordered that all of the artillery of Poitou be sought out, for he was advised that one would be unable to take the castle without batteries of engines. So it happened that the fifth day after that the Duke of Bourbon had taken the city of Montleun, and as yet awaited his engines, suddenly out of the skies there came a tempest which commenced between Vespers and sunset, so bad that it was a torrent instead of drops, for there were marvelous thunder, and massive lighting flashes which struck terror. Afterwards there was very great wind as great as any ever seen, so horrible that it knocked houses down, rendering them uninhabitable, and at two o'clock in the morning hailstones fell, of such tremendous size that they knocked down trees in the woods and flattened the grain in the fields. In this tempest were killed more than a hundred horses of the duke's men, and some pages by the houses whose stones fell on them. So it happened from this terrible tempest that at the castle which was situated on high ground, there remained no trimmings, awnings or coverings which had not fallen, so too a large portion of the wall had fallen, so that those inside were fearful and dismayed. It was proposed to those within that they should surrender, to which they responded defiantly that it seemed to them that even if all the walls were knocked down, the place could not be taken. So the Marshal of the Bourbonnois answered that, since they would not yield to reason and surrender the fort, he would venture no further talk of treaty, and so if they were taken there should be such punishment that others should take it for an example. For the Duke of Bourbon would have them all hanged by the neck. After the Marshal said this there was a great division among them so that inside of three hours, they came to request the treaty. So the Duke of Bourbon ordered them to take heed of that which he wished to say: The conditions that those in the castle required were that they should freely leave with their persons, their horses, their harnesses and that they could bring with them all the goods that were within, and that they would have two days grace to bring them out. This was reported to the Duke of Bourbon who sent it to the council of the knights of Poitou, who said to the duke: "My lord, by God take the treaty and let them go, for this is one of the most perilous places in Poitou, seeing that it sits but a dozen leagues from Bordeaux. We never would have been rescued from it if not by you. My lord, we beseech you that before the treaty is made, let them with dignity collect their foodstuffs, for we need you to send people to guard it at our expense and supply it well." So the Duke of Bourbon responded to them: "You ask that I send there under the castle garrison at your expense and that you will supply it well. But if I allow the taking of the foodstuffs perchance, before you will have provisioned it, those from Bordeaux could have removed it. For that reason, without exception, I do not wish that they take any foodstuffs from there." So Marshall of the Bourbonnois, Sir Jean de l'Aye, responded to the companions how it was, that the duke wished that they should not take any foodstuffs but that they should depart from there themselves, with their horses and harness, about which they were happy; and by this the castle of Montleun was delivered; and the Duke of Bourbon sent the garrison inside at the request of the Poitevins, and gave the place to be guarded to Bouteillier, in the name of the Duke of Berry.

XLVIII. How the Duke of Bourbon besieged Vertueil, and how the mine was ordered to be made there.

Because the strongest place was yet to be delivered, it appeared to the Duke of Bourbon, that he had not done anything, if he did not take the place called Vertueil. He went to besiege it with a noble company of Bourbonnois, Poitevins, and Frenchmen. It was one of the most beautiful places and the strongest which anyone may see, and it sat on a high rock; and there were inside fourscore men-at-arms, Englishmen and Gascons, and a good fifteen arbalestiers; and the captain of this castle of Vertueil was a young Gascon squire named Bartholomew de Montprivat, a man of great enterprise, who was not present there at all. At the siege with the Duke of Bourbon were the Sire de Parthenai, the Sire de Poulsauges, and the Sire de Torsay, Sir Gui de Cousant, Sir Renaud de Roye, Sir Robert de Chaslust, Sir Gaultier de Passac, Le Borgne[17] de Veaulce, Sir Boucicault, L'Hermite de la Faye, his marshals, Sir Jean de l'Aye and Sir Blain Loup, Châteaumorand, Sir Renaud de Bressolles, Sir Jean de Tilly, Sir Robert de Damas, who in his time carried the banner of the Duke of Bourbon, Sir Pierre de Fontenoi, Guichard Le Brun, Bertier de Nasselles, Tachon de Glené, which for his good customs people called "the good bailli of the Bourbonnois." And Michaille was there, and others in great numbers. Thereupon, the Duke of Bourbon and his men set up camp on one side, and the Poitevins on the other, and when they were installed in this way, the Duke of Bourbon consulted with the seigneurs of Poitou and their counsellors at that very place, asking them by which manner one should overcome it, whether by ladders or by mine. Despite this, the duke went about the place on horseback, having been well advised, and it appeared to all that it could not be taken in any way but by mine. And to this advice, the Duke of Bourbon responded that to him it appeared to him to be truly said. "But good seigneurs," said the duke, "this mine will need to be cut very long, through rock, and will be very costly, we will have to stay a long time until it is finished." The seigneurs of Poitou responded: "My lord, for God's sake, what with all the good things that you have done for us, you needn't fear that you won't have this place before you leave. It is the most dangerous place which exists in these marches, for its garrison before you arrived was constantly raiding Couhé and Poitiers, and could destroy everything if it remained uncaptured." And then the Duke of Bourbon went to visit the place where he would make the mine, and sent two captains to oversee the same mine, each one having ten men-at-arms under him. These captains were the lord of Torsay and Le Borgne de Veaulce, who brought equipment and a great deal of construction materials to the front of their mine, which was quickly begun. And, in order to be

17 "Borgne" was an obscure title.

better prepared for the strategy, the Duke of Bourbon sent one of his marshals, Sir Blain Loup, with a good hundred men-at-arms, before the gate of the castle, for within there were a great number of people. The mining took six weeks before it was entirely dug, and those in the castle countermined strongly against them. And during the three weeks which the Duke of Bourbon was there, the king sent him three messages, each saying that he should let it all go and come before him, because the king had learned that the King of England was attempting to take the seacoast castle at Écluse[18] in Flanders, which Philip, Duke of Burgundy (the uncle of the King of France) had rebuilt in order to guard the port of entry to the realm in that area. And all the more the Englishmen coveted the city of Écluse, if they were able to have it, to hold it in their guard and subjection like Calais. And to accomplish their intention, the English had sent a great army by sea to Écluse, under the captaincy of a young English knight named Sir Jaques d'Andellée, who zealously carried out the commands of the king his lord. And the King of France, fearing that the castle and town of Écluse might be taken by his enemies, seeing as that the Flemings were not in good accord with the count Louis of Flanders (who was wed to the daughter of Duke Philip of Burgundy), desired to go there in person and remedy the situation. Therefore, the king commanded the Duke of Bourbon, who held the siege before Verteuil, with these words: "You know, good uncle, that if Écluse should be taken, this would be the destruction of our realm: for this reason we do not wish you to fail, and come immediately." And God knows that the Duke of Burgundy, on whom this matter touched, should hasten to the king.

18 Called "Sluys" in English sources.

XLIX. How the Duke of Bourbon was unhappy about leaving this siege of Vertueil, and for this reason sent his excuses to the king.

The Duke of Bourbon, who at great cost and effort, had faithfully held siege before Vertueil, in order to honorably take it, hearing said news from the king, was preoccupied and thoughtful, and he called to his private knights and servitors, and to them he said "You see here one of the great dilemmas which I have for a long time endured. For this touches my honor in two ways; first if I leave this place, I leave to my great dishonor; and if I do not obey my lord the king some people will be able to say that this is badly done. Concerning these things, I have many thoughts and not at all without cause." Further the duke said to his knights, from whom he was taking counsel: "Here is my thought concerning this matter: if it seems good to you and most honorable, at my advice I will send two knights to my lord the king, to show him that I have a great desire to accomplish his commands and to tell him that I have great sadness and displeasure if I go from this city and castle of Vertueil so shamefully, which touches strongly on my honor." And to carry out this ambassadorship, Sir Jean de Châteaumorand and L'Hermit de la Faye went from the Duke of Bourbon to the king in Paris, and conveyed to the king their lord's regrets.

Concerning this the king took well their coming; and in the king said to them that he needed his uncle the Duke of Bourbon to come to him, letting go of all his business. The two knights responded to the king: "Sire, you know that it would be dishonor for this lord if he should leave this place without taking it; and also he has not got the wherewithal to lead the Poitevins, who are great in number. So you advise what is to be done; for the Poitevins have at their expense made war of which my lord your uncle, the Duke of Bourbon, is chief." And the knights said to the king to make a delay, in order that their lord, the Duke of Bourbon, should accomplish his affairs in taking the castle of Verteuil and that he should be able to come honorably before the king. So the king answered to the knights: "Ha ha dea! He will not stay away because of money! Before you leave, I will send the finances by you to my good uncle, with which he will be able to come." So the knights were overjoyed by the king's response, which quickly they sent to the duke at his siege of Vertueil, and that he should hasten as much as he was able to take the place, for they had learned from the king how necessary it was that they should return. But as much as the knights had done for the king, the duke had to wait three weeks for the money which the king had said that he would send, that is, fifteen days before it was disbursed, and eight days before it would reach his hands. But the knights said to him: "Hasten to finish your work, so that when we get there, you can come with us." The Duke of Bourbon having heard the report from his knights, and doubled the number of workers to finish the mine, it transpired that when the knights came to the siege, at its completion, they related to the duke how the king and the Duke of Burgundy had left Paris, and were able now to be at Écluse, to oppose the English army, which had landed there. And as the knights had sent to the duke to come to him, he had managed it so well that he needed no more than two more days to complete the mine.

L. How the Duke of Bourbon fought in the mine at Vertueil, and how he got the castle.

The mine was finished so it could safely be entered and fought in, and the knights Torsay and Le Borgne de Veaulce who were in charge of it, came to the Duke of Bourbon saying to him: "The mine is ready, come when you please." "Good," said the duke. But the next day at Matins, the English inside, who saw that the mine was broken through, thinking to stop it made a sally against the guards of the Duke of Bourbon. So the English were repulsed so heavily by the guards that five men-at-arms were taken and four killed; and on our side the lord of Marueil was killed and the lord of Treignot was wounded so that it was necessary to carry him, and two squires of Poitou were killed and fine fighting was done there. Thus this skirmish; and the same day the Duke of Bourbon took a dozen knights and some squires with him, saying: "I wish to go see the mine"; which he would not have done if he had no hope of combat there. So the duke went putting himself right up front, and put Le Borgne de Veaulce before him and said to him: "Borgne, go ahead since you know the people of this castle, and tell them inside if there's a knight there he should come forward, and he will find who will receive him to fight in the mine." Then Le Borgne de Veaulce called to ask if they did not have knight who wished to perform arms. So they told him no, but with them was a high gentleman who had a good company inside, and was lieutenant of the captain and was all ready and prepared to perform arms with whomever wished to come. To this Le Borgne de Veaulce answered: "Come forward and see one here who is ready," not wishing to name his master. Then the Duke of Bourbon advanced in the mine, and likewise did the squire which those of the castle had mentioned, who was called Reynaud de Montferrand, from the other side. They struck each other with thrusts of their swords against one another and mutually there were none who (by way of intervening) could help but say: "Bourbon, Bourbon, Notre Dame," which much astounded the squire Renaud de Montferrand who stepped back and said: "How so, my lords, is this the Duke of Bourbon?" "Yes indeed," said Le Borgne de Veaulce, "it is him in person." Then said Reynaud de Montferrand: "I ought to praise God well, since he has today given me such grace and honor to perform arms with such a valiant prince, and you, Borgne de Veaulce, tell him that I request that it please him that in this honorable place where he is that he should make me a knight by his hand, for I will never have it more honorably. For his honor and valiance I am ready to surrender the place to him." When the Borgne de Veaulce had spoken to the Duke of Bourbon, who observed that all these things were to his great honor, said that he was well content if Montferrand brought the keys to him for the opening of his mine. Montferrand agreed with him and gave them to him and surrendered the keys, and right there the duke made him a knight; and the said Montferrand requested on his part that he would give him the prisoners who had been taken in this skirmish where Marueil died and the Duke of Bourbon was very content; and he ordered that Montferrand would surrender the place the next day. Further it was ordered that the knights and squires who were there with the Duke of Bourbon should bear arms the next day inside their mine with those of the castle, one side against the other, which Sir Jean de l'Aye, the marshal would oversee, so that each one would be content to have fought in the mine. The knights and squires who bore arms against those inside were the lord of Parthenai, the lord of Cousan, Sir Regnaud de Roye, Sir Robert de Chaslus, Sir Jehan de Châteaumorand, Le Borgne de Veaulce, the lord de Torsai, Sir Guillaume de la Fourest, Sir Blain Loup, Marshal of Bourbonnois, Sir l'Hermite de la Faye, Sir Jehan de Saint-Priest called the little marshal, Sir Boucicault, and the squires Michaille, La Jaille, Perrin d'Ussel, Bliomberis Loup, Tachon de Glene, Guichart Le Brun, and others, and they were not able to fight except with swords, because the opening had a width of only a foot and a half; but each one did his duty well, one after the other, according to the place, which was narrow and because the night grew dark, the companions returned to the tents. The next day the Duke of Bourbon sent one of his marshals, Sir Jean de l'Aye, to the castle to Montferrand, lieutenant of Bartholomew de Montprivat who had not yet returned from England, to summon him to surrender the place, which he surrendered just as he had promised, and came out with all his men armed and mounted in good order and came before the pavilion of the Duke of Bourbon and dismounted, who was well accompanied by knights. So Reynaud de Montferrand knelt before the duke and said to him: "My very redoubtable lord, I thank you most humbly for the benefits and honors which have come to me from you, to be a knight by the hand of so high and valiant a prince as you are; so it is an honor to me and all my lineage forever." The duke answered: "Sir Regnaud, chivalry is very strong in you for you are a valiant man of good lineage." Immediately the duke sent to find a beautiful courser which was very close by, which he gave to him, and had Sir Guillaume de la Pierre, his chamberlain, bring a great gold belt, weighing ten marks of silver, which he also gave him, about which Sir Reynaud de Montferrand held himself to be much honored, and he said before all that never in his own person would he arm himself and go against the Duke of Bourbon. Then Sir Regnaud took leave of the duke who put in the castle the lord of Toursay and twenty-five men-at-arms to guard it in the name of the Duke of Berry, and thus having taken Vertueil, the duke left with all his company and went to Poitiers, wishing to go to the king. When he was at Poitiers the Poitevins made a request of him: "My lord, we ask you by the honor of God and the good things which you have done for us, since you are leaving, that you should leave us half of your men; there are three places between Limousin and Poitou on the river Dordogne which are destroying the countryside; in them are captains Bernard Douat and Gabillon, and the three places are Courbies, Les Granges and Montvalent." The Duke of Bourbon responded then to the lords of Poitou: "You are six hundred men-at-arms, and I have another six hundred from my household which I lead, and your six hundred will be well able to take those three places." So the Poitevins said to the duke: "We are not able to do anything without your people, give us a captain to lead this thing: they will be well paid. We will take your ensign, and six or seven from the people of your house." Then the Duke of Bourbon made his arrangement, that he should leave from his people two hundred men-at-arms, and two hundred of the Poitevins whom he would lead to go to the king. The Duke of Bourbon left six hundred men-at-arms in Poitou, and to lead them Sir Jean de Châteaumorand, who carried the ensign of the duke, Sir Regnaud de Roye, Sir Boucicault, the little Marshal, the Borgne de Veaulce, Sir Pierre de Fontenai, Sir Robert de Damas, Sir Robert de Vendat, Sir Ouldrai de la Fourest, along with Michaille, Guyon Gouffier, Bliombéris Loup, all from the household of the duke, who accompanied his pennon, and others of the Bourbonnois country. The Duke of Bourbon left with six hundred men-at-arms, and went very quickly towards the king who was at Écluse.

LI. How the men of the Duke of Bourbon, in his absence, and the Poitevins conquered Corby, les Granges, and Montvalent.

While the Duke of Bourbon had left Poitou to go to the king to organize the affairs concerning the matter of Écluse [Sluys], it happened that the Poitevins did not wish to waste time, nor did the men whom the Duke of Bourbon had left behind. So the Poitevins said to the Bourbonnois: "There is a place twenty-two leagues from here called Courbies, which we could sneak up on, without them suspecting anything. Nearby, about a bowshot away, there is an abbey where they go to hear the office at Christmas; and anyone who put an ambush there, would not fail to take the better part of the garrison, and to do this but a hundred men-at-arms would be needed to do the sneaking. And from now to Christmas is but three days, for which reason the thing is just at the right moment." This was decided upon and some hundred men from the Duke of Bourbon's house volunteered. In command were Sir Renaud de Roye, Sir Jean de Châteaumorand, carrying the pennon of the duke, Sir Boucicault, and Sir Robert de Damas, who were all well mounted. They rode those twenty-two leagues in one day and one night with guides from the country leading them, and set their ambush in the woods two hours before daylight. This Christmas Eve, a little before the sun rose, the captain of Courbies, his wife, and the majority of the people of his side sallied out, to go to the abbey to hear the service. At the height of the service the Duke of Bourbon's ambushers, who were in the woods, sallied out and took the captain, his wife, and the other people, and led them from that place to make them surrender, or to cut off their heads. Very quickly the captain agreed to the surrender, if only that he and his wife should be safe, so it was done. He surrendered the place to a hundred men-at-arms who took the others away as prisoners. The booty of Courbies amounted to a hundred men-at-arms just as many prisoners of the robe,[19] a good four thousand francs, and they made the men-at-arms raze the place and they returned back to their companions, whom they had left behind, to whom they gave a good part of their profits. Having assembled, all of one accord with the Poitevins, they went to besiege les Granges, which was in the flatlands, of which the captain was Gabillon, who had a good twenty-four combatants. The place was entirely built of brick, which the Cardinal of Limoges had made, and there were no complete ditches on one side. Immediately Poitevins and Bourbonnois made military equipment of wood to come to the foot of the wall of a great tower which was there, and there they began to mine. The garrison did not dare to sally forth, and could not do so because they were entirely surrounded by the Poitevins and Bourbonnois, and they defended the tower the best that they could. But the tunneling progressed

19 Nobles of the robe owed their noble status to holding administrative or judicial office.

so enthusiastically that with two days and two nights the tower was mined, and a breach made at the end to start a fire, which thus made it fall. Half of the tower came down, which killed a good twenty men on that side, and those who remained on the remnant of the tower clasped their hands together, as a sign to those without that they prayed for mercy. So it was done except for the traitors, of whom there were four, who had their heads cut off. The Granges were delivered, and Gabillon and the English prisoners whom they had destroyed, were taken by those of the Bourbonnois to the lords of Poitou, who gave to the companions, for their good service, three thousand francs. The companions of the Bourbonnois and of Poitou, headed to Montvalent, which Bernard Douat held, but when Bernard Douat knew that they had come, he left the city to go gather men, and to defeat the army if he was able leaving in the city as a guard some thirty combatants. When the army came before them they had consultation between them saying "No place holds before the Duke of Bourbon's men, and they hate our captain mortally, for the taking of the duchess his mother; and if we are taken we will be killed for that reason. So it would be better that we should surrender ourselves to my lord the Duke of Bourbon." That was done, and Bernard Breschard, a captain for the Duke of Bourbon placed Montvalent on guard and he guarded it well. From Montvalent the Duke of Bourbon's men took their leave from the seigneurs of Poitou, to go to their master, seeing that they had achieved the conquest which they were obliged to do. And leaving the seigneurs of Poitou, thanked them much for their help, and paid them for a month on top of their salary, and they went very quickly to their prince, who they much desired to see; and on the road they found many messages which increased their haste, for the Duke of Bourbon always strongly cherished the people of his own house and those of his country. So the companions rode on their journeys so that they should come to Écluse, where the Duke of Bourbon their master was with the king, and they found that the English had landed in great power before Écluse, and ere besieging it with a force of vessels before the new castle of Écluse which sat on the sea, and which Duke Philip of Burgundy had built. So the company was well received and feasted by the Duke of Bourbon because they, together with the people of the king, amounted to fifteen hundred men-at-arms and all men of value in the army of the king said that the Duke of Bourbon had made the best deliverance of a castle which one could do; for in combating in the mine in person at Verteuil against the noble man Renaud de Montferrand, who guarded the place in the name of the King of England, had surrendered that place to the Duke of Bourbon, with Renaud requiring him that he should be made a knight by his hand. Concerning which the people in the army said: "See that for a great thing! The Duke of Bourbon had there in Poitou six hundred men-at-arms who have taken three good places, and have come in good time to fight against the English."

LII. How by the intelligence and advice of the Duke of Bourbon the English left their siege in front of Écluse.

After the taking of Vertueil, in the year of grace 1382, the King of France was at Écluse, together with his uncles, the dukes of Burgundy and Bourbon, to counter the attack of the English army, who had descended upon those parts to conquer the castle of Écluse and the city. The master and captain was Sir Jacques d'Andelle, who there had anchored his ships, and landed a siege from these ships, and no one could relieve the siege arriving by sea, nor could they do so by land, because the land force was palisaded. Duke Philip of Burgundy, who saw this as infuriating, and was afraid for his castle and the king's city, commenced to say to the Duke of Bourbon, in the king's presence: "Good cousin, you have done good things in Poitou, and so too have your people, and you do not seem abandoned, for you have good company." The Duke of Bourbon responded: "My lord, we and my company are at the command of the king and of you and to this we have come. But, my lord, it seems to me that the king and you are consigned to remain here a long time, which cannot work out otherwise. You see that the English have landed and have besieged your castle and the city, and so you do not have provisions." And then the Duke of Burgundy said: "What does it appear to you good cousin, that we should do?" "My lord, it seems advisable to me that you ought to round up all available seamen, of whom there are some good ones in the Isle of Cagen, which is yours, to determine if there be no vessels there, for there are none to be had here." So said the Duke of Burgundy in the presence of the king that this was well said, that on this he had taken counsel, where it was reported by those of the coast that in the Isle of Cagen there were eight vessels, and two in dry-dock outside the harbor of Écluse. And it was concluded in the council to have five hundred men-at-arms and four hundred arbalestiers in the Isle of Cagen, and that one should put two hundred men-at-arms and a hundred arbalestiers on two vessels from Écluse, which would do great damage to this army because most of the English were landed before the castle, where they had commenced to dig a mine and they were more at ease on land than at sea. So the Duke of Burgundy said to the Duke of Bourbon: "Good cousin, let us send in from this our island five hundred men-at-arms—250 of yours and the same of mine as well, together with the arbalestiers—and they should come here within two days, and go confront and fight the vessels of the English sailing on the sea adjacent to the castle, whilst the English remaining ashore are intent on preparing their mine. With those of the island there will be the people of our two vessels which are here to support them." And so it was accomplished. For the dukes of Burgundy and Bourbon sent to the Isle of Cagen five hundred men-at-arms and five hundred bowmen, to whom was said that they should come on the second day at dawn, as they had been charged to do, to strike the chain when the vessels of the English were arranged between two towers. So the companions hastened, and went to the isle and prepared and that evening they made a great guard of the lords' men, namely the Duke of Burgundy's and Duke of Bourbon's men with those of the king, at the hour which the men-at-arms had been ordered, they left the Isle of Cagen and came to strike at the chain which the English had stretched from one tower to another. When Sir Jacques d'Andellée saw this, he commanded his English to leave the land, and they gathered in their vessels in great terror. But they were not able to gather as quickly as our people, who had left the Isle and having embarked on some of their vessels and fired them. Then sixteen vessels were taken and burned, and the English were most embarrassed by this loss. So they gathered all together, and in four hours they had raised sails so they could go on their way, and there was great joy in the army at the damage done to the English at their going. The king and seigneurs ordered great measures to be taken at Écluse, for fear of the return of the English.

LIII. How the Duke of Bourbon retained Lord Norris in his service for the government of his country.

The King of France having arranged the guard of Écluse, he left with his uncles and went to Paris where there was news of the beginning of a conjuration, rebellion and murmuring against the nobles which also was likewise happening in Flanders. But in France, the king carried himself in such a way that by God's mercy nothing further happened, and the murmuring was pacified, and the king in Paris made some grand ordinances, and the dukes his uncles of Berry and Burgundy, who organized to hold the estate of the king so grandly, and the same of his brother the Duke of Orléans, who was reasonably young. Further they ordained that Duke Louis of Bourbon should have the guard over the person of the king, without moving, as the grand chamberlain and peer of France which he was. These had the rule of the realm and of its finances after the person of the king and they established their pensions recording which each one ought to have. After these ordinances the Duke of Bourbon saw that he had to stay and pay attention to the protection of the king. He thought to put his country in order, and that for this it was necessary to have a wise knight, who represented his person and the government of his country and in imagining that the Duke of Bourbon said to the people of his council: "I very often heard the praise of a knight of Nivernois, namely Lord Norris, and I am informed that he is a good knight, a gentleman and very wise and concerning this I have heard many good things from the seigneur of Mesonconte, and the lord of Montmort." The Duke of Bourbon said to the lord of Montmort: "He is your neighbor, I wish to send you there, so he will come speak to me, for I much desire to see him." So Montmort responded: "My lord, I am ready to do that which you have pleased to command me." Then the lord of Montfort left and came to the Nivernois, and reported to Lord Norris what he had discerned from the Duke of Bourbon his lord, and Lord Norris went willingly with Montfort to Paris, to the Duke of Bourbon, for the great good things which he had heard spoken of him. Lord Norris, on arriving in Paris, he being inspired by the deeds of the Duke of Bourbon by means of his knights, and the reasons the duke had sent him inquiries; but notwithstanding this, the duke wanted to speak to him from his own mouth, and he said: "Lord Norris, considering your intelligence and gentility, I have sent to ask you to take the government of my country, where I have need of a good governor." And to this Lord Norris answered "My lord, those who have spoken to you about my intelligence are badly informed. But as far as gentility goes I wish always to be a gentleman, and believe that what small affairs are mine, I will handle with the best of my ability, the most loyally as I can. But in regard to your affairs which are so great, these will be a great burden on me: for I doubt that I know how to do it any better." The Duke said to him: "Lord Norris, you will do it well enough, for I am greatly confident in your good sense, loyalty and gentility, and that you will make a good chief. And I have, by the way, two or three loyal officers, who are gentlemen, and who will serve you well and show you all the ways of my country." Thus, the Duke of Bourbon retained Lord Norris who made an oath to the duke, and the duke sent him to his country. So much came to be heard of the excellent ordinances which Lord Norris made while he was in the Bourbonnois country.

LIV. How Lord Norris employed himself in the service of the Duke of Bourbon, and what he did.

Sir Pierre de Norris, when he was at Molins, took the government in his hand as the duke had charged him to do and the first ordinance which he made was that all the finances of the Duke of Bourbon should be received by one man alone, and to do this Lord Norris appointed Lorin de Pierrepont, who was a gentleman, and who knew the customs of the country, and who loyally had served the duke. And Lord Norris established, in the chamber of accounts, one who had good memory named Gaiget, who was a clerk with him, and a most subtle man, and one of good habits. And by these ordinances that Lord Norris made, the finances of the Duke of Bourbon were kept in order. And after Lord Norris had put the country in good order, both in its finances and in justice, he raised a wall for Villefranche in Bourbonnais, which was a beautiful city, but until then lacking an enclosing wall; the wall resulted in a great profit to the country. And he also enclosed Feurs in Forez, which was a great merchant city without fortifications, and by the methods and devices at his disposal, this cost the Duke of Bourbon nothing, and it was agreeable to the people, for he was loved by everyone. And with this he was generous with his own, and he lived grandly and held a very fine table. He also began the castle of Montluçon, and it is well said that before he had remained nine years in the service of the Duke of Bourbon, Lord Norris found the ways and means for his master the Duke of Bourbon to acquire Chastel-Chinon, one of the best castles of the duchy of Burgundy, and worth five or six thousand livre of rent, and was given in recompense to the Queen Blanche Créel, who wanted to take only three hundred livre of rent, and so sold it to the king. Likewise Lord Norris recovered the land of Combrailhe which was worth 2000 livre of rent: that which was bought by Sir Pierre de Giac, chancellor of France and that said land had been sold formerly for the marriage of the Queen of France and the dauphin of Viennois, for which the chancellor had given twenty-five thousand gold francs. So Lord Norris found ways and means by which the men of the Bourbonnois were content to pay the said money to the chancellor and by the time he had retired, his master the Duke of Bourbon had been well served. During all these services the Flemings commenced to make a great deal of unrest, as did a party in France, which the king had not been well able to pacify. And because the Duke of Bourbon was most careful to guard the person of the king where he was, he ordered this Lord Norris to send him nobles from his country, armed and mounted, and to punish any that refused. Lord Norris did this, and led them to the duke himself, as he wished to be in the battle, if it came to that. And when Lord Norris was at Paris, the Duke of Bourbon said to him that he had done due diligence to lead his people to him: "Since when it's you who has come here, I am very happy about it, for much good has been reported to me concerning your works, which very much pleases me.

However for the present you are unable to come with me, for I have heard about the great unrest at Clermont-en-Beauvaisis, to which places it would be best that you should go, and that you should take twenty-five or thirty of my people so that you will be well accompanied. For you know that those of the Beauvoisin are accustomed to do evil things and raise any rebellion whatsoever, and you see that this city of Paris grumbles all sorts of bad things, and the Flemings have indeed chased off their lord the count, who is likely to lose everything, if the king does not hasten to go and succor him. The Flemings are allied with the people of Paris, which is renamed a commune." On account of this Lord Norris went by the command of his master into the Beauvoisin, greatly regretting the need to leave him, and by his intelligence appeased the people of that country, and, as much through justice as through sweet words, put them in good grace and obedience to the Duke of Bourbon their lord.

LV. How the King of France undertook an expedition to Flanders.

The current year 1383 was not yet finished when a conjuration was agitated in Flanders, of the communes against their lord the count, and the insurrection was thus. For the mayors and échevins of the cities having the protection of privileges of their franchises showed how the Count Louis their lord had trampled and oppressed them and did not let them enjoy their normal and traditional ways to which they were accustomed, but instead had broken them and brought them to naught, as they said. And all wanted their due from him, and wished him to uphold the laws and customs that they ought to retain, but the count wanted to exercise all the power of justice himself, by placing his officers among them, which was a great harm to the commoners, who were accustomed to live by the laws of the city, and to be subjects to their lord by consultation, and to be subjects of the seigneur by reason; for this feeling being very aggravated by his bad lordship, they rebelled all with one voice against him and threw him out of the county, and choosing one of their accomplices named Jacques d'Arteveldt to sustain them they said to him: "Count Louis has harshly taken war against us to trample us underfoot and hold us in servitude; while he says nothing of it, we well know that he has already married off his daughter in France; what good is it to tell us how to govern ourselves, when the count is always here?" Jacques responded: "For so much as we are in agreement, we are strong enough to resist him. Let us defend ourselves from those who come to attack us, and I am the one who with a good heart, will undertake the responsibility of the office to defend and guard you with my power." All the towns of Flanders ordained that their leaders of ten should raise taxes, fortify their towns, and put in place great numbers of men in the field to fight whoever came to assail them. And as soon as the Flemings had put themselves to the fore, Count Louis, the lord they had chased away, left the country and passed into Artois, and went to Hesdin, looking to find Duke Philip of Burgundy, who had married his daughter. So he was told that he had gone to Paris to the king. And when the count went there, he found the king and the Duke of Burgundy, his son, and said to them: "My sovereign and very dread lord, my lord the king—the land, seigneurie and county of Flanders, which is mine, I hold from you in fief and sovereignty, from which cause I am a peer of France; and the dean of the peers who is here, your uncle, the Duke of Burgundy, has married my daughter. Now just as the people of my country are rebels against me and have chased me out, not at all through my fault, but theirs, since they have never been able to put up with hardship; they are so rich and sleek that they are not able to endure anything. I advise that if they have great power, since they have thrown me out of the country, they will endeavor to throw out others, and conquer their lands. For which, my sovereign and redoubted lord, I have come to you and your uncle, my son, for refuge; that you ought to remedy this, and put me back in my seigneurie, as a good lord ought to do for his loyal vassal." Then the Duke of Burgundy took up the talk and said to the king: "My lord, my father-in-law of Flanders speaks well; summon your people and let's go fight this rabble." "You have reason, good uncle," said the king, "and in order that we follow you swiftly, we will leave here tomorrow, and set out for Flanders." That same night, the King of France sent letters to his men-at-arms, who in many quarters were loyal to him, that they might follow him, and that all should come together at the bridge of Commines, at the river by which one enters Flanders. Thereupon all the captains made haste to join him.

There was, namely, the Marshal of Sancerre who had a fine company of more than six thousand men-at-arms, the lord of Clisson, Constable of France who had many men, the lord of Sempy, the lord of Saveuse, the lord of Renty, the lord of Aussy, the lord of Fosseux, and the lord of Longueval, all from Picardy, and many other captains, so that the king had a good six thousand men-at-arms, who were lodged in his tents along the same river, near the bridge of Commines; and the Count of Flanders was personally with the king and the Duke of Bourbon had many people close at hand, and this host assembled at the bridge of Commines with the bishop of Langres, who was a very valiant man, and had a good company as well. Meanwhile, the aforesaid Jacques d'Arteveldt, leading the commune of Flanders against his seigneur, ordered one of his followers, named Piètre du Bos, to position himself near them, at the foot of the bridge of Commines, so that the French were not able to pass; and with Piètre du Bos were a good ten thousand men.

But that night it happened as the Marshal of Sancerre was lodged on the river that his people, who were far from useless, found a good man who apprised them of three small vessels, standing in the water, sunk. Hence, the Marshal had them taken out of the water, and his people were able to cross throughout the night, a good six hundred men. At dawn they went to attack the Flemings, commanded by Piètre du Bos, who maintaining guard of the bridge, and this they did not anticipate. The Duke of Bourbon's people, whose chief was Robert de Chaslus, together with Sir Gaulchier de Passac, Sir Jean de Châteaumorand, the lord of Saint-Priest, the little Marshal, Sir Boucicault, Sir Robert de Damas and others, with the bishop of Langres, of the household of Rougemont, who all were armed, carried out the Marshal's plan. At the hour which the Marshal attacked the Flemings, those of Bourbon lowered their bridge and attacked those from the other side, with his good six hundred men-at-arms, and with this assault two thousand Flemings were drowned, and in all, four thousand killed. Thus it transpired in a single battlefield, where the Marshal of Sancerre was, on the bridge, by the efforts of the Duke of Bourbon's people, the good marshal, and the bishop of Langres; and Piètre du Bos fled, woebegone, with only four thousand men remaining, toward Jacques d'Arteveldt, his captain. So the news was taken to the King of France, the Duke of Burgundy, the Duke of Bourbon and to Count Louis in their tents, who were very happy and praised God for such a good beginning.

LVI. How by the good advice of the Duke of Bourbon and of the lord of Couci, the King of France had the battle against the Flemings at Roosbeck.

The King of France, who had known how his people had dealt with the past night against the Flemings, was overjoyed; and for this next morning he broke camp from the place where he was and with all his people passed the bridge of Commines, and they went to Ypres, which opened the city to him, and the king was lodged in Ypres with this army all around. With the king being at Ypres Sir Guillaume de Neullac made an enterprise, together with the Duke of Bourbon's men, where there were Sir Gaulcher de Passac, Sir Blain Loup, Marshal of the Bourbonnois, Sir Jean de Châteaumorand and Sir Guichard his brother, the lord of Saint-Priest, the little marshal, Sir Jean de Saint-Priest, Sir Robert de Damas, Sir Robert de Vendat, Sir Michaille, Guyon Gouffier, Tachon de Glené and many others to ride out all night to go attack a town which had made no attempt to defend itself, and was only five leagues away, a town called Poperingues. Neullac and the Bourbonnois arrived there, one hour after midnight, and found the town watch guarding the barrier. So the companions boldly attacked the watch, of which they killed a good half, and the remainder fled. Soon there were many dead, both of the watch and those of the town, four thousand people, whom they put to flight. And there were many rich jewels of the womenfolk and vessels of silver draperies and other goods which they found there, which were marvelous. So they turned back with all of the profit to the king who gave them good cheer, and in the next morning the king decamped from Ypres to go towards Bruges. However they did not know that three leagues from the plains of Roosbeck, Jacques d'Arteveldt, who well knew of his coming, was above them on the mountain of Roosbeck, with all of forty thousand men-at-arms. The French seeing this, as the communes prepared to fight them, they put their battle in ranks, and put themselves into good order, of which they made three orders: in the avant-garde were the Constable of France, Clisson, and the Marshal of Sancerre well accompanied with a good retinue; and in the king's battle on the right there were ordered for his guard the dukes of Burgundy and Berry and the Count Louis with their people, and in the third were the Duke of Bourbon and the lord of Couci in good company ready to do well. But when the battalions were arranged to fight the Flemings the Duke of Bourbon said to the lord of Couci: "Good cousin, see here the constable and marshals who are in front; and we are not able to attack our enemies if not through them which is a very extraordinary thing." Then Couci said: "My lord you tell the truth! It appears to me that if we go between the king's battle like a wing and take the mountain we will make today a good battle if it please God." Then the Duke of Bourbon said: "Good cousin, that's good advice." Then the banner of the duke which Sir Robert de Damas carried began to go forward, and the Duke of Bourbon and the lord of Couci with all their people after them until they climbed the mountain behind the battle formation of the Flemings, and adroitly with great shock of lances, with blows with axes and striking of swords they came to clash in the middle and from this beginning the French arranged them thus that they repelled the Flemings in their vanguard, which fell back more than six arms' lengths. But because in Froissart one finds the valiance of the courageously enduring knights and squires and their names both those of the king and those of the lords the dukes his uncles, following the constable and the marshals and the lord Couci who acted in the affair valiantly there is no need to say more. But to come to Duke Louis of Bourbon concerning whom this chronicle is made, there should be named some who were with him in this combat: Sir Guy, lord of Cousant, Sir Hugues de Chastellus, the lord of Châteaumorand, together with his sons Guichard and Jean, knights, Sir Le Barrois, Sir Robert de Chaslus, Sir Blain Loup the marshal of Bourbonnois, Bliombéris his brother, the lord of Saint-Priest, Sir Gaulchier de Passac, Sir Boucicault, L'Hermite de la Faye, Robinet de Vendat, and Oudrai de la Fourest, knights, Sir Robert de Damas, who carried the banner, Sir Regnault de Bressolles, the lord de la Fayette, the lord of Chaugi, and squires, Guichart le Brun, Michaille, Guyon Gouffier, Perrin d'Ussel, Tachon de Glené, the bastard of Glarains, Philippe Beraud, Baudequin Meschin, and others in good number who cruelly made acquaintance with the Flemings and fought so well with blows, that there was nothing to criticize.

So then the Duke of Bourbon and the lord of Couci who with all their people attacked the Flemings from behind on the mountain of Roosbeck, forcefully conducted themselves to the clash; many a lance was shattered and many hauberks split or cracked. There one could see many a man fallen down, heads sundered, and hands cut off and scattered in the field. The French and Flemings fought with very great force and then the Duke of Bourbon performed marvels of arms: with axe in hand, he struck Flemings right and left, and none that he struck rose up again. And the valiant prince plunged among the Flemings, so much so that he was thrown to the ground and wounded, but he was quickly rescued by the good knights and squires named above and others who strove to relieve him, while all the while withstanding the swarming and murderous Flemings. Thus was the Good Duke remounted by the lord of Châteaumorand and Michaille, and again fiercely they returned to the battle. He who saw the lord of Couci scatter the throng and strike down Flemings, killing and chopping them up, would thereafter remember him as a valiant knight. So much did the two lords accomplish, by the effort of their people, who fought vigorously, that their enemies turned in flight—even those who had until then held fast as bravely as they could. So they made their great slaughter, and so much of it there was that some upset the others so that they fled. So the captain Jacques d'Arteveldt was killed and his banner knocked down which banner was borne by an armed woman called Big Margot, who there remained dead. And it was commonly related that in the battle against the Flemings that the battle was won by the Duke of Bourbon and the lord of Couci with the help of their people because they had pursued boldly from behind. At this battle on the mountain of Roosbeck sixteen to eighteen thousand Flemings were killed, and the remainder fled. And when the lords of Bourbon and Couci and their people had sufficiently killed Flemings and finished the battle they came to their horses which they and their people mounted in haste and ran after them in the hunt and killed a good two thousand and a thousand were drowned in the pond; and the duke and Couci pursued others so far that they encountered Piètre du Bos, who was in a small grove with a good three thousand men, and there they attacked him and assaulted him fiercely; and Piètre du Bos and his Flemings sold themselves dearly and defended themselves courageously; relying on the advantage of their location. This melée was brutal and grievous, for the lords of Bourbon and Couci, together with their people, made an effort to eject them from the grove, doing this to put themselves in a position to rout more people on the mount of Roosbeck. And so valiantly did they plunge in that they cast them out of the grove, and had the better of it. And there, because Piètre du Bos was killed, the Flemings lost their nerve, and were so full of fear that at no time was any blow struck by them, so there were dead and taken, four thousand men. The Duke of Bourbon had but three of his dead and Michaille grievously wounded. And at the time which the Duke of Bourbon returned from this affair with the lord of Couci, the bastard of Flanders came before him, crying: "Ha! My lord Bourbon, the remaining Flemings have escaped and are going to Courtrai, give me some of your people and let us pursue them!!" To this, the Duke of Bourbon answered: "Sir Jean de Châteaumorand, you take my banner and you such and such and go after them." So his men went in this pursuit along with the bastard; and the Duke of Bourbon and the lord of Couci turned back to the king who was with his battalion at the foot of Roosbeck, who out of joy wished to embrace the lords Bourbon and Couci and praised God for the victory which he had given through them and their people.

The people of the lords Bourbon and Couci rode swiftly after the Flemings of whom they found very great troops on the road so they killed plenty of them and the French and the Flemings entered Courtrai: and the Duke of Bourbon's men took, after the killing was done, the great Street of the Bridge where were the most beautiful houses of the city where they lodged and gained many goods, and sent news to the Duke of Bourbon, their lord, about what had happened, about which he was very happy. And the duke ordered them not to move from where they were, and they obeyed him: for with the victory of the battle, the Duke of Bourbon had the renown of having taken Courtrai, and found his lodgings grandly furnished when he got there. The next morning King Charles came to Courtrai and the duke of Burgundy and his father-in-law of Flanders also the Duke of Bourbon who found his lodgings well made up, and a great supply of victuals. The King of France stayed two days in Courtrai where he found in the belfry of the city three hundred golden spurs of the knights of the Count of Valois which the Flemings had killed [in 1302]. Because of this there were great exhortations to level the city. The Duke of Burgundy prayed that this not be done for it was one of the fine cities of Flanders, and only those who lived there could accomplish this.[20] And then the ambassadors of the commons of Flanders came, each from his proper town, to request from their lord, Count Louis, in the presence of the king, mercy for their forfeit. And the king made peace between the count and his people and gave it back to the count in full sovereignty.

20 Meaning only they could create such a town.

LVII. How the king on his return from Flanders entered Paris which the Duke of Bourbon entered first.

During the year 1383 after the battle of Roosbeck in Flanders and after the King of France had restored the count of Flanders his vassal to his complete lordship, the king left the country with the Duke of Bourbon and all their people. The king rode cheerfully by daily stages, until he came before Paris, because of the rebellion; and the Duke of Burgundy with his father-in-law the Count [of Flanders] and his company went to Bruges to put the city in order. So the king was in fine battle order before his city of Paris and doubted whether he should enter for there were still in the city a good eighteen thousand men in harness to take up arms against him. So it was arranged that the Duke of Bourbon should enter first with a full eight hundred men-at-arms because he was loved by the people of the city, and the duke entered with the vanguard, a good battalion and the rearguard; and finally the duke sent certain people to the crossroads of the city, because there was no point of assembly. The duke went straight to the Palace in this manner, and then to the Louvre, where he put men, and likewise to the Bastille of St. Anthony, and the good people knelt before the Duke of Bourbon as before God, for which he had great pity. The duke returned to the king and said: "Sire, enter your good city of Paris when it pleases you, for you will be met gladly, and if there are ten or twelve who have done evil, the others haven't done anything." Then the Duke of Bourbon went before and in the same order as he had entered the first time, with king after in good order, who went to the Palace, and the Duke of Bourbon passed beyond with his people in the city to find out if there was anything bad taking place; and this night certain captains were ordered to go all night through the city with three hundred men-at-arms. The three captains were the Gallois d'Aunai, Châteaumorand, and Le Barrois, who kept watch this night and in leaving the palace they had assembled the watch and come to the Châtelet, and from Châtelet, to St. Paul at the house of Cudo where two Breton servants had broken in. Inside there were some women, who cried out "Murder!"[21] Hearing this, the guard descended upon the place, and entered, and the two servants were caught loaded down with women's robes, money, and jewelry, especially one of them, since the other had done no wrong, according to the women. And the one carrying the robes, Gallois d'Auni, Châteaumorand and Le Barrois chose to hang from the transept, and the other had his ear cut off and was sent on his way. And that servant stayed hanging there for two days, and everyone came to see, saying that it was the best justice that they had ever seen done by men-at-arms. The captains went to St. Paul, and to the Bastille St. Anthony and turned back to St. Innocent and into the great

21 Similar to the English call, "Help! Murder! Police!" Movie, 1914; song by Thursday's Children, 1966; song by the Fuzztones, 2001.

street of St. Denis. Their valets, who had gone before found there the valet who had plundered a tradeswoman of headdresses, with a good two hundred pounds of jewels. So the malefactor was taken, the jewels upon him, while consorting with his pals, where Châteaumorand, Le Barrois, and Le Gallois d'Aunai found him. The same people hanged him that night from the pillory of the Temple, where he hanged for three days; and the furor was so great in Paris about the justice they had done that it was marvelous. The next morning it was ordered, that wherever one found servants doing evil that one should hang them on the spot without taking them to the gibbet.

LVIII. How the weapons of Paris were taken to the Louvre, by the command of the king, and who received them; and how the Duke of Bourbon spoke fine words to Lord Norris.

Because the King of France was more secure in his city of Paris, and so that the inhabitants should not have cause to move themselves to make conspiracies and to rebel, it was announced by the king after his return from Flanders that every man who had harness should carry it to the Louvre on pain of being a false traitor against the king. On the morning when the announcement had been made, Le Barrois, Châteaumorand, and Le Gallois d'Aunai were at dinner with the king, who much praised what they had done, and the king gave the three of them fines or forfeitures[22] of fifteen hundred gold francs, and the king asked them to go to the Louvre to see the receiving of the harness, and find out the number. They went there and were there for two days by the command of the king. So you should know that inside of three days there were brought to the Louvre fifteen thousand harness of arms without mistake. Insofar as these arms were received there were instructions given concerning those who were in agreement with the rebellion, whom they had drawn as traitors through Paris, and cut off the heads of up to a dozen; and this was shown to the king and further they said that they would cut off the heads of all the slackers, of whom they had many. Those who were in charge of finances said that it would be better if the king would make a requisition of funds to cover the expenses in Flanders, than to proceed any further in a criminal case. The king gave heed to this advice and made an outlay of two hundred thousand gold francs and the king dismissed the men-at-arms for the time being. And Lord Norris, who knew that the Duke of Bourbon was in Paris, left Clermont, and went to him and said heatedly to the duke that he had made him miss this fine expedition in Flanders. "Don't concern yourself," said the Duke of Bourbon "you will be sent on others. And I have good need of you, there where you are going." Then the duke asked him how the land of Beauvaisis was faring: "Quite well, my lord," Norris said, "and I have there acquired six hundred pounds of rent, which have cost you nothing, from the town of La Hérelle; And I have begun a pond which will not be smaller than Gouveulx when it is finished." So the duke was very happy and recommended that Lord Norris should go bastaging[23] in the Bourbonnais and raise money in profusion: for the king who had done such great things hoped to do even greater ones. So Lord Norris went to the Bourbonnais in this official capacity, and the duke remained in Paris in the personal guard of the king, as he was commissioned.

---

22 The king is using money confiscated from his enemies to reward his supporters.

23 Fee due for a loaded pack animal; collecting such a fee.

LIX. How the duke Philip of Burgundy took passage to England.

Charles King of France and Louis Duke of Orléans, brothers who were both young princes at this time gave themselves over to joy and happiness for the victory against the Flemings; in the city of Paris at the Sainte-Chapelle, for this victory the king and the princes of the royal blood made orisons, offerings and praise to God proceeding to Saint-Denis where lie the bodies of the most Christian kings of France. Even though the king was young, the well-advised princes, the lord dukes his uncles, Berry, Burgundy and Bourbon had ordained such sound and mature counsel, as much in the court of parlement, as in the offices of the realm and likewise in reforms, so that the public affairs were well governed and also the king and the lords were very content concerning God and the peace which by His grace had sent them, seeing that, by His help that the English, their ancient enemies had been chased completely out of the realm; and subsequently, it appeared to the Estates, which they sought to enfeeble, that fortune was bitter and sweet in turn. And in this prosperity the glory of France conducted itself for the space of three years where every party came to look favorably on the majesty of the king, as much for his renown as to seek refuge, and to have safety with him, equally the royal constitutions, laws and ordinances which in his parlement addressed and which they saw willingly and governed in their countries according to these; and the ambassadors who came to France from many regions, because of the sense and worth and honor which they knew to be in Duke Louis of Bourbon, came directly to him for he had the administration and the guard of the person of the king, about which he dealt with summarily according to their cases and many were content with his way of speaking. During this time of prosperity Duke Philip of Burgundy, this valiant prince who undertook many good things like the battle of Flanders, and the deed of Écluse, who saw the King of France his nephew grow and have the strength and majority of a man and recalled the conquests, exploits and valiant deeds which former kings of France had accomplished in upholding their rights and on this one day among the others he went to Paris to the Palace of the dukes of Burgundy where there were many lords, and began to say to the king: "My lord, the kings your predecessors have accomplished many a good thing as much in enlarging the realm as in guarding and defending their rights and therefore in these times of peace which we have, you and we of your blood can make an accumulation of men-at-arms and provisions, so that none should attack us." Then the king said to the Duke of Burgundy: "You may well say this, good uncle, but why do you say it?" "My lord," said the duke, "I will tell you: It seems to me that what is not done forcefully is as well not done at all. These English have made war on my lord your father for a long time, and on you, and they don't do anything but cross over often to this side, and they are but a little people. Leave off all these little enterprises, do one that will be remembered forever. You are the greatest living king, and you have more people, and it has often occurred to me that we should undertake to cross to England and to strike down the great pride of these English. To do this, my lord, it is necessary to command all your vassals and subjects who are your loyal servants and also your allies and pensioners, and first of all the counts of Hainault, the Duke of Juliers and the Duke of Brittany, who is very powerful and will willingly come to serve you, and your good cousin the Count Amé of Savoy, son of the Green Count and of the sister of the good cousin of the Duke of Bourbon, who will serve you with a joyful heart. Inside half a year I will come to the port of Écluse with vessels for the crossing of ten thousand men-at-arms but my lord it is necessary that you should send to the high master of Prussia, who indeed is your ally, that he should send this number of vessels which he is able, and I know that with your good cousin of Hainault and your cousin of Brittany together with the power of Flanders we will lack for nothing." So was this speech of the Duke of Burgundy to the king's council very well heard and received gladly by all the valiant knights and worthy men present. They spoke with one voice to the king: "Behold a high and most honorable and just enterprise, my lord of Burgundy has told you a very valiant one and he is able to do more than any other to help you. For he is a high and powerful prince and is a great lord over the sea in the province of Flanders." And the Count of Tancarville, who spoke afterwards to the council said that it seemed good to him that the king and the Duke of Burgundy should choose up to eight knights to put this affair in good order and that was executed, and all the finances of the realm were accumulated to put that into effect, which was one of the more difficult aspects of the affair, and they were put in sure hands so that nothing should be spent if not on this army, and further it was said that the king sent orders through all the countries that anyone in arms who wished to serve in arms on this expedition, and take his pay, should come to him at Écluse, and there he would satisfy him entirely. For he wanted it known that he was crossing over to conquer England. The King of France arranged a time of eight months when all those of his command should find him at Écluse as he had ordered. The knights said to the Duke of Burgundy that he should go towards his county of Flanders, to assemble his fleet, which was very strong. He replied to the king in his council that he indeed had a strong fleet and a great many troops: "And you, sire, and the others who remain here should apply diligence, each according to his undertaking that, on the named day they should be in place; because by lack of ships there is no chance that the journey will be accomplished."

So it was decided to conquer England by crossing the sea; and the Duke of Burgundy left to go to Flanders, and the dukes of Berry and Bourbon remained with the king, to put the rest in order, together with the eight knights who had been chosen in council to do this. In this council it had been set that the Duke of Berry should have government of the realm during the expedition, concerning which he said that he was not at all happy to remain, and that certainly he should go with the king in his power, all the way to Écluse, in hopes of going to England. The Duke of Bourbon who was chivalrous and had long thought on his matters sent to Lord Norris who grandly governed his affairs, he should put all his finances together, and further bring for his garrisons to Paris two hundred barrels of wine and two thousand pieces of salt pork from the forest of Tronçaie, and that all this provision was taken to Clermont in Beauvoisin, where he too received the wheat to make his biscuit and another two hundred barrels of wine and the lord the Duke of Bourbon commanded all these orders to lord Norris who did it, in such a way that the provisions of the Duke of Bourbon were the best one could ever see.

LX. How the crossing to England was broken, and how the Duke of Brittany made an agreement for the English of Bourbourg to leave.

During 1386 the King of France who was young and very determined to do things which led to renown had already made his command for war to the lords named above and to many others, and announced his move to cross to England. For this he left Paris in noble trappings and went to Écluse, first, to wait for his people. Now the time came that the king had ordered, and there were never such good men as these who voluntarily made their way to the Channel, in hopes of sailing by sea to England. So vassals, noble men, and allies came to this command, so that the king had in his company a good twenty-two thousand men in leg harness, and eight hundred archers; and the valiant Duke Philip of Burgundy, Count of Flanders and of Artois, who had not been asleep, had indeed assembled sixteen hundred great vessels all with sails of which there were a good eight hundred boats with two sails and all the other cutters and good passenger boats, and everyone said that they had never seen such a line of battle on the sea for a prince, nor a greater army since Troy the Great. There were vessels assigned for each and every seigneur; and it was said that the Duke of Bourbon would have the vanguard in this army, and his vessels were delivered to him, where there was a fine company of knights and squires and other men-at-arms who willingly served him and followed him for his good name. The knights who commonly had served him in his journeys were Sir Guichard Daulphin, the lord of la Tour, Sir Hugues, lord of Châteaumorand and Sir Jean his son, who carried the pennon, the lord of Saint-Priest, Sir Blain Loup, Marshal of the Bourbonnois, and Bliombéris, Sir Guillaume de Garret, Sir Jean de Saint-Priest, called the little marshal, Sir Le Barrois, Sir Jehan de Bonnebaut, Sir Gaulchier de Passac, Sir L'Hermite de la Faye, Sir Robert de Damas carrying the banner, Berthier de Nasselles, Phelibert Beraud, Guichart Le Brun, Baudesquin de Vessée Michaille, Guyon Gouffier and others. Beyond this it was said that the dukes of Berri and Burgundy took over the guarding of the king and they governed him because the Duke of Bourbon was commissioned to leave the vanguard notwithstanding that the Duke of Berry was ordered to govern the realm, where he did not at all wish to remain. Both the harbor of Écluse and the port were beautiful to see with the king's army floating on the sea and the equipment inside which the lords had ordered to be brought. Insofar as the protectors and administrators of the sea made haste to hoist their lines and raise sails and cross over the sea it was made known to the king that the English, who began every day with great malice, and were very certain about the king's crossing, to obstruct him crossed to this side to Flanders at Bourbourg, by the advice of some who never loved the realm, and there was a great clamor at Écluse among the lords who said: "What are we doing by going to England? See our enemies, who are over here in force! Do we want to go to conquer the realm of England and lose our own?" So said those who had never wanted to cross over anyway. From this came such a great commotion among the lords that the army was broken by it and it was decided to allow the vassals leave to go, and to go by land to where the English were in the Valley of Cassel, where they had taken two cities, Bourbourg and another one. So a great part of the king's men-at-arms headed to that area and others went unhappily; and the king rode to Bourbourg. So he had it besieged all around with his men, and inside Bourbourg were a thousand English men-at-arms and a thousand archers. There was one part of Bourbourg enclosed by a stockade, but there were moats full of water, and the king kept his siege before Bourbourg, some of his captains supplied with troops, together with those of the dukes of Burgundy and Bourbon with up to two thousand combatants, and the French left the lodgings and went before the city up to the stockade in an assault, to see what those inside would do. The lord of Tremouille was the first to enter the ditches and the pennon of the Duke of Burgundy next, and that of the Duke of Bourbon, and other people surrounding the ditches, who fought very well at the stockade; and during this fighting at the stockade fire was thrown into the city of Bourbourg, which was covered with straw, and the fire was so horrible that it burned everything; so that the English demanded a treaty and requested to speak only with the Duke of Brittany. The king who knew this prayed to the Duke of Brittany to go speak to them concerning which the Breton duke said to the king: "Sire I will not put myself at such a risk if you do not make a complete withdrawal." The king ordered those who had already knocked down a great part of the stockade and indeed burned half the city to pull back. So the Duke of Brittany went there and agreed that the English should go free and clear, and that the city, already burned, should go to the king; and this the duke brought back to the king. Concerning this the dukes of Burgundy and Bourbon said to the Duke of Brittany: "Why should my lord the king give them permission to go free? The city is half taken, and burned and the English have no victuals!" The Duke of Brittany replied to the king: "My lord they still have a quarter of the city where they have collected their victuals, and before you have taken them you will have a great loss which will be very damaging to you, and they have promised me that they will go without making war." The Duke of Brittany was heeded, who arranged things so that the English left freely, which was a great loss to the king, as has been recalled many times.

LXI. How two knights were sent into Spain by the counsel of the Duke of Bourbon to help King Henri with his war.

The high barons, the Count of Hainault, of Ostrevant, Duke of Holland, and lord of Zealand, also following the dukes of Brabant, of Lorraine, of Bar, of Juliers, of Brittany, and the Count of Savoy, who had all made great expenses to accompany and serve the King of France in this army and to cross to England and conquer it, when they saw that the enterprise was broken took their leave and returned to their countries and the king still remained in Flanders with his uncles, the dukes of Berry, Burgundy and Bourbon. And while the king was there the archdeacon of Cordova came to him at Bourbourg from King Henri of Spain and the archdeacon prayed to the King of France that he should send to King Henri his lord, two thousand men-at-arms paid for two months up to a hundred thousand francs, though this he was loth to do, for he would thence be greatly beholden. And when the men-at-arms came into his presence, he was satisfied as to their value, and sent back money to the King of France, who was well pleased. And finally the archdeacon said that there was a very great danger if the King of France was not able to help the King of Spain who was his ally, for the King of Portugal had already made a great march against the Spaniards and was certainly known to the King of Spain that for the glory of this victory that the King of Portugal had committed himself to make the English army come to greatly lay waste to Spain. Through it all the archdeacon asked from the King of France nothing but that the Duke of Bourbon should have this responsibility to go to Spain; for he had been there before. But the Duke of Bourbon who had consulted with his knights said that this army could not be accomplished with so little money and gave these reasons: two thousand men-at-arms paid for two months amounted to eighty thousand plus twenty thousand which had to be provided to other captains and allies. Thus the Duke of Bourbon said to the king: “My lord, consider two valiant knights, and that each lead a thousand men-at-arms, and they will be less costly than me. Nevertheless I announce that I will go at my own costs and expenses for I prefer to spend my own on my honor rather than that I take the responsibility which I am not able to carry out.” The king said further to this: “Good uncle, who would seem to be the two captains to be sent?” “My lord” said the duke, “I don’t know for you have an abundance of valiant and good ones,” (and the Duke of Bourbon named many) “but my lord among the others you have here two most enterprising, who have served you very well in all your affairs: One is Sir Guillaume de Neullac, and the other Sir Gaulchier de Passac, and they are servants of my lords your uncles, Passac to my lord of Berry, and Neullac to my lord of Burgundy. They are knights who do loyally that which you command them for they have been in my service where I have frequented with them and they have served me very well, and it seems good to me my lord, that the people whom you will order to go to Spain in arms and in particular the captains are from the countries and households of my lords your uncles which is a fine thing, since the King of Spain will see that you and your uncles wish well to do his pleasure. Also I pray you that you be pleased that I will give them two hundred gentlemen of mine to the end that I will go over there. I will find them there notwithstanding that I know well that the two knights will serve me with a good heart." Then the Duke of Burgundy said: "My lord, good cousin of Bourbon has well thought and well advised in this need to your very great honor and we are very content, good brother of Berry and I." Then Sir Guillaume de Neullac and Sir Gaulchier de Passac were named, who took the responsibility by commandment of the king, who told them: "Good cousin of Bourbon has advised us on this account of your valor." Then the knights told the king: "Sire, we are not at all worthy of so great a responsibility. But we are ready to obey you in all things which it pleases you command us." The king told them, "Go to our good cousin of Bourbon and he will tell you what has been arranged." They went there to thank him, and they said to him: "High and mighty prince, we thank you humbly for the honor which you have done us, for you have given to us who are two poor knights the enterprise, which was ordained for you who are such a prince as everyone knows, and which is too great an undertaking for such poor men as we are. It is a formidable thing for two knights to lead two thousand men-at-arms as far as Spain, a journey of two months, all without your good counsel and inspiration: presuming that your pleasure is to give us five hundred men-at-arms from your country, with some from your household, that will be for us a great honor and a great renown for you."

So the Duke of Bourbon replied to the knights: "I do it very willingly and perhaps you will see me very soon." To which they reply "May God wish it! For if you come, you will find us your good servants!" Sir Guillaume de Neullac and Sir Gaulchier de Passac left to take their road; and the Duke of Bourbon ordered that with the knights should go on his part Sir Jean de Châteaumorand, and the Sire de Blot who had under their direction four hundred men-at-arms from Bourbonnois and Forez. The duke gave them leave to gather the men and most of the Bourbonnois went there with them namely Sir Guillaume de la Fourest, the Sire de Saint-Geran-le-Pui, the Sire de Chitain, the Sire de Chazeul, Le Borgne de Veaulce and all the good companions of the Bourbonnois.

LXII. How the Duke of Bourbon went to Spain the second time.

Sir Guillaume de Neullac and his companion, their men-at-arms together with those of the Bourbonnois were not able at all to be in Avignon, when news came to the King of France how the navy of England had crossed to Spain led by the Duke of Lancaster. So the Duke of Bourbon was much troubled about what he should do and decided that he should go to Spain. So he took leave of the king to go to the Bourbonnois to gather men, and take his road and order everyone in Beauvoisin and elsewhere that whoever wished to come and serve him should follow him. Many came at his command, for the good that they knew in him, and likewise the great ones of the king's household came to him. Duke Louis left Paris and went to his duchy of Bourbonnois with so many men, where he found Lord Norris, who had amassed a great amount of money to make the expedition and the king indeed paid for three months for the men of his household, a good six score gentlemen and so that the Duke of Bourbon staying in Bourbonnois found as many of the people of the king as of Berri on top of his own, a good two hundred noblemen. The duke set out to catch up with the others. But in all lands everyone heard it said "The Duke of Bourbon is going to Spain," each took after him to such an extent that before he reached Navarre he had a good three hundred gentlemen, knights and squires. Staying in Navarre the duke heard say that the Duke of Lancaster with his Englishmen and abundance of Portuguese were besieging Burgos in Spain, which was the city of King Henri. The two knights Sir Guillaume de Neullac and Sir Gaulchier de Passac whom the King of France had ordered to go before, who were lodged at St. Domingo de la Caussade, learned reliable news about how the Duke of Bourbon had come into Spain and they were overjoyed and sent to the Duke of Bourbon that he should hasten: so there he was with them inside of three days and the duke having come, there was great joy and it was considered what should be done and the knights said to the duke: "My lord, see here that the embassy of Burgos is here, who says that the English have besieged the city, and they say that there has been a great mortality among them. So advise us what to do." The Duke of Bourbon answered on his feet: "Since they are dying it is good that we should go and help them die some more. It seems to me that the sooner the better, for they have no point of retreat from here to Portugal which is a long way." His words were very agreeable to all, being of the sensible counsel of the Duke of Bourbon who finally said, "Let's go from here to the queen's hospital which is but three leagues from Burgos, and let's send people ahead to find how the English are lodged, so that tomorrow at dawn we can go and attack them straightaway; and everyone said that it was well taken, and that one could not do better.

LXIII. How the Duke of Lancaster raised the siege of Burgos in Spain; and how the Duke of Bourbon followed him into Portugal where he was not willing to consent to a treaty of the King of Spain with the English.

The Duke of Lancaster, who was besieging the city of Burgos, was unhappy that he had been unable to take it and was very troubled by the mortality that had run through his host; but even more he despaired because the Duke of Bourbon was lodged near him, three leagues away, in great strength. Since he didn't wish to wait until the Duke of Bourbon moved against him, and knowing that the entire French army was lodged at the hospital, he decamped with his Englishmen that evening around midnight, and rode a good dozen Spanish leagues to the city of Medina de Campe, and the next day to Saint-More, then they crossed the river and went to Chassel Rodrige, which is in Portugal. The Duke of Lancaster and his English staying in Portugal believed themselves to be safe, but the Duke of Bourbon who had a great heart for the affair went with all of his men after them day and night: in such a way he came to St. More a day later. He gave an order to cross the river which divides Spain and Portugal and to pursue the English, that the seneschal de la Jennete who was a valiant man and a thousand men-at-arms should ride and hit them hard, so that the English were in disarray and so it was done. At dawn the French and Spanish attacked them in their camp and a thousand English were taken there and a great many were killed; and having made their assault, they withdrew to their side of the river, whither they led off to the army some good prisoners. The King of Portugal who knew of this defeat, put together a great many men, a good four thousand men-at-arms to aid the English who were of his party. For he married the daughter of the Duke of Lancaster. Then the power of the two countries' armies stood, French and Spanish on one side, and English and Portuguese on the other, with just a river between them, and news came to the princes of the armies, the Duke of Bourbon, the King of Portugal and the Duke of Lancaster that King Henri of Spain had passed from this life, and left the young son Dam Johan as his successor and heir. For some days, with the battalions standing across from each other, there was talk of a treaty, which came from the English and which the King of Portugal presented. You should know that it appeared to him if Dam Johan Infante of Spain, the new king, had married the second daughter of the Duke of Lancaster, who was there and already married to the sister, in his view there would be no longer any war between Spain and Portugal and they would be like brothers, and also that as a result of this marriage, the King of England would not stir up war anymore. These lords wished to charge the Duke of Bourbon to make this treaty which he said he would not do it all for the following reasons: "First because the King of Spain was allied to the King of France, by faith and by oath, and now the King of Spain is allied to the King of England by marriage, which is an alliance of blood relation. I do not know by what means the King of Spain should not fail one or the other and for this reason, I do not wish to be involved." The Duke of Bourbon said to Johan the new King of Spain about the late king Henri that the Spanish had made: "Sire, consider well what you do: for you are allied with the greatest living king, and who well has demonstrated it to the late king, your father, and to you and I take leave of you and go to him." For which reason the King of Spain put great effort to keep him but he did not wish to stay any longer; and the Duke of Bourbon left the kingdom of Spain [with seven hundred men-at-arms, those who had come first with Sir Guillaume de Neullac and the Sire Gaulchier de Passac and some of his own whom he had led, up to seven hundred men-at-arms] and crossed to the king of Navarre, Charles, whom he ought to lead to France, to the king and the Duke of Bourbon said, on leaving Spain, to Sir Guillaume de Neullac and Gaulchier de Passac: "Cross by the mountains of Roncevaulx, and go to Orthez, to Count Phoebus of Foix and wait for me there; for I will be there soon and we will do something worth remembering on our return." So the knights replied, "Willingly, my lord: But it will be convenient to delay a little so that we will receive pay for the rest of the two months that the King of Spain owes us." So the knights and their men remained in Biscayne near Nadres, near the enemies, and the Duke of Bourbon entered Navarre and went to Pamplona where the king [received him and entertained him well. The duke remained there for eight days and the king] discussed their affairs together. Then the Duke of Bourbon received news of the treaty between King Johan of Spain and the English by means of the king of Portugal.

LXIV. How Count Phoebus of Foix entertained the Duke of Bourbon at his city of Orthez as he was going homeward from Spain.

The Duke of Bourbon, staying in Navarre, thought that he had spent too much on the expedition to Spain and not achieved in any way as much as he had wished. He came to the conclusion that, as he had a worthy company of men, he ought not to waste any time in employing them in some honorable exploit against the enemies of the King of France, his sovereign lord. And to do this, and so that the men-at-arms should not leave him, he sent Sir Jean de Châteaumorand to Orthez, to the Count of Foix, to ask him if he would lend him fifteen thousand écus; and it was the intention of the Duke of Bourbon to make war on the land of Médoc, between the Gironde and the sea, quite close to Bordeaux, where most of his people would follow him, as well as those who remained in Spain, for whom he would wait to arrive. And be it clearly understood that at the same time the Duke of Bourbon left Saint-More in Spain, the Duke of Lancaster and his English left to make their voyage to England, and things were looking good, for the Duke of Bourbon brought some ladies there in company with the duchess, who trusted in the duke's good honor, and went to him for the great advantage which they could plainly see. So they were richly married afterwards to some valiant knights of the French realm, that is to say Dame Ysabel de Ferriers, whom the duke gave as wife to Renaud de Roye, and others whom he married well. Sir Jean de Châteaumorand and Sir Le Barrois were at Orthez with the count Phoebus to seek in the name of the Duke of Bourbon their lord this loan, to which he replied that he would do it very willingly and all that they wished; so that the knights Le Barrois and Châteaumorand turned back to their lord the Duke of Bourbon who was departed from Navarre, reported to him what Count Phoebus had said to them and that he and all that he had was well at his command; about which he was very happy and joyful and hastened to Orthez. God knows what cheer Phoebus Count of Foix made to him; and he defrayed all expenses in his city of Orthez for the Duke of Bourbon and all his court for the eight days he remained there, for which the Duke of Bourbon gave thanks and he was grateful also for the money which he had lent to him. The Count of Foix told him that beyond this he also wished to do something much greater for him. As the duke was at Orthez one of his knights and chamberlains, the lord of Chaugny, died, who was laid to rest there with the minor Friars. Count Phoebus, who had left Guienne, through having certain lands on lease there, knew that the French captains would return from Spain. So he doubted that they would pass through without ravaging them. For this he asked earnestly to the Duke of Bourbon that it might please him to order Jean de Châteaumorand and Le Barrois to the captains up to the foot of Roncevaux against the lord of Saigne, to obstruct them so they should not enter at all into the land of Solle, nor of Mauléon which were on their guard: for Count Phoebus had thought that they wished to come to ransom them. So the Duke of Bourbon acquiesced to him, that some of his knights should go to the captains and he ordered Châteaumorand and Le Barrois to go there; they said to the duke that it seemed to them that the count Phoebus ought to give them one of his gentlemen, to report the news to him, and the diligence which they had exercised. So Count Phoebus gave them Heliot de Coppene, one of the best squires of Gascony, to do this and to be there with them, and the knights left, and they found that already the captains were past four hundred men-at-arms, from this side of Roncesvaulx, who no longer wished to wait for their payment from Spain, but desired to return from them to their homes. So the captains led the four hundred good men-at-arms to the Duke of Bourbon and said first to the captains, Sir Guillaume de Neullac and Sir Gaulchier de Passac, that the Duke of Bourbon prayed them that they should not enter the territory of Solle nor Mauléon, and they obeyed his command, and the duke and Count Phoebus were very happy with those who had come to him, and Count Phoebus gave each captain a fine courser for his diligence.

During a hunt, Queen Jeanne de Bourbon meets her mother, the Duchess Isabelle de Valois (wearing a veil and wimple for mourning). Jeanne's brother Duke Louis II, kills the stag. Count Phoebus of Foix was a renowned hunter and author of the Hunting Book. *Louis was no stranger to hunting himself. Surely in his eight days of hosting the good duke, the count could not resist arranging a hunt. A seventeenth century copy after an original destroyed by fire in 1737. Alamy stock image.*

LXV. How the Duke of Bourbon warred against the Bourdelois by the advice of Count Phoebus and what happened.

When Duke Louis of Bourbon had his people with him he was much pleased; so he reflected that he had sojourned a long time and because of this one day he said to the Count of Foix: "Good cousin, since our people have come to me, I don't want to wait anymore to do something, and I wish to employ myself well, by your good counsel, in what I wish to do, and secretly, for that which you tell me should not be revealed for you are very close to the frontier." Count Phoebus said: "My lord, when you leave here, I suggest that you go to the Bourdelois to a city called Brassempouig, which is a city where there is an abundance of villains, who have no care for the garrison, but govern everything themselves. And you will find them bold villains, and part of the city is enclosed with a stockade, and I believe that they will not be able to hold out against you. When you go there you will find a strong house which is from Perrot le Biernois, which cost a good fifteen thousand francs from the funds which he acquired at Chalusset. And I think that if you burn the house, that would not be a bad thing. In addition to that, in taking this town of Brassempouig you will have conquered the lord of Lescar, who holds it for the King of England." The Duke of Bourbon left Count Phoebus, and with his company went to the house of Perrot le Biernois, an Englishman, and burned it and demolished and destroyed all the gardens, and Perrot was deprived in that hour of all that he had amassed, pillaged, and robbed in his time. From there the Duke of Bourbon went with his company before Brassempouig and parlayed with those of the town concerning their surrender, about which they replied very proudly, and said that they were good Englishmen and true Englishmen should die. The Duke of Bourbon ordered an assault and then the men-at-arms dismounted and at all costs Duke of Bourbon's men and those who were returned from Spain commenced a rough and strong assault and the men-at-arms began to enter the ditches, and to break the stockade and the villains against them defended vigorously and the French strove so much that they got rid of the stockade. The first who entered there was the lord of Roche-Guyon, and there was a cry from those in the town that they had killed him; immediately when the French heard this cry, Le Barrois and Châteaumorand, who carried the pennon, entered and those in the household of the duke followed them, Sir Blain Loup, Bliombéris his brother, the little marshal, the lord of Chitrang, Sir Robert de Damas, Sir Guillaume de Garet, Perrin d'Ussel, Philippe Beraud, Guichard Le Brun, Baudequin de Vesse and afterwards there was returning from Spain Sir Guillaume de Neullac and Sir Gaulchier de Passac who with all their brigade splendidly entered by force and when they were in, they killed many in the town, and took prisoner the rest, and Roche-Guyon was unharmed. So the town of Brassempouig was taken, because of the evil name that it had. From there the Duke of Bourbon headed to the town of Lescar, which was taken by a fine assault on his arrival as it was assailed roughly and there were forty combatants inside and that night they lodged there, for the lord of Lescar had left to go to Bordeaux to seek help against the Duke of Bourbon. On the morrow the duke stayed near Lescar, and ordered his standard through all the country of the lord of Lescar, and his men burned towns, cottages, and houses so there was nothing left to burn, and they returned to their master. The Duke of Bourbon left Lescar, and went before a town called Ayenmal, located in the marshes, which had belonged to the King of France and the seneschallate of Toulouse, but the lord of Lescar held it in subjection with a great tribute for which reason it happened that the people of Ayenmal held to his party. When they saw the French before them, they surrendered to the Duke of Bourbon, praying that he would put a garrison in the town to guard them from the lord of Lescar, and they would be true subjects to him and the King of France for they were by rights part of the seneschallate of Toulouse. To another town nearby named Moncuc, the duke sent some of his men, and that town made obeisance like Ayenmal. The duke sent garrisons of his men to the two towns as long as Sir Jean D'Azay, seneschal of Toulouse sent there men to guard them for the king. The Duke of Bourbon in returning from Spain destroyed two towns of the King of England in the Bourdelois, and won two others there which thereafter held themselves as good Frenchmen.

LXVI. How the King of France went to Germany to war upon the Duke of Juliers, and how the Duke of Bourbon had the castle of Dul by means of one of his valets of the wine cellar.

The Duke of Bourbon who in the Bourdelois had finished what he had undertaken and had nothing more to do, sent two of his knights to the King of Navarre as he left the Bourdelois and found him in Toulouse, just as the two of them had agreed. So the king of Navarre left Pamplona and came to where the Duke of Bourbon was, and both set out, and they went to Paris to the King of France who made great cheer to the Duke of Bourbon for the conquest which he had made in the Bourdelois and the king received the king of Navarre in his grace, and retained him for his council, at the prayer of the Duke of Bourbon, because the King of Spain Henri, recently departed, who had married his sister had requested it of him long ago. Further the king said to the Duke of Bourbon: "Good uncle, I am very happy that you have come; you have come at just the right time. For the German dukes of Guelders and Juliers, who were accustomed to be our allies, have defied us in the matter of Germany. We have hope that we and good uncle Berry will go see them and you will be there because we very much want you to be part of the company." So commenced the expedition to Germany of 1388, by the King of France, where he led six thousand men-at-arms and ordered the Duke of Bourbon to lead the vanguard on this expedition. So the king rode by day marches just as he entered Germany in great power, and rode up to Juliers, where he placed a siege and the foragers were sent through the country to plunder, as was the custom. The Duke of Bourbon, who led the vanguard saw a very fine castle, nearby, which sat on high and is called Dul, of which the nobles inside inhabiting it carried the arms emblazoned in gold and red, which the King of Aragon of old shared with them, and it appeared to the duke that whoever had the castle could do great damage to those of Juliers, to his vassals; and also in this thinking of it, a subtle German varlet employed in his wine cellar, who had served him for a long time, came to him and said: "My lord, I am from this country, and you are well able to have faith in me. I love your household for I have been raised up in it, and you have done many good things for me. Give me up to sixteen companions and I will go lie in wait, so that it will be possible for us to do some harm to those who enter the castle or to those who sally out." Further the valet said to the Duke of Bourbon: "My lord, if I see my occasion, I will take three or four of my German companions and go to the gate of the castle of Dul, which you see, and say that the Duke of Juliers has ordered us there to be in the garrison with them and to guard the place against the French who are in the country." So everyone in the household of the Duke of Bourbon said this was a good strategy of war, seeing that in this time everyone was dressed like a German. Then the duke said to the valet that he could depend upon his life being well provided for if he did this. That valet together with his German companions left from the lodgings of the Duke of Bourbon and came before Dul, an hour before day and they called out the captain in German saying that the Duke of Juliers, their lord, had sent them to be in the place with him in the garrison. So the captain believed them because of the language they spoke, came down from the castle, came to them and led them in because of the trust in the assurance they gave concerning his lord. When they found themselves stronger than the captain, they took him, and imprisoned him and that night mounted a good guard. The Duke of Juliers who knew how often the French came before his castle of Dul, so that it should be better guarded in the night, sent eight gentlemen who came there in the morning and they, thinking to find the captain who they knew, found the servants of the Duke of Bourbon who led them into the castle and held them prisoner. In the morning the valet of the wine cellar descended from the castle and came to the Duke of Bourbon his master to tell him how he had opened the castle of Dul to him, and that it was now his. So the Duke of Bourbon was very happy about this, and ordered troops to guard it, and the king with the Duke of Berry who were before Juliers rejoiced greatly in the taking of the castle of Dul, and the Duke of Juliers was sad about it and distressed, not without cause for it was the master castle of his country, and he feared that because of this castle his town of Juliers, which was strong and beautiful was doubtless to be lost by the long stay which the King of France took in the marches as he wished. After this the Duke of Bourbon had Dul in his hand, and a knight came to the king and the Duke of Berry, who were in their tents before Juliers and said to the king: "Sire, the duke your enemy is in his town of Juliers, thinking about what he wishes to do." So it was decided that two heralds would be sent to him to see what he wished to say. So the heralds said to him that he should perform obeisance to the King of France. So the Duke of Juliers remained that day without giving any answer to the king, and the next day his response was that he was not able to make a treaty without the Duke of Guelders, or the Duke of Guelders without him, for they were allies on these points and on this promise, and that the king ought to go to the land of the Duke of Guelders and whatever the Duke of Guelders did, the Duke of Juliers would hold as done. He said this because it seemed to him that no Frenchman would dare to enter the land of the Duke of Guelders who was able to harm him.

LXVII. How the King of France went to make war on the Duke of Guelders, and how that duke and the Duke of Juliers came to an agreement with the king.

The dukes of Berry and Bourbon told the king that it, the response of the Duke of Guelders was possible and if someone put one of them into obedience the other would not contend with the victor. For they decided to make war on the Duke of Guelders who held great lands; and on this the king left Juliers and he went with all his host to the middle of the country to the Duke of Guelders, who marched between Juliers and Cologne on the Rhine, holding to the Marquis of Moravia, to whom the archbishop and the marquis with the Duke of Brunswick were allied. But the King of France remained in the duchy of Gueldres for just four days, where the French went to invade up to the gates of Aix in Germany, in Moravia and in Brunswick. Most of the invaders were the Duke of Berry's men and on their return they brought back great pillage to the host, and took many prisoners, and were all rich from the great profit which they had made in this raid. Those having come were well received by the king, and by the Duke of Berry their master for the great chevauchée[24] which they had done. In the morning, the king made a good arrangement that before three places of the Duke of Guelders, which were two leagues from the host of the king, a thousand men-at-arms were to be sent before them and two thousand were to ride through the country and three thousand should remain in the host with the king without budging. It was said in this manner the duchy of Guelders was put in subjection. So the king remained eleven days in his army and during this time the three places were taken by force of arms from the Duke of Guelders, and his country was overrun, burned, and laid waste by the Duke of Berry's people. Then the Dukes of Guelders and Juliers saw that evil came to them and their countries were devastated in all parts, and sent ambassadors to the Duke of Berry that by God they should treat and they made their peace with the king. So peace was made just as you have heard. The Dukes of Guelders and that of Juliers promised never to go against the King of France, nor his realm, on behalf of no person who lived except the Emperor whom they were not able to exclude. Neither the king nor his council took much account of this, because the emperor was uncle to the king and the dukes or their procurators made their oath to the King of France on that promise, and gave letters sealed with the seals of their lords the dukes, with the Duke of Berry and the Duke of Bourbon being present, and those places were surrendered. The treaty was accomplished which was very grand and honorable and the king left Germany to his high honor, having put

24 A large-scale raid, generally meant to disrupt an enemy countryside.

his enemy in subjection, and passed through the forest of Ardennes, with all his army and then gave leave to his men-at-arms and returned to France to his hostel in Paris, where he was given high honor and great fame for the good of the realm.

LXVIII. How the king and the Duke of Bourbon gave men to the Constable Clisson, to aid the Count of Penthièvre, against the Duke of Brittany.

Sir Oliver, lord of Clisson, Constable of France, who had remained for the fighting in Brittany, knew that the king had returned from Germany and remained in Paris together with the dukes of Burgundy and Berry and Bourbon so he went to the king complaining that the Duke of Brittany had taken trouble to try to destroy the Count of Penthièvre, and said to the king: "Sire, the count is your subject and ally and holds the greatest part of his lands in Brittany from you, and so if the Count of Penthièvre is destroyed, you will lose the greatest of your allies in Brittany." The king replied: "By God, Constable, I will not lose him at all for I will help him." The lord of Rivière came along with the Constable to make this request, and he was in complete agreement. "Although," said the king, "I have had great expense in Germany and now I do not have nearly as much money as I would like." "Ha! Ha! Sire," said Clisson, "don't worry; for the men whom you will give me, I will pay for two months in this town." Those who heard him say this were very eager to go there. The King of France gave to Clisson his constable eight hundred men-at-arms to go to Brittany against the duke, of which the Duke of Bourbon gave two hundred, the chiefs being the knights Le Barrois and Jean de Châteaumorand; and Sir Guillaume de Layre who was from the household of the king with another two hundred; and little Sempy two hundred; and Moncavrel, who was a knight of quality and honor in the king's household, also had two hundred of them. So the king and the Duke of Bourbon gave eight hundred men-at-arms and four captains to the lord of Clisson, who at once paid the captains to deliver the men-at-arms and to make their musters, by his treasurer the Sire Jean le Roi, who managed the finances at Notre Dame at Paris and gave the money for two months, and gave orders to muster at St. Brio des Vaulx. Clisson immediately left the king to make his way with his men-at-arms and went straight into Brittany before St. Brio where he had two of his captains waiting for him to start a siege. They were Raul de Carselio and his brother who held Guignant for the Count of Penthièvre the two of whom had there a good four hundred men-at-arms who were Bretons speaking Breton.

LXIX. How the Constable Clisson dealt with this war, and how St. Brio surrendered to him.

The lord of Clisson, who came well accompanied, went to besiege St. Brio de Vaulx of the Duke of Brittany, and God knows he was equipped with artillery, bombards, and siege engines. He remained in the siege for five weeks and put the town in such a state by the beating of his engines and assaults that it no longer could be held. During this time of the siege the Duke of power of men that he was able to assemble and to come and raise the siege and he went to lodge at Piédreuch a quarter league from St. Brio with three thousand combatants of whom there were two hundred men-at-arms and all the remaining ones were men on foot. On the morrow the duke left Piédreuch. When he was before the army of the lord of Clisson, he put his men in battle order. The constable Clisson, who was a valorous knight of bold enterprise, went boldly from his siege camp with his men arranged to give battle to the duke if he dared to wait. The Duke of Brittany seeing the battle order of the lord of Clisson, told his men: "My lords and companions, see Clisson there has arranged his companies and desires nothing but battle. I would not willingly refuse that at all but I see that he has arranged a great wing of his men who are mounted on great coursers of superior quality. Our horses are small; and those who are over there will come charge us and we will not be able to withstand them; and things will be the worse for us." For this reason the duke retreated that day with his men to Piédreuch, which he had left, and Clisson to his lodgings. When Clisson was lodged, he called his captains and told them: "Good lords, I know well that the Duke of Brittany will order an attack tomorrow before Montcontour, which is of the county of Penthièvre, so pillage the country, for there is much there to be had. It is my intention to send Beaumanoir, who is here, all through the night between Piédreuch and Montcontour, and you Le Barrois and Châteaumorand, take thirty companions mounted on the best coursers you have, and you Sempy and Montcavrel also and you Guillaume de Laire and your companions also. None but the best horses should be employed in the affair. Beaumanoir will lead the remaining men of my household for I do not wish that you should be any more than 150 men-at-arms for you are plenty for six hundred horses of Bretons and as God wills, the horses of the Bretons will be useless, and it seems to me that you will not fail to find your adventure, and you will be able to take it or destroy it, as you see fit.[25] The lord of Beaumanoir and his company went to set an ambush between Piédreuch and Montcontour. So it happened that on the morrow, between daylight and sunrise, the lord of Chastel and Sir Pons Perilleux left the Duke of Brittany to go and ride to Montcontour, and the Duke

25 It is unclear what they hoped to take. St. Brio? Montcontour?

of Brittany was to follow to besiege it, and these people were to be organized as a vanguard. But Beaumanoir—who was in his ambush, and saw them coming from far away with their companions, all with lances in hand—charged fiercely right into them, so the result of was eight score Bretons dead and wounded, and the remnant escaped by burrowing into the great and deep forest and among the others who were taken were the lord de Chastel and Sir Pons Perilleux, brother of the viscount of Rodes in Aragon and other good Breton prisoners. Beaumanoir with his company went back to Montcontour, where they hoped the duke would come to harm them if he could. But the Duke of Brittany who had said this left in great haste and made his way with all of his men to the bridge of Lanion, which is a bridge on the seashore. Beaumanoir and his people who knew that the duke had crossed the bridge, left Montcontour and went after Clisson whom they found before St. Brio, prepared to fight at the crossing of Lanion where he had crossed, and there the constable Clisson went to offer battle and so the two armies saw each other on the bank of the sea and in their encounters both sides did good deeds of arms, and fought good big skirmishes. When it came to the middle of the day, the lord of Clisson said to his men: "My good lords, you are well mounted, the horses of those over there are small, charge into these Bretons and push them into the duke's battalion." They did just that and in this melée a good hundred Bretons of the duke's party were killed and a good hundred horses gained; inside of two hours later the Duke of Brittany went to St. Lormech, and the constable, the lord of Clisson back with his chivalry and his people to his siege before St. Brio des Vaulx, whose inhabitants surrendered to him the next day, seeing that the duke who ought to have delivered them had failed to rescue them from the siege.

LXX. How the constable Clisson warred on Brittany, and how the duke Philip of Burgundy in a good way reconciled the Duke of Brittany and the Count of Penthièvre.

The Constable of France, the lord de Clisson, had sojourned at St. Brio for four days and had garrisoned it with his men, and to do the worst to the Duke of Brittany who he was waging war against, he sent out raiding into the forests of Quintin where all the livestock of the country was and also the hunting reserves of Angoillo from which he led away more than ten thousand head of animals, which the lord of Clisson shared out and gave to all of his companions. From St. Brio Clisson went to Poirier, which belonged to the marshal of the duke in his war, Sir Bertrand Goyon, and the place was assailed on all sides until it was taken and leveled. From this place the lord of Clisson ordered the captains that the king had given him to the port of Lanyon which the Viscount of Coymen held, and there were eight hundred men-at-arms, and they went there in good order, but they did not find the viscount, for he had gone to the duke and had left his place unprepared like a fool. It was taken by assault as was the Viscountess of Coymen his wife, and he lost everything that the viscount had there and the lady prisoner to Chapelle, the niece of Châteaumorand who was not detained, for she was given her robes, and went off to her friends and a garrison was left there in the port of Lanion for the lord of Clisson; and in returning the house of the bishop of St. Brio was taken which was very strong and near the cross of Malchalt where Merlin did marvels. From there the constable Clisson and his army went to Quintin which is at the entry of the forest of Broceliande, which town surrendered to him, and then to Loheac, where he collected all his men wishing to do some further great thing. But while the Constable was at Loheac, news came to him of how Duke Philip of Burgundy was at Angiers, which the Duke of Brittany had planned for a long time, and so Sir Jean de Hangest and his brother, brothers of the bishop of St. Brio-des-Vaulx, were requested to make peace between the Count of Penthièvre and him. The Duke of Burgundy, who was at Angiers, sent his ushers at arms to the constable lord de Clisson and to the captains whom the king had given him, with letters patent from the king and his people which were presented to him, while saying that they and the Duke of Brittany acted treasonously at Angiers towards the Duke of Burgundy, who was charged with making this peace and that during the agreement and the negotiations neither Clisson nor the captains should perform any exploit of war, for the king forbade it and also likewise to the Duke of Brittany that all together had vowed to obey the Duke of Burgundy, because he had been sent to these parts by the king and while saying that they and the Duke of Brittany were charged to make this peace, and Clisson should not bring to Angiers more than one hundred men-at-arms in his company, nor the Duke of Brittany one hundred or six score, and they should lodge in Angiers, one on this side of the river and the other on the other side so that there would be no quarrel there. If I have told you a long story, know that peace was made there and sworn by the Duke of Brittany and the Count of Penthièvre in this manner. For they promised in the hands of the Duke of Burgundy that in regard to all the debates which might happen between them, they would not make war without the permission of the king or of the Duke of Burgundy representing the person of the king; and so their oaths were made. It was said that this was a very honorable peace which the Duke of Burgundy had made which was not to appear partial to one side or the other, but so honorably executed this deed for the king that one could not name a better or more honorable peace. The Duke of Burgundy wished that peace pact should take place in sight of the two parties before the captains of both the king and of the Duke of Bourbon who were with Clisson and the others in order that each would witness the treaty. The Duke of Burgundy asked the Duke of Brittany if this treaty seemed good to him and the other party likewise: so they were content with what had been done in the name of the king, whence the Duke of Burgundy, who was, as everyone knew, a wise and valiant prince, said: "But I want also to say to you one word more which I have been charged to do by the king. For I assure you by my faith before all the chivalry, that the first of you who breaks this treaty and wages war, my lord the king will come against him to his destruction." So the Duke of Burgundy left Angiers and the Duke of Brittany remained in peace and the Duke of Burgundy headed with all the other captains towards the king their sovereign lord, who was at Paris, and the king and all the other lords were well content with the peace which the Duke of Burgundy his uncle had made and the obeisance which the Duke of Brittany and the Count of Penthièvre had made to him.

LXXI. How the king went to visit his country of Languedoc, accompanied by his brother and the Duke of Berry and the Duke of Bourbon.

Not long after Brittany was pacified, the King of France received counsel and advice to go to Languedoc where he had not been since the death of his uncle the Duke of Anjou, which is one of the good countries for money that the king had. And at that time, the king, who had a happy and joyous heart gave and spent so much that he was not able to provide for his own needs, and he was advised that it was for the best that he should head into those parts to collect funds for he had a good need of them and it was the country which was most able to aid him with funds, because it was located in the marches and confines of Guienne and Bourdelois and other provinces which were most able to harm the king and for that it was necessary to go there.

Orléans, brother of the king, together with the Duke of Berry and the Duke of Bourbon went with the king accompanied by four hundred men-at-arms. When everything was arranged the king left Paris and went to Mehun-sur-Yèvre, where the Duke of Berry feasted him grandly and then to Gannat, where the lord of La Tour with the ladies and demoiselles of the country happily feasted him. The king left Gannat and went to Puy-Notre-Dame, where all the people came to see him, and the king stayed in the town for three days, where he was given many beautiful presents and some great gifts. From Puy the king took the straight road to Carcassonne, which is such a city and town that one ought to know it, where he stayed eight days to visit the fine castle and city which is there. The king had it announced that everyone who had committed a crime should come to him, for he had come to the country to do justice to each one; and in this town he carried out much business, and for that which remained to do he appointed a time to everyone who had come to him at Toulouse where all of Languedoc attended him, and he was received and feasted so grandly that it was marvelous to see the delight. There were so many people in the streets to see him that no one could pass. So the streets by which he passed, were adorned and decorated with ornaments rich and beautiful, and the consuls of the town were dressed in royal habit and carried the canopy to the king, and little children came forward and carried in their hands little banners of the fleur-de-lis, crying "Noel! Long live the king!" So the processions of the university and the other clergy followed, of which there were a great many. And after the king were the dukes of Orléans, Berry, and Bourbon, and far enough behind them the barons and seigneurs of the country, then the seneschal and the magistrate of those parts, and then the people of the guilds followed in their proper order, dressed in livery and carrying the banner of their offices. And wherever the king went in Toulouse, tables were set up, where all manner of men drank and ate in passing. In this joy the king went to the major church to praise God, and from there to castle Nerbonnois, his royal hostel, where he stayed a month, to learn how well his officers did, and to hear accounts and from there to rule on the quarrels of the country. During the time that the king remained at Toulouse his vassals came to him, he sent for the Count of Armagnac and the count of Foix and also there were the knights and squires of the country. The king had it cried around that all who held fiefs with him should come to Toulouse and he would receive them; and more, that each one who knew himself to be forfeit, he would give law and justice, and for this cause, he had come to this country; the words were well and gladly taken by the whole people, who said: "The king is well come." And then when the king had received his homages and the country was put back in good order by the good advice of his uncles, the dukes of Berry and Bourbon, the city of Toulouse made a great contribution of dishes, and the townsmen made some big requests, to which the king granted those which seemed to him good, and the others not. The country of Languedoc gave the king in all three hundred thousand francs of good money.

Tomb effigy of Olivier V de Clisson in Basilique Notre Dame du Roncier, Josselin, Brittany.
Wikimedia Commons, public domain.
Paul Barlow photographer.

LXXII. How the embassy of the city of Genoa came to the king to petition that he would be pleased to give a power of men to cross to Africa.

The renown of the government of the realm of France ran everywhere, a result of the good sense and honesty of the lord dukes his uncles. For everyone who heard of it praised God for the good justice which reigned there, for which God suffered the realm to be at peace, and indeed the valiant French knights entertained themselves with long voyages to have more honor; and those from other realms came to France to see the king, who gladly received them and gave them generously from his own. The knights said that prosperity sat well in the realm for a fine prince was king, a capable knight, strong and agile, well-prepared to conquer great things; and when they had returned to their countries, they highly praised the sayings and deeds of the King of France. At this time the city of Genoa governed itself by a commune, and the people chose one or the other to be duke for a certain time, to govern the town inside and out. Insofar as they governed themselves by this policy they were united and prospered greatly and conquered overseas many towns and castles. Now in this season when the King of France was still at Toulouse the city acted as I have said. At that time the Duke of Genoa was a very subtle man, wise and well-spoken, named Sir Antonio Adorno, who if he thought to bring to a good conclusion the enterprise he wished to accomplish he did not know any prince to whom he could so quickly ask for help than the King of France, who had the heart for great things, and was at peace, so that no one made war on him. Therefore the Duke of Genoa sent a notable embassy to Toulouse to the King of France, supplicating him that it would please [the king] to help the Genoese, who were his well-wishers, and grant them men of power to go against the infidels. That they knew a town in Saracen lands which was at one of the points of the sea of Spain and that of France called the town of Tunis in Barbary, which provisioned three Moorish kings, who did not have enough if it weren't for the town from which they received victuals, from the people who brought them there by sea out of avarice for in all their countries no goods crossed because in their lands there was just a beach and there were three Saracen kings. First is the King of Tunis, the second the King of Tlemcen, and the third the King of Bougie. "And let us have no doubt," said the Genoese ambassador to the King of France, "that if Africa was in the hands of the Christians, which we will indeed take if it pleases God, and the three infidel kings and their lands are destroyed, they will thence take to the Christian faith, which would be a fine achievement for your reign, demonstrating that you are the greatest of the Christian kings, and will thus have great renown. If you undertake this affair here, we offer you, Sire," said the ambassadors, "from the seigneurie of Genoa, to all those whom you please to send there, to deliver to them vessels and biscuit, and that all the seigneurie of Genoa in this expedition is ready to live and die with you." This speech was well received by the king and the chivalry because of the fine offer of the Genoese. All the knights said to the king: "Sire, see here one of the best types of expeditions which one could ever see, and the prince was well-born in a good hour, that he should undertake such a good work for the honor of God and the good of Christendom." The King of France said to the ambassadors: "Your promises are good and honorable, and your request just and reasonable; and for this I will respond to them here in two days."

LXXIII. How the Duke of Bourbon undertook the expedition to Africa, and such lords offered to go with him with whom he was content and he retained them all.

During the space of two days which the King of France had to make a response to the Genoese through their embassy, the valiant prince Duke Louis of Bourbon came forward who said to the king: "My lord, I beg you that for all the services which I have always been able to do for you it please you to give me this charge, which I am able to do for you, and in your name, in God's service: this is the one thing in the world I most desire and after mundane deeds it is a good thing to serve God." Then the king said to the Duke of Bourbon: "Good uncle, you know the great affairs which we have to deal with, also you will find with great difficulty men who want to go so far. For this reason you will not want to undertake this voyage." The Duke of Bourbon replied to the king: "My lord, I have the knights and squires of my country who have never once failed me, nor in this affair will they fail me now, nor will I deny them their share of glory." And so much did the Duke of Bourbon press the King of France, his lord, that he was obliged to concede this to him. In the morning the Genoese came before the king to hear their response, and the king said to them that he had well known and seen the honorable expedition which they had proposed, "and for this reason," said the king, "I give you for your chief my good uncle the Duke of Bourbon, who is such a knight as you know, and I cannot give you any greater person of my blood, unless it would be the other dukes, my uncles of Burgundy and Berry in hopes that the thing should take place." The ambassadors of Genoa fell at once on their knees before the king giving thanks very humbly concerning whom he gave them to be with them, the prince which they most desired; and so the people of Genoa left very happy and so joyous that it appeared to them a gift from God and they hastened energetically to go prepare the army and there was a great uproar at Toulouse in the country of Languedoc and not even in Languedoc alone but also at Bordeaux and in Spain and also in Aragon concerning this expedition that the Duke of Bourbon would go against Saracens. It happened that the Souldich of Estrau, one of the best knights of the world who was from the Bourdelois, sent his embassy to the Duke of Bourbon begging and requesting that it would please him to obtain a safe conduct from the King of France for him and ten gentlemen so that he could go in his company on the expedition to Africa and the lord of Castillon-entre-deux-mers did the same, to whom the Duke of Bourbon sent safe-conducts of the king so they could come to his service; and the Viscount of Roddès who was a very valiant knight of the realm of Aragon, and the lord of Saigne were sent to beg from the Duke of Bourbon that it would please him that they should be in this army in his company. The lord of Couci who was in Picardy and knew about the enterprise of the Duke of Bourbon also the Count d'Eu sent to him that they had their retinue of two hundred men-at-arms which they led, and likewise the lord of Graville, a Norman, who had thirty men-at-arms to serve him. And the Duke of Bourbon was very happy about all this and he retained them all. But it happened that some strong noble Englishmen at Calais who knew about the movement of the Duke of Bourbon namely the lords of Clifford, Climbo, Neufville, Cornuailhe, Jeannicot d'Ortenye, Sir Jehan Franc, sent to the Duke of Bourbon requesting that he would be willing to receive twenty-five gentlemen and a hundred archers in his army if the duke would be content; and the lord of St. George who was of the county of Burgundy sent to ask the duke that he should retain twenty-five gentlemen; so the duke did this and God only knew whether the noble men of the household of the king, likewise those of the dukes of Orléans, Berry, and Burgundy, would offer their service to the Duke of Bourbon. So then the Duke of Bourbon thought: "So many people have been offered to me that I'm afraid I will not have enough ships" and then he had it put down in writing those who would go with him and he found that there were fifteen hundred gentlemen. Then the duke took one of the masters of the household and one member of the Chamber of Deniers[26] and five others of his officers to send word to the Genoese the number of men which he would be leading, informing them that he would have with him a good fifteen hundred gentleman so that they should know to have enough ships and also he sent them to get provisions of salt meat, biscuits, fish and other victuals which were appropriate for going by sea. So the Genoese sent word to the Duke of Bourbon: "Sire, we have enough vessels to lead six thousand men-at-arms if you bring them, there is no lack of horses and we are happy and overjoyed about what you sent to us. Bring what you want: for we have twenty-two galleys and eighteen ships and they are well lodged, please God, because let it please you that you and all your men should be at Genoa the week after St. John's Day[27] and there you will find us completely ready to cross over." This having been decided, the king left his country of Languedoc, and he went to Avignon to see Pope Clement [VII], and the Duke of Bourbon with him, who went willingly to ask permission from the pope to go against the infidels and that he should give absolution of punishment and sin for him and his people. The Holy Father did this with a good heart for the Duke of Bourbon and his people and the Genoese and for all those who went in the army and the king was grandly feasted by the pope who blessed him and went to Paris together with the Duke of Bourbon, who took leave from the king, his brother and the lords and he went to his country of the Bourbonnois where he organized the honorable things which he had to do both for the ordering of his country and for

26 The deniers were the standard coins and the Chamber of Deniers was a financial body of the royal government.

27 June 24.

the army under him. He being resident in the Bourbonnois, he had all his good servants come to him to put in order the affairs of his country, which he ordered immediately and in this ordinance specified that Lord Norris should have the government of his lands.

A 15th century depiction of Duke Louis landing in Africa.
British Library, Royal 14 D VI f84v.

LXXIV. How the Duke of Bourbon sent two knights to the king who agreed with him about what the Genoese asked; how he responded; and how the duke came to Marseilles.

Sir Antonio Adorne, Duke of Genoa, who well knew the goodwill and great diligence which the Duke of Bourbon put into the deed going to Africa, said to him that the army was just about ready and he lacked nothing for the day which had been set. But the Duke of Genoa said to the Duke of Bourbon : "Sire, the commune begs you that you should obtain from the king that he will be willing to give them certain consignments of wheat and wine, for money, in his country of Provence; for the country of Genoa is poor and lacks the resources of other countries. We of Genoa asked him but he is not willing to grant it; for that reason the army might break up. Accordingly, sire, we implore that you attend to this yourself." When the Duke of Bourbon had received the letters from Genoa he was afraid that the army of Africa would be broken, concerning which there was a great rumor, and immediately having heard his counsel he sent Sir Charles de Hangest to the king to ask him for that which the Genoese had asked him, and that it would please him to grant two thousand barrels of wine and four thousand loads of wheat to put in biscuits. Further the knight was charged to ask the king that the whole army which was going to Africa should come to Marseille and at the town should be surrendered to the Duke of Bourbon and to all those whom he would put there and the Duke of Bourbon worked hard to repair the evil which could happen. Furthermore, the duke asked that it would please the king to assign some men there to be charged with making sure that the price of supplies was not excessive, considering it was in the service of God which they were going. All of these things were entrusted to Charles de Hangest and his men to report to the king, whom he found at Beaucaire. So the king received him grandly and saw the requests which the Duke of Bourbon made of him, to which he responded as you will hear. "The expedition," said the king, "which our good cousin the Duke of Bourbon has undertaken is very grand and very honorable and everyone ought to help him with the great honor that he has undertaken, but when it is at the request of the Genoese I wish that my good cousin of Bourbon should know that I don't love them a little bit and that they should not have any victuals of mine unless they pay a great tribute, for this is the custom. But notwithstanding this, for the great expeditions and service of God which the good cousin has undertaken this and more I will grant him and all the other things which I am able to do to please him." Sir Charles de Hangest left the king and took his letters with him and went to Genoa by way of Marseille who waited for them to have the letter of their treaty which they were as happy as they were astounded, and the ambassadors together with the Genoese undertook that the twenty-two galleys and ships should come from Genoa to Marseille to collect the Duke of Bourbon and his people. It appeared to them for the better, and also provided them with a very big market for victuals. So the Genoese praised the statement of the ambassadors from the Duke of Bourbon who departed from Marseille and went to the duke their lord to whom they recounted the answer of King Louis and that which they had accomplished with the Genoese who concerning this were more happy and joyous than one is able to say. So the Genoese praised this statement; and the duke said that God directed the affair and immediately sent through all countries of which he had news that everyone who intended to cross with him to Barbary should come to Marseille on the first day of July and then they should find the navy ready to go when they would be able to embark and cross over if it please God; and at once the Duke of Bourbon who was meticulous about everything heeded the advice that he had ten days beforehand to organize his navy and to plan what he should do in each day and also if the Genoese should hasten to come there when they knew that the duke had come to Marseille. So he did, for he was there on the chosen day well accompanied by men of his household and country. With the Duke of Bourbon at Marseille, the Genoese advanced to lead their navy to him, as much as to show they would not fail to honor their commitment as to collect their victuals. After they came with their galleys and ships, the Duke of Bourbon had counsel with the Genoese about how many men each galley could carry. And for this the duke told that they should put in a roll all their ordinances and how much each galley and ship could hold of men and victuals, and the course which they ought to set. And this the valiant Duke of Bourbon did, so that when his men had come they should know where to be and what to do. And the duke commanded further to his quartermasters what to do, and how to do it, ensuring that the lord of Couci, the Count d'Eu and other lords and men of good name who followed him, were thus lodged honorably at Marseille as they were. But the Duke of Bourbon did not remain six days in Marseille which those who had requested it did not come from all sides and others who had not asked him for anything, like the Count Daulphin, the Viscount of Uzès, lord of Caillart, who had a good company, and many others. Why should I tell you the whole long story? So that the lords with their men came, the Duke of Bourbon, as they were, had them assigned to the ships in order that each one provide that which they were lacking notwithstanding the promise of the Genoese which was a good ordinance and well conducted by the Duke of Bourbon. Beyond the provisions of the Genoese the Duke of Bourbon acquired and put in his vessels two hundred barrels of wine and two hundred pieces of salt pork with a lot of pottages and such provisions which are carried on the sea. He put two thousand chicks in his ships in case of maladies. When the men were all come to Marseille each one found his lodgings prepared and ready for them to go on the sea.

LXXV. How the Duke of Bourbon departed from Marseille, went to Genoa, and how in good order he landed before Tunis and besieged it; and how the Saracens were rebuffed.

In the year of grace 1390 this noble and valiant prince, Louis Duke of Bourbon left the city of Marseille to make the voyage which he had undertaken with the lords who for his sake had come to accompany him, and embarked on the sea on the day when they were supposed to go according to the ordinance which they had written before. After the army was on the sea all of the ships and galleys were loaded at Port-Vendres with meat and wine, fresh water and armor and everything which was appropriate and necessary for an army to carry a nobleman in such an affair. The Duke and the other barons took their assigned decks and forecastles in the ships and galleys, while the knights, men-at-arms, and the sergeants of which there were many, and the arbalestiers lodged where they were ordered. Then the galleys and ships sailed by the wind which filled the sails, along the coast of Genoa; and it was ordered that the army should not disembark at Genoa, but should be on the sea for three long leagues, and the Duke of Bourbon entered there, for they had requested to see him. He entered there together with the Count d'Eu, the lord of Couci, and the Souldich de l'Estrau, and he was grandly received and feasted by the people although he hardly stopped there. On his departure they gave him large supplies of spices, syrups, plums of Damas, and other liquors which are good and strengthening for disease, for which he very much thanked them, and he left Genoa and went with to his army on the sea where there were twenty-two galleys and eighteen ships both of war and of voyaging, where there were hardy bachelors and good knights and valiant men-at-arms from many countries and able seamen who were sufficient for a fleet bound for finding a port and taking it. The Duke of Bourbon who was on his galley much enjoyed seeing galleys and ships one near the other for the weather was gentle and calm so that the sea hardly moved. The Duke of Bourbon entreated the young men that they should keep up their instruction and discipline of arms from the gentlemen and old warriors who were already proven men, and he entreated the old ones that they should instruct the younger ones who were most teachable. Then the Good Duke saw his people well encouraged to fight, and that he was ready and able to undertake a great affair and do it with their support he took the route to Africa, since the waves of the sea showed that the wind was up, hence they were able to sail as desired. So they navigated by the coast of Sardinia where there were plenty of good towns to better refresh themselves without wasting their victuals. The names of towns are: La Guillasse, Castle à Caligari, La Mousière, La Coniglière, which was but sixty leagues from Africa. At La Coniglière, a plan was made to land before Tunis with the vanguard, the battle, and the rearguard; and it was ordered that the lord of Couci, who was a very valiant knight and a good captain, should have the vanguard with him and the Count d'Eu to be the first to land, with a good six hundred men-at-arms that the Duke of Bourbon would give them and a thousand arbalestiers from Genoa and elsewhere to complete the company, and the Duke of Bourbon with those of his household and his country should disembark afterwards with his battle and the Souldich of Estrau, the lord of Castillon, and the English with the Count Dauphin together with the Genoese who were in the army should follow them in the rearguard. The lord of Couci and the Count d'Eu and their company landed before Tunis near a mosque of the Saracens where they made themselves battle-ready, to wait for those from Africa who were to assault them but no Saracens appeared to attack them and seeing this the Duke of Bourbon quickly debarked from his galley with all of his own battle and all of the rearguard. And by nightfall, the Christians were facing before this city of Tunis in good order, with their whole navy behind them. The next day the siege was organized by the Duke of Bourbon and the Genoese and he sat before Tunis on the land side and the Genoese on the sea side. The siege which the Duke of Bourbon set was along the land from the sea on one side to the sea on the other side where the Africans had three gates, and on the sea side they just had one and the Saracens of Africa, twelve thousand of them when they saw their town besieged by the Christians didn't wait a second to attack the lodgings of the Duke of Bourbon and the others, from their three gates, all to inflict great damage on the Christians with one stroke. So they waited three days without coming out, uncertain of how much those outside would do. And after three days had passed, at the time when the host took its meal, when the Saracens did not see any of the men, they sallied out of Africa by the three gates with the intent of running beyond the houses; but with this the Christians kept on their guard, each one remaining fully armed. So the Saracens failed in their enterprise, for those of the army who were prepared and armed repulsed them so heavily that the Saracens had three hundred men killed and those at the lodging of the Duke of Bourbon advanced so far in this muddle, where the good gentleman Sir Hugh de Chastellus, lord of Châteaumorand who never in his life did voyage save at his own expense, nor was he ever content to remain in the court of the lord, and after him his two sons Jean and Guichard, knights, the lord of Négrepelisse, who was of the household of the duke, the lord of l'Espinasse, the lord of Chastel de Montaigne, Sir Le Barrois, Sir Blain Loup, Marshal de Bourbonnois, the lord of St. Priest, Sir Renaud de Bressolles, Sir Robert de Damas, Sir Guillaume de Garet, Sir Berthomier du Vernay, the lord of St. Porgue, Tachon de Glené, Michaille, Phelippe Beraud, Guichard Lebrun and many others of that household whose names I don't know with many others who acted in such a way that they killed many Saracens at the gate of Tunis with the result that the Saracens had such fear that they did not sally out for three weeks, but gave thought to fortifying their place.

LXXVI. How the Duke of Bourbon spoke to the council before Africa and how the siege camp was enclosed, and the organization of guarding it.

The Genoese, who knew the Moorish Coast, had sent ahead and commanded two of their speedy galleys in the Saracen marches to spy out the country, and they returned to the siege camp and reported to the Duke of Bourbon and the whole army that the King of Tunis, the King of Bougie, and the King of Tlemcen prepared vigorously to combat the Duke of Bourbon with a good sixty thousand horses. To which report the Duke of Bourbon replied: "They are badly come! They should consider what they want to do." Then the duke called the lord of Couci, the Count d'Eu, the Count Daulphin, the lord of Graville, the Souldich of Estrau, the Viscount of Uzès and others. And the Genoese captains and the duke told them in council that three Saracen kings were coming against them and what they ought to do. Concerning which some said that was a great thing to await these kings and their power and of those who were before Tunis; and others said they preferred to raise the siege and depart to leave shamefully when the Saracens were coming in such great numbers. To which thing the Duke of Bourbon was unable to restrain himself but responded to the latter: "My lords, I greatly marvel that you fear what you have not seen, and you don't know yet if they are coming. It appears to me that if the Saracens are coming we are strong enough to have a good fight against them, with God's help." The duke said to some of his relatives: "You, good Cousin d'Eu, and you good cousin Couci, what do you say about this?" They said to him: "My lord we think that what you have said is good, and very honorable. For to say that you have come from so far a country to gain honor on this side, and that honor comes, and you have lost it, you have made dishonor out of your honor." Then the Duke of Bourbon said: "My lords, you speak well. It seems to me that it would be good to enclose our lodgings with some light fencing, because the Saracens don't fight except on horseback." The lords said: "My lord, you speak well, and we also wish to say it and a little enclosure will be enough. And it was said by the Genoese that it would suffice that the enclosure be made of ropes which spanned from one sea to the other, enclosing the siege camp, which would be four feet high, so the horses would not be able to jump it. That should suffice for this rabble. But at this assembly there were some wise Genoese who said that when the rope was stretched out oars from the galleys should be placed between the ropes so that the arbalestiers would be able to shoot better and more forcefully against the Saracens if they attacked the army and also against the push of lances. So this discussion was well heard and heeded by all which much pleased them, and so the army was enclosed. Afterwards the Duke of Bourbon ordered where the captains of the Genoese army should be, which guard each should have in the manner which you will hear. First each who had a hundred men-at-arms and fifty arbalestiers should be established to guard twenty-five fathoms which order was given to each lord or captain having charge of men-at-arms. Further after mature deliberation it was ordered that the Duke of Bourbon should have with him a thousand combatants under his banner, which Sir Robert de Damas should carry, and Sir Jean de Châteaumorand should carry his pennon, who held themselves in formation at the duke's command in front of one of three gates of Africa, and five hundred arbalestiers to aid and secure where there were needs most pressing and to repulse the Saracens if they sallied out of the town. In such was the order so good and fine, they all said: let the Saracens come when they wish!

LXXVII. How the King of Tunis, a Saracen, accompanied by two other kings, came before Africa: the skirmish that took place there; and how the Duke of Bourbon and the lords skirmished there one day after another.

The Saracen king of Tunis, the principal one in Barbary, knew that his city of Tunis was besieged by Christians and was prepared to relieve his town with men-at-arms, or raise the siege, if he could, but he felt that he was not strong enough to do this, and called upon two allied and consort Kings who at his command came to Tunis in great strength, to whom he said: "You my dear brothers, and perfect friends, King of Tlemcen and King of Boulgie, you have known how the people of Genoa by their presumption have for many years warred upon me, and presently have done worse to me. The duke and rectors of their city have caused the Christian prince to come, the prince of the blood royal of the great King of France, namely the Duke of Bourbon. And then if he should take my town, which he and the Genoese are besieging, this would be a great loss for me, and you should be impoverished, because your soils are poor and sandy, and not well-provided with resources, save those that come by sea from my port at Tunis. And to this I say: do not for long suffer an enemy's rule that you could remove by stratagem or force. Confront them, knowing what sort of people they are, and fight for our freedom." And the King of Tunis, having finished his speech, the other kings agreed with him. Know then that eight days did not pass before the King of Tunis, the King of Tlemcen and the King of Boulgie assembled at Tunis, each in their formations, according to their custom, with all their trumpets, drums, cymbals, fifes and clarions, ready for battle. And they were indeed a good 60,000 persons, on foot and on horseback, and they were as close to the Christian army as only one shot of an arbalestier. At this hour from there sallied out from the army two stones' throw, a thousand combatants and six hundred arbalestiers: and seeing this the Saracen kings ordered their own knights all well accompanied with horses to clash with the Christians but they did not dare to approach because of the shot; and the Christians saw their cowardice, advanced, especially those who had been ordered to this, and struck them vigorously and the men-at-arms and the arbalestiers behaved so well on this charge that they made the Saracens retreat by chasing them well, and by force of shot; and the skirmish was so good that the Saracens lost there sixty good horses and a hundred men dead. And the Saracens, seeing themselves routed in this way, forced themselves to enter battle with the Christians, because they could see how few they were compared to their own large number. Many valiant knights and reliable heralds later claimed that if the night had not come so quickly, and if the rearguard had joined in the battle, that the infidels would have there lost their advantage, and been turned back to their shame. But the Duke of Bourbon, who was experienced in battle and war, seeing the night approach, did not want his people taking such a risk, considering that those in the city could launch a surprise attack. And so, night fell and passed, and the three Moorish kings and their men went to camp near Tunis on some high ground, which was quite close to the army of the Duke of Bourbon and of the Genoese, where the Saracens put up their tents and pavilions; those in Tunis greatly rejoiced in their coming that night and when the Christians saw their situation it was ordered by the Duke of Bourbon his council and the Genoese that they should place six hundred men-at-arms and three hundred arbalestiers to stand guard on a little hill about two stone-throws in height, in case the Saracens should venture out to skirmish; and was well put into effect. At this time nothing more was done on either side and so the Saracens withdrew into their tents and the Christians into their lodgings and they ceased their labors and the others who had been given the responsibility went on guard. The Christians went out against the Saracens into battle each day to defy them and ran right up to their tents to skirmish. The Saracens seeing this came out from their lodgings and fought skirmishes with the Christians so it happened that sometimes the Christians repulsed the Saracens, penetrated right up to their lodgings, and likewise sometimes up to their army: for such is the profession of arms.

The lords who had come with the Duke of Bourbon said: "My lord, we have been informed, and rightly so, that you intend to take the city of Tunis, and these kings who are here wish to prevent that; and this siege will take some time, because they do not wish to engage you in [full] battle, but instead, little by little, come every day to skirmish, hoping to starve us or find us in disarray. Therefore, we suggest that you and your men initiate raids of our own against these infidels." This was very pleasing to the Duke of Bourbon and he granted it to them with a good heart, so skirmishes of the Christians and Saracens commenced on that day. First, Lord Couci and the Count d'Eu with their people fiercely fought, and on the morrow the Count Dauphin, the Viscount of Uzès, and the Viscount of Roddes and the lord of La Saigne of Aragon, who with their people performed well. Following the next day that valiant knight the Souldich of Estrau of Bourdelois and with him the lord of Castellon together with their men, valiantly conducted themselves in there. The fourth day the lord of St. George with the lord of Graville and their men performed very grandly. After this, as the days passed there were in their turn, the lord of Clifford, Jean Franc, and the good squire Jennicot d'Ortenye with Cornuaille, who therewith claimed his eminence amongst their Englishmen, who really performed well. And each one did his turn according to the coming day. And the Duke of Bourbon, seeing that the others had done their turns went there in person with the knights and squires of his household, who skirmished there vigorously, and those of his company. And so too did the Genoese captains and the men-at-arms, with their arbalestiers, who killed many Saracens, and it was one of those skirmishes that had to cause many people on both sides to be killed and wounded. For forty-two days altogether without any delay they skirmished with each other. And it frustrates you or I to single out any one of these valiant knights and squires for their audacity, or strength, or prowess. So well did they do it that each of them was worthy of being praised; for the nub of it was that twenty Christians took on thirty Saracens with lances and shot.

LXXVIII. How the Duke of Bourbon and his company made the assault against the town of Tunis; how the Saracens maintained themselves against the Christians.

The Duke of Bourbon taking into account the deeds of Saracens and their comportment sent a query to the lords of his company and the captains of the Genoese to whom he said: "My lords, you see the power of the Saracen people. As I long as I have your government, they're not so much to fear as people say for I see that our people get the better of them every day in every skirmish and because of that I think that since we have come before this town of Tunis we have not put any effort into the assault. So it will be good to consider how one can take it. We will be famous if before such power of our enemies we are able to take it." And the lord of Couci, the Count d'Eu and the other barons said that he spoke true, and further the Count d'Eu and the lord of Couci said: "My lord, you will do well to ask the Genoese if they carry any equipment of war and see what they think of it." So they sent to the Genoese captains of the ships and galleys to whom they made this request: then the Genoese responded: "My lord, we have in our ships a scaffolding three stories in height and three fathoms and a half in width, and couldn't we bring forth this scaffolding on little rollers, since some of our factors living in the town's merchant quarter have told us that we would not fail to take the town by land with such a tower, the might of which the Saracens are unaware. And on the other side by the sea," said the Genoese, "we have the intention to build on four galleys two *becs de faulcon*, and on each *bec de faulcon* a watchtower in which to put fifteen men-at-arms and ten arbalestiers. Each *bec de faulcon* should be as high, and no higher, than the tower of the gate, which is quite strongly defended. If we are able to take this tower, we will then win everything else."[28] The Christians of the army were so happy and joyous about this, since it appeared that all was ours. The Duke of Bourbon asked the Genoese when this equipment would be ready. The Genoese did not ask for a term of more than eight days when their affair should be ready, about which there was great rejoicing. And without fail, the Genoese had their scaffolding prepared, and were ready to bring it up near to the city tower, where it was intended, and the *becs de faulcon* to be brought on the galleys as well. The people of Tunis, seeing the preparations being made to attack, no longer trusted the Christians remaining in the city, as a point of security, and restricted them to their homes, for the Saracens greatly feared

28 *Bec de faulcon* or "falcon's beak" was a phrase used to describe anything that resembled a beak, especially a pole weapon with a sharp point on one side and a hammer on the other. Here it describes a siege weapon mounted on a galley. The siege engine had a tower garrisoned by twenty-five men, and was big enough to support a large hammer.

this scaffolding which approached their walls. So they put all the bombards of the town, and they had good ones, on the top of the tower of the gate, to shoot at said scaffolding, and the Saracens covered the stones which they shot with inch-thick tow, on which they spread a powder with which to set fire to the scaffolding, and such stones arrived all ablaze. And the Saracens of Tunis flung so many stones that they burnt down the scaffolding within one day and one night, which much enraged the Christians. But during this the Duke of Bourbon and the knights who were there that notwithstanding the risk, advised that all the company should go in good order to assault the town, at the three gates, on land in order that the *becs de faulcon* which the galleys carried by sea should do something, and so the assault was ordered, and the *becs de faulcon* ordered to do their duty. On the morrow the assault began, with the *becs de faulcon* doing what the Genoese had undertaken. But the Saracens of the town made an engine of war on the tower in opposition to the *becs de faulcon*, as you shall hear. The Saracens who maintained a rearguard of the town including undoubtedly the tower of the gate, set aside all the defenses in order to build a wooden platform at the highest point; without apparent defenses but with holes about three fingers wide placed at intervals, and this having been done, placed some of these Saracens beneath the platform. All the Christians who crossed onto the platform from the *becs de faulcon* had their feet pierced by the Saracens who were beneath them, these Christians being unable to see the Saracens, and the Christians had so many wounded that it became necessary for many to jump down from the tower and so ceased the assault of the *becs de faulcon*. And near the gates, on the ground, where the Duke of Bourbon was, together with the companies of the lords who were with him, each in the place to which he was ordered, and the Genoese with their countrymen (leaving a guard sufficient for a retreat), the attack was so fierce that one of the gates was burned. But the great multitude who were inside blocked it up so that none could enter. And during the assault the three Saracen kings named above and more than 46,000 men were in range of an arbalest of the Christians—who shouted: "Brace yourselves!" nastily at those of the town. And they did not dare approach that army, on account of the strong rearguard which watched out for any Saracens fleeing. It was a fine thing for the Duke of Bourbon and his company to attack so strong and good a town on the sea like Tunis was, before the power of three Saracen kings who at the beginning had sixty thousand horses not including the power of the city.

LXXIX. How the Duke of Bourbon went to make Boucicault the younger retreat, and how the duke attacked the Saracen tents with his men.

The darkness of night required the Saracens to retreat into their lodges and the Christians into their enclosure, and so the day passed. But for eight days afterwards while the Christians and the Saracens were facing each other it happened that Boucicault took his turn at the watch, which was always drawn up between the army and the Saracens. Boucicault was a chivalrous man who, through some interpreter made a request in the skirmish where he was whether there was any Saracen who wished to combat him on foot or horse. They replied no. Then Sir Boucicault said if they wished to perform arms ten against ten or twenty against twenty he and his company would be ready. So the Saracens responded no, not if the kings their lords did not want them to. When Boucicault saw their refusal he said to them that he would fight them in a secure field, twenty Christians versus forty of their Saracens. As long as this conference lasted it was ordained that they should not make war on each other. With difficulty were these negotiators, Christians and Saracens, brought together, which astounded the Duke of Bourbon, the lord of Couci, the Count d'Eu, the Souldich of Estrau, and the other barons, for the whole army ran to this assembly so that the lord of Couci, the Count d'Eu and others who saw the army taking leave of its senses said to the Duke of Bourbon: "My lord, the people run like beasts over there with Boucicault and they are not able to keep guard and it seems to us that if you do not order some to retreat, things will turn out badly for us." Then replied the Duke of Bourbon: "I can't send a better message than one from me. I'll go there myself." So he asked for a mule he always had and it appeared good to the lords, that he was not able to send a better message to make them retreat. So the duke mounted his mule, left his tent and went off with the people of his household. It was not long before more than three hundred gentlemen were following him. The Saracens who saw the Duke of Bourbon—whom they recognized by his coat of arms—coming to join Sir Boucicault with many men-at-arms, began strongly to retreat towards their tents, and Boucicault and those with him to chase them. Sir Boucicault who saw the Duke of Bourbon coming, gave himself over to pride and chased the Saracens more boldly and the Duke of Bourbon with his company went after to bring about a retreat. When Boucicault was at the tents, the Moorish kings and their Saracens put themselves in battle formation outside their lodgings, and Boucicault put himself in battle formation with his men, awaiting the Duke of Bourbon and those who came with him. The Duke of Bourbon caught up with those whom he wished to make retreat, and he very violently spoke to Boucicault, concerning his great follies. But the Duke of Bourbon seeing that there were a good two thousand combatants following him, and seeing also the Saracens who had abandoned their camps and put themselves in battle order all outside, said: "My friends, since we see the lodgings of the Saracens abandoned, let us go by God and charge among their lodges and if the Saracens are worth anything they will come and defend them." The duke forbade anyone should be so bold as to ignore his order and think about pillage, but they should fight forcefully and at the first sound of the trumpet which he would have sounded, everyone should pull back to his standard. Then the Duke of Bourbon first and the lords and the captains each in his place, with their men-at-arms and arbalestiers of Genoa charged among the tents of the Saracens, attacked all the lodgings and cut the ropes of the tents and set fire to the lodgings of straw and the Duke of Bourbon remained for an hour in the middle of the Saracen lodgings with his standard of the belt of hope. During this the Count d'Eu arrived with a good seven score combatants who came from the other side, by the shore, which made those who were already there very happy and joyous. Because he was late, the Count d'Eu said to the Duke of Bourbon: "My lord you see the finest thing one can see, and I thank God that I am found in your company, but for God's sake, let's go back, for it is evening and if the Saracens attack the lodgings there's only the lord of Couci with a few men, and a bunch of those are ill: so he will be completely lost." So the Duke of Bourbon said to the Count d'Eu: "We will go there immediately, please God." Then he had the trumpet sound and put himself in battle order, all outside the tents they had attacked a stone's throw away, and the duke ordered that in case the Saracens advanced to attack them that they should attack them en masse without chasing them; and the Duke of Bourbon put four hundred Genoese arbalestiers and two hundred men-at-arms with them like a wing. So the Saracens came four or five times thinking to strike in the rear, but they were fiercely rebuffed and lost their people, and accordingly the duke repaired to his lodgings in battle order, without loss of men, except for six gentlemen who had died in the Saracens' tents from lack of air or from dust, from which they did not recover, because they were very heavily armed; one of whom was lord of Vailly, brother of the Count of Sancerre, the second Sir Geoffrey de la Celle Guenon, and four of their squires. And the duke came to the lodgings and found the lord of Couci in good order, and he was very sad that he had not been in the Saracen tents with them. So each returned his place and order, and the Saracen kings whose lodgings the Christians had attacked went to camp a half a league farther away, and the Duke of Bourbon, after all this, remained before Tunis fifteen days, where on one side and the other as much by our Christians as by the Saracens there were fine exploits of arms for the Christians used some arms of the Moors against their enemies and the Saracens strove to fight with some arms of the Christians likewise.

LXXX. How the Christians' departure from the siege of Tunis took place and their good manner of leaving.

The Duke of Bourbon who was besieging Tunis greatly desired to have it. So it would turn to a great victory for himself if in the presence of the Moorish kings he would be able to take it and he dedicated himself to this purpose and so did the lords and men-at-arms of his company. So that the goal of his desire should come more quickly he spoke to some of the captains and patrons of the Genoese army about this. They replied: "Sire, this city is marvelously strong as you see and it is very well supplied with men and there are these kings with very great troops who in our opinion will not move to the field; you can do nothing to make them give battle and they delay us to make us eat up our victuals. Also in our warships we have neither ram nor rock thrower, neither any siege engine to take to the wall. Our siege tower is burnt and the becs de faulcon are exhausted: so we don't know what to say about this." The duke said: "There is only one thing more to do." And all the while that the Genoese spoke of this necessity to the other military commanders and galley captains, they were asking those of Africa for a treaty, by the terms of which the Genoese would lift the siege by the Duke of Bourbon and all the others, and that the Africans should do the same with the king of Tunis, with his army doing no harm to the Christians for ten years. So the Genoese willingly revealed this message to the Duke of Bourbon and his chivalry; that thus did it in the presence of the companions. Then a response was given by the duke to the Genoese, who boldly said to those of Africa, the Christians had not come there to pay tribute but to conquer them. Further they said to their king that the Christians had nothing to do with him, that he was worth nothing. On this the Genoese made a response, which much alarmed the Africans, and the Genoese were also alarmed, who had nothing more to maintain their fleet and also the chivalry had nothing to eat. The Genoese, seeing that the Africans wished to negotiate with them, proposed another treaty with them namely: that the payment which the King of Tunis took each year in Africa they would pay for fifteen years without said king taking any of it and within the year they should pay to the duke and the commune of Genoa twenty-five thousand ducats to pay them off from the army and they should give good and strong security such as they should demand. The security which the Genoese demanded, in answer to them and to guarantee the said treaty were Catalans, Neapolitans, and Sardinians, who were rich merchants living in the city, and they would guarantee the treaty; and the treaty between them should last for four whole years, which the great rich merchants did not want, but when they had enough debate on the subject they saw that all which they had that was worthwhile was in the town, some very great riches of all three countries, and that if the town was lost they would be ruined, seeing that the king gave them little aid. So they agreed to the treaty, which the Genoese reported to the Duke of Bourbon and his knights: and the Duke of Bourbon brought all the chivalry, French and English, together to know whether this treaty was honorable or not; and when they were standing in council the Duke of Bourbon wished that the Souldich de l'Estrau, from Bourdelois, who was one of the oldest in the army and one of the most valiant knights one could find spoke first. When asked his advice about it; the Souldich said that there was no reason that he should speak about it first and he had hardly seen any such thing in his time, but however he spoke willingly about what he knew, and that little which he had seen in his time, which he did not wish to praise. So he said that this was the best place he had ever found himself in his life, to have held out in the field against the power of the three kings for two and a half months and assailed the town, before them without them having sent remedy and since they had gone on to attack their tents, and had thrown them out by force which is a much greater thing than the greatest battle that one could ever see. "About the treaty, which those of Africa offer," the Souldich said further, "it is also as honorable as if the town had been taken: for you put them in tribute and in servitude, and they are not able to refuse and it is made in the face of all their power; and as for me," the Souldich said further, "who am nothing but a poor knight, I hold this thing as honorable as though I had been in three battles."

After the Souldich, Jeannicot d'Ortenie, an Englishman, one of the most valiant knights anywhere, said he held to the opinion of the Souldich d'Estrau and that certainly he did not know anything to say but to repeat it. Afterwards the lord of Clifford, chief of the English came, who said when asked that he held to the statement of the Souldich; and that was the opinion of the English. So after that the Duke of Bourbon asked the advice of the Count Dauphin, who told him: "Sire, it appears to me that the things that have been done are so great and good up to now, and the treaty so honorable, that you ought not to refuse it." Afterwards the lord of Couci spoke, and said plainly to the duke: "My lord, this voyage in which you have come is so grand and so honorable for you and for all those who have been on it, that one cannot say better as to such power as of the three kings and as to such great things which you have done. For they have not dared to fight you, they have lost every time and you have had the advantage, and moreover have taken their lodgings from them, which amounts as much in honor as a good battle, and it is a bad defeat for them. But you have such a great treaty by which they are so strongly enslaved, and whereby you are able to leave as honorably as though you had taken the town. And present such power as you see before us, and also my lord, and your people have a lack of victuals, and they have among them many diseases, from which you may lose many, because you have stayed too long; and you will be remaining for no good reason for you have the best treaty that one is able to obtain for you and for your company." Afterwards the judgment of the Count d'Eu was asked, who said that, after the lord of Couci he had nothing different to say.

Also it was put to the lord of Graville, who held to that opinion, and the lord of St. George, the lord of Castillon, and all other knights, of which there were many. And during this negotiation the Genoese had taken the surety of their treaty, nothing remained at all then but to order the departure and have the fleet prepare to leave on the third day. And on this third day the Duke of Bourbon ordered the vanguard, battle and rearguard to enter the vessels, and the duke said to the lord of Couci: "Good cousin, you were the first in the disembarkations when we came to Africa; I wish to be the last to climb into a galley in the departure." And so he did and sent the Duke of Bourbon to a mosque, behind an old wall where there were two hundred men-at-arms and a hundred arbalestiers and they were ordered on pain of their heads not to embark, they were there two hours before day; and at sunrise the duke sent his rearguard to the port and had it announced everywhere that each should withdraw to his vessels, just as had been ordered in the evening.

So they did, and those in Tunis who saw the retreat of the Christians, despite the treaty they had with the Genoese signaled to their army that the Christians were retreating. So all the Saracens came in battle order to the port, and despite this the Duke of Bourbon retreated in good order, each in his galley, turning their faces to the enemy so that there were not but two hundred men retiring with the duke. And when the Saracens saw that there were hardly any people left to retreat, the kings sent six hundred men on horse to attack them there, who made a great cry, and the Duke of Bourbon held his ground and revealed his ambush and attacked them, whom they drove off so heavily that a hundred or six score were killed in this charge and then the duke returned in his place, where he remained for half an hour, together with his ambushers, whom he ordered to withdraw with him, to see if the Saracens could be drawn in once again. However they did not come anymore. So the Duke of Bourbon retreated at a leisurely pace, along with his men, meeting no opposition, to his navy, and installed himself in his galley, floating upon the sea, with his army comingled with the Genoese. On this day, they went to the island of Connillière, where they stayed all the next day. And the Moorish kings, who knew that the issue of Africa was settled, headed back, each to his own country, with their Saracens. They had before doing this informed the Christians that this path would be the most honorable, and proposed it to the Duke of Bourbon through the knights of France and others connected to him, and said to the Genoese: "My good lords, see here the great lords, knights and others who have served their honor and you on your enterprise. They've come from afar to seek honor, and for this I pray you my friends if you know towns or places under the infidels where I and this fine company can employ ourselves, while we are together, name it, for I am ready to exert myself there and they are too. Then the captain of the Genoese army, Jehan de Oultremarine, answered: "My lord, we know of no place where you can better exert yourself than by going from here to Sardinia, where there is a castle which from all parts resupplies the kingdom of Tunis, where the merchants of the country come, and is called the Castle of Cagliari. And he who is able to take it will do a great injury to the Saracens and much good for the Christians: for Sardinia is a rich country which resupplies them."

Ships of the Mahdia Crusade-fleet with her leader, the Duke of Bourbon, and the Oriflamme (1390) as depicted in a 15th century manuscript. In the foreground is a galley while the rest of the ships appear to be cogs.
British Library, Harley 4379 f. 60v.
Wikimedia Commons, public domain.

LXXXI. How the Duke of Bourbon on his return from Africa took some places in Sardinia for supplying victuals to the Saracens, and how by chance he arrived in Sicily where the lord of Clermont feasted him; how he placated the lords of Plombin and de Lerbe against the Genoese and then went to Marseille.

Since the Genoese had assured and informed the Duke of Bourbon concerning that castle he and the other lords said: “Let’s go!” And from that island where they were the whole fleet sailed to Sardinia before Caillé and openly entered the port where there were very large ships which were taken by force of arms as was the lower town of the port. And the next day the Castle of Caligari surrendered to the Duke of Bourbon, where there was a captain who he declared to be for the Viscount of Narbonne, who did much evil, and was a man of that same country. And the Duke of Bourbon handed over the said castle to the keeping of the Genoese, whom he made to swear and promise that no victuals should go to Tunis; and the Genoese promised the duke that they would guard it well and loyally for the Christians, and on this promise the Genoese requested from the Duke of Bourbon the following: “My lord, there is near here another place that is more at fault than this one in resupplying Saracens, namely Guillastre, and is not so strong, such that it might be taken on the first assault, if they don’t surrender in the first place.”

So immediately the Duke of Bourbon and his chivalry said: “Let’s go there,” and they went, and after that they made the appearance of assaulting it, those of Guillastre did not wait at all for the assault but surrendered to the Duke of Bourbon who took it on condition that he grant them mercy. And he put them under the authority of the Genoese, whom he made promise that they should do nothing to displease those of the town: and they made an oath likewise as to the people of the castle of Caligari, and from there, the Duke of Bourbon and the Genoese set forth, and planned to head to Naples, to show them the treaty they had made with those who had provisioned Africa. But that night took place the most terrible disaster on the sea which ever a Christian saw, and they believed that all the galleys would sink and the ships perish. By fortune the Duke of Bourbon arrived at the island of Sicily, at a city called Messina, which belonged to a great baron of the country named Manffroi, lord of Clermont and many of his galleys were scattered and they came to arrive in many places, and of all the galleys of the army he lost at sea that of the Souldich d’Estrau and of the lord of Châteaumorand, which were broken by the force of the wind that went to the port of Tropez. They were so well helped by the men that those in the galley were not drowned, though they lost their baggage. And the next day the Duke of Bourbon (to whom was reported the news of the lost galley, on which had been some of his good servants), sent his own personal galley straight to Trapani, it being but three leagues away, which retrieved the good servants and brought them to him at Messina, where the duke remained eight days to refresh his people and put his vessels in order. Manffroi, lord of Clermont—who was in those days lord of Messina, Trapani and Palermo and a good bit more than half of the island of Sicily—because he was gouty in his feet, sent a message by his people more privately to tell the Duke of Bourbon that he was welcome into his country and all his army; and for all these days the duke sojourned in the island and the lord of Clermont feasted him well and paid his expenses so that the duke remained there eight days, together with the lord of Couci, the Count d'Eu and the Count Dauphin.

When the Duke of Bourbon wished to leave Sicily the said Manffroi lord of Clermont asked whether it would please him to make [Manffroi] a knight, for a more valiant prince there never could be. The duke was very pleased about this request, and made him a knight, for which the lord of Clermont thanked him and on departure gave the duke two beautiful coursers of the race of Clermont, near Palermo, to the lord of Couci one, the Count Dauphin one, and to the Count d'Eu one more, and to the galleys and ships of the Genoese, biscuits, salt meat, and other provisions, and commanded further to other vessels that victuals should be no more expensive. It was made so by his command, and the Duke of Bourbon regarding the pleasing services which had been done in this country sought to bestow great honor upon the lord of Clermont to whom on his parting he gave a gold belt with his device of hope. More, the Duke of Bourbon asked the Genoese what voyage they were making so they told him: "Lord, on leaving here we will go by sea and we can go before a town which is held by a despot of Romania, called Terrassine and there is a good seaport, and those they provide victuals to Africa, no more nor less than the island of Sardinia. So you can do no better than to go assail them and destroy them, and it appears to us that it is good to go there." Then the Duke of Bourbon and his knights boarded a galley and his men and his fleet left from Messina and sailed by sea with both sails and oars until they arrived at the port of Terrassine and in fact entered it, and took the lower town and besieged the castle.

And within two days the castle surrendered to the Duke of Bourbon who granted it to the Genoese to guard, under the agreements and promises which they had made for Castle de Caligari and la Guillastre and the army left there and went to Plombin near Pisa; and the lord of Plombin was a grand gentleman and there had been a great war between the lord of Plombin and the Genoese which still continued. And the Duke of Bourbon having arrived at Plombin those of Genoa pressed him strongly, because of the old war which had been between them and the lord of Plombin they wished to destroy him and they insisted on it.

So the Duke of Bourbon responded: "I am not come to make war on Christians but if it is a matter of peace which I am able to employ myself I will do it willingly, and I will set out and seek it; you will say your case and he will say his: and, if any way of agreement can be found there, I will do my duty with a good heart: and here a great number of knights and wise men who know well how to organize your conflict." So the Genoese said: "Lord, we are well content that you are pleased to take charge, and we thank you." Then the Duke of Bourbon sent a message by some of his knights to the lord of Plombin that he should speak with them. So the said lord gladly came to the duke who welcomed him with good cheer. Then the lord of Plombin shared with the duke the causes of the war and what claim he had, and the Genoese likewise, which the Duke of Bourbon put to the council with the noble chivalry who were with them. Without making the story too long, the duke put them from their dispute into such good accord as if they were brothers, and ended a great dissension. From Plombin the army went to the Isle of Elba, where the Genoese were said to have some right which the lord of Elba had taken from them, and it was quite true; but before the duke left he sent them so good an accord that they were content with it, and the Genoese obtained their rights. The army left Elba, and arrived at Portefin very close to Genoa around to the south. From there a great party disembarked not including the Duke of Bourbon who did not wish at all to disembark at Genoa —nor did the Count d'Eu, the lord of Couci, nor the Count Dauphin about which the Duke of Genoa and all the commune were displeased, for they really wanted that he should disembark, to make him some great gifts gold and silver and vessels. But never did he partake in any greed. So they urged him very strongly to disembark, to which he answered: "My lords, you take me to Marseille and from there I will return if you please; for when I left there I had vowed to God and St. Louis of Marseille, that this should be the first port on my return where I would re-enter the realm of France." Then the Duke of Bourbon and the lords to the satisfaction of the Genoese left and went to Marseille and all the others disembarked at Genoa to restore their health from the mortality in some afflictions which they had had at the siege of Africa, and on the sea, from which there were a great many deaths among the Genoese and others. At Genoa the lord of Saint-Sévère died, and Sir Guichart, son of the lord of Châteaumorand and a dozen Englishmen. There also died the lord of Castillon, a Bourdelois, and the lord of Caillart; and the Souldich de l'Estrau, the lord of St. Georges, and the lord of Graville and the others who were rested left Genoa and went to their homes.

LXXXII. How the Duke of Bourbon after his return from Africa, made his declaration to aid his sister the Countess of Savoy concerning her dowry about which she had been wronged.

The Duke of Bourbon stayed at Marseille, where he remained for ten days to rest himself and his men who were very tired from the effort and the great suffering which they had had in this noble expedition. During this the duke sent to Forez where he had but four days' time at the side of the duchess his wife, and in Bourbonnois in the company of Lord Norris, to seek his horses and his other equipment which he needed and gold and silver of which he needed a great amount, much of which had he had spent honorably. When the horses had arrived, and those which he had summoned, the Duke of Bourbon left Marseille and went on a pilgrimage to St. Antoine of Vienne to Notre Dame of Puy and then to his country of Forez where all the people came out to meet him making great cheer for him and the greatest honor one could make everywhere he went. He stayed in his town of Montbrison eight days with the duchess his wife; both of them loved each other with true love. Their beautiful children John and Louis were there, whom the duke was cheered to see. And while the duke sojourned there news was brought to him how Bonne de Bourbon his sister, the Countess of Savoy, had been removed from the government of the count and of his country, (which count was her son by her husband [Amédée VI]), known as the Green Count, and who, in addition to this, refused to return her dowry. So Duke Louis was very unhappy about this especially about the dowry being wrongfully retained and he said: "Since one must stand by a fair sister, I should remedy it;" then he immediately ordered the barons, knights and squires of his country who were with him to come to him on a set date. So Duke Louis left Montbrison and rode in good company to the city of Grenoble where there came at his prayer to be at the aid and relief of the countess against the Savoyards many lords of Dauphiné, namely: Sir Aimaird de Clermont, banneret, together with three knights, fifteen squires and a hundred men-at-arms; the lord of Montchanu with two knights and thirty men-at-arms to Clermont; the lords of Giers and of Riage with forty companions, well mounted and armed; Sir Henri de Vallins with twenty-two men-at-arms; the lord of Mont Rigaud and Gilles Coupier, knights, with nineteen companions. The lord of Marmai and Vachon d'Asses, squires, came there with thirty men-at-arms, Francois de St. Andrew with ten men; and Robinet de la Chassaigne, lord of La Moulierre in Auvergne, who had come there at his expense to twelve men-at-arms for which the duke was grateful. Then the duke took it upon himself to say to his men-at-arms: "Since we are here together with the valiant knights of the Dauphiné who have come out of their goodwill to accompany me let us do something, please

God, so that my beautiful sister of Savoy will not be completely abandoned." Then the knights, both from Dauphiné and those of the duke, said that he should send defiances to Savoy; for they were ready to enter the country in arms, so that the good lady should receive her right by force; that was her dowry, which had been taken from her wrongfully. But count Amé, who was then the premier duke in Savoy, had ascertained that the Duke of Bourbon was so close from him for him to move war, made to assemble his council where there were Sir Jean de Beaufort, chancellor, the seneschals and marshals of the country, Sir Boniface de Chalant, and Sir Gaspard de Montmajour, and this notable squire captain of Pimont, Henri de Colombier, who had supported the good widow lady always and against all and always increased her honor. They negotiated to such an extent that thanks to this wise squire expostulating to the count his lord about the evils which could follow from this war, a noble embassy from the count to Duke Louis of Bourbon was sent to the town of Grenoble. There the letter of defiance was made which two squires carried from the Duke of Bourbon; one called Ponsard de Grantval and the other Jean du Bois from Limousin, a squire from the office of warhorses. When these ambassadors presented themselves before the duke they announced to him that by God he did not wish to make war on the count his kinsman and what had been done to turn outrage to the countess his sister was not coming from the count nor from the three estates. Duke Louis was able to hear enough of the ambassadors' presentation who spoke further not to wish to displease the duke concerning the government and administration of the country and the county which for a long time had been refused to the lady Bonne his sister. "For likewise lady Bonne of Berry, mother of our lord the count, wished to have it, which seemed to us to come from hatred and envy between the noble ladies; for this event had been discussed in council that the count ought to assume the governance of his country, and to lady Bonne of Bourbon Countess of Savoy our great lady," said the ambassadors," will be awarded, and duly assigned a stipend, to be annually paid out of the total dowry that she is owed. The count, our lord, and the three estates have so ruled, unanimously." Then Duke Louis of Bourbon, as would any reasonable prince, agreed to the terms proffered by the ambassadors (for in this way one held true to one's sister), went to Chambéri to inform the count and council of the settlement with the Duke of Bourbon, who was very happy with this agreement. Thus it was established that the agreement concerning her dowry and arrears was well and truly secured to her satisfaction. So she left the country, for she did not wish to remain there anymore, and she went to Mascon, where from then on she followed a very saintly and honorable way of life. And Duke Louis, her brother, who did not want to leave Grenoble until his sister was content, thanked the lords of the Dauphiné and all the others, and gave leave to his men-at-arms except for those of his household. Then he repaired to Montbrison, from which he then proceeded to his duchy of the Bourbonnois, to Molins, where he found Lord Norris and his council, who were very joyful and happy with their lord as were all the people.

LXXXIII. How the Duke of Bourbon went to Paris to the king to whom he strongly discouraged the expedition to Brittany.

When the Duke of Bourbon sojourned for some days in his town of Molins, Lord Norris went to speak to him. "My lord, you have reached an apogee, thanks be to God, for you have arrived at great honor and very great renown, both for your expedition to Africa and for your rescue of your sister. And also, the King of France has made the most important appointment that he has been seen to make in a long time, of which I am certain that you will soon hear news, seeing that the king knows of your coming." And then the Duke of Bourbon asked which direction the king wished to go, and his council told him that they had heard he was going to Brittany. Then the duke said to them: "Are the truces broken which my lord of Burgundy made between the Duke of Brittany and the Count of Penthièvre?" They said yes and that Clisson and La Rivière, who governed the throne, had broken them all. So then said the Duke of Bourbon: "It is badly done and very badly advised." Nothing remained but that the King of France should summon the Duke of Bourbon. The king knew well of his coming; his letters containing that, after the honorable expedition from which he had come, he wished to go to him quickly. So the Duke of Bourbon did it, to obey the king and also because he had a great desire to see him, and he went to Paris where he had great cheer from the king and everyone who was there; and for two whole days the king and the duke spoke of nothing but the adventures he had had. And the report of this honorable expedition to Africa which the Duke of Bourbon had much pleased the king, and they had good cheer for those two days; and the third day the King of France told the Duke of Bourbon: "Good uncle, we wish to tell you some great things which we have undertaken against the Duke of Brittany who every day cannot help but displease us." To which the duke responded: "My lord, if you don't have a great cause, it is badly done; for you know that my lord the Duke of Burgundy your uncle, who made the peace between the two of you will not be at all happy; and perchance those who are always with you who have counselled you on this, are partial, and look to their own benefit and very little to yours. For which you have to put this matter in great deliberation before you undertake the deed." And the king said hastily: "Good uncle, we have deliberated everything, and our command is that you be at Le Mans within a fortnight. So we ask that you will accompany us, in full strength, and be there with us on that day, and in this matter, we appeal to your honor." Then the Duke of Bourbon said: "My lord, I will do what you ask. But I suspect you are heading into trouble; and I do not know if my lord of Burgundy has consented to this." And the king quickly replied: "We have not taken any counsel at all from our good uncle of Burgundy." Then the Duke of Bourbon said to the king: "My lord, it appears to me that this is not to your advantage. For Clisson makes you partial to the Count of Penthièvre against the Duke of Brittany, who is a great lord, and who is able to serve you well; and you are not taking this seriously enough. Rather, you ought to take pains to defend them from all assault, for they are your vassals. For this reason the Duke of Burgundy made the treaty at Angiers, which you ought to hold to, and not follow any partiality."

John the Fearless in a portait by an anonymous painter executed in France, possibly Burgundy c.1404. Wikimedia Commons, public domain

LXXXIV. *How the King of France went into Brittany to make war on the duke; and how from a malady which came on him, it was necessary for him to return.*

Charles King of France when he had heard the salutary speech which the Duke of Bourbon had made to him, did not want to listen to him anymore about that, but said to him completely excessively: "Good uncle, certainly we have promised to go there; so we will keep it and leave Paris four days from now to be in Le Mans eight days to the rallying-point in order that everybody who knows that we will be there will go there more willingly. And for this, prithee, good uncle, that you will come with us step-by-step and send one among your knights among your people, rallying them to join with you on the day appointed. And also our good uncle Berry will be there, and our good brother of Orléans will come with us." Then the Duke of Bourbon who could not hold back the king, sent a knight to his people, so they should follow him; so they did that, and the King of France was already departed from the city of Paris and went to Le Mans in 1392 where he remained twelve days, meanwhile awaiting there all the great strength of his forces which came to him from all sides and when they came the king wanted to leave from the city of Le Mans to go to Angiers; and Marshal Boucicault went before La Flesche to make lodgings for the king and from there to Angiers and in the next day the king left to lodge at La Flesche, and passed by the plains of Pont-Valain where the Constable, Claquin, had once defeated Sir Robert Knolles. And on this plain the king suffered a sudden malady, which caused him to put his hand to his sword and attack everyone and those who were able to flee from him, hid, for he was a good knight in body and limbs well-proportioned and strong, and on account of this he was well to be feared. The good Duke of Bourbon who saw the king in this condition was very sad, so he took twelve gentlemen and went to him, and told him: "Ha! Ha! my lord, is this well done? You are doing well! You dishonor yourself." The king, who loved and feared him, was completely ashamed. So the Duke of Bourbon pulled close to him and said: "Sire, put away your sword." The king did not want to. When the duke saw this he said to the king: "My lord, give it to me." So he did, and then the Duke of Bourbon told four squires, his men, who were well armed, that they should take the bridle of the king's horse, and turn back the army from Pont-Valain; and the king, who was in a great fury, was brought back to Le Mans. For there was a great heat of the sun, it became so hot that it was a wonder of the world; and because he was overheated it was necessary to remain at Le Mans for thirteen days because he was in constant fever. Nevertheless, he did his novena to glorious St. Julien, patron of that city, and everyone who had come at his command was allowed to return home. And after the thirteen days by the mercy of God the king got much better, and the Duke of Berry and the Duke of

Bourbon led him to Paris where he remained sick for a long time. For he recovered for a month and the next month the malady was back, and this illness remained with him the whole year, and in truth at other times all his life, which was a long one. Because of this infirmity the princes of the blood royal, especially three of them, namely Duke Louis of Orléans, brother of the king, Duke Jean d'Berry and Duke Philip of Burgundy, his uncles, said that a regency was needed in the kingdom of France, about which they were in debate. For the Duke of Orléans said that because he was the brother the king the regency belonged to him. The Duke of Berry who was the oldest uncle, said also that likewise he ought to have it. And Duke Philip of Burgundy who was a very great and able lord and also uncle of the king, said that the government should belong to him, and from these debates and strife sprang dissension.

LXXXV. How the author speaks a little concerning fortune, and how it appears to him.

The author has many times thought of the little he has seen and less retained on the fact of fortune, and what it is. This has established his opinion, saying that fortune is nothing else if not permission from God, seeing that in this mortal life many kingdoms by division fall into miserable ruin, in which the great and the inheritors were expelled or dead, and others raised to their seats and obtained their lordship. For the poor pilgrim has a good memory of the years from the chapter above up to the eve of the ascension of this year, 1429, and of the diverse ways that fortune by its mockery turns things topsy-turvy and is never stable, showing under heaven nothing is firm; and of this the excellent poet Boccaccio speaks in his book *De Casibus Virorum Illustrium (The Fates of Famous Men)*, where each prince holding lordship ought to watch out for himself, so that he not be brought down by his own scheming, as is described in this volume, which speaks of little else but the miserable end of the very great ones who have not heeded it. Even the Greek philosopher Sophocles, in his great old age, wrote in verse diverse tragedies in which he described the bad and disorderly deeds of kings and high princes of the world. Wherefore I willingly recount this to give understanding to all that fortune is mutable therefore nothing ought to be trusted but only God, from whom all good things come. And the crux of the matter was, there was more than enough uncertainty and bitterness among the gentlefolk of France, the clerical estate as much as the nobility, being put into a cruel bind, when one of the proudest and most valiant knights of the world, Prince and King of this land, by reason of this devastating illness could not rule his kingdom; therefore it came to pass that the dukes, his brother and his uncles, had among them a bit of envy out of ambition to rule. But the very honorable prince and valiant lord, Duke Louis of Bourbon, went from one to the other, admonishing them that fear and obedience were due to the king, just as much then as before, and that the lords should be careful that other nations not ridicule their division, and take advantage of it to invade the kingdom, especially their old enemies the English, whom they had expelled with such great effort, and who would invade again if they saw a second opportunity. This, and many effectual words, the good Duke of Bourbon spoke to the other princes, who were slowly brought, without realizing it, into compliance, and in the end he governed well enough that most were satisfied. Notwithstanding the king's illness, there was good peace in the realm, attributable to this good and honest prince, the Duke of Bourbon, who labored hard to maintain it, for which he was extravagantly praised, honored and loved by all in Paris and everywhere else. During this good peace, the kingdom flourished in good things, many of the great lords made war in other lands, and for this they sent into France (where there was the glory of chivalry) their special messages to the dukes, the lords in France, ruling

the kingdom that it might please them to send knights to aid them, who went there with a good heart and willingly employed themselves in the expeditions so as not to be idle. The first of the lords to make war at this time was Jean of Hainault, Duke of Holland who called himself King of Frisia, and undertook its conquest, where also the noble chivalry of France went. A little later the high baronage of France and elsewhere also went to Hungary and passed the river Danube, in which place a Saracen Turkish prince named Basac[29] won the battle against them, in 1396, by which Christendom was very much diminished because of the nobles who died there. Soon after that King Richard of England by the ties of marriage and fleshly alliance had taken to wife the daughter of the King of France, Ysabeau, and from this marriage it was believed that peace
was made between the two kings for all time. But fortune, which is variable, marvelously turned its wheel against this King Richard. For when he thought to be at the height of his glory, he fell and was found dead. Some said that he was killed by a conspiracy of the greatest in the land; and others said that he was dead in prison; but whatever the manner of his death the queen his wife was returned to France and the Earl of Derby, Henri, was chosen King of England, named by the barons of the land.

29 Commonly known as Bayezid.

LXXXVI. How the Duke of Orleans was killed at Paris and how the Duke of Bourbon had bitter sorrow over it.

In the following matter, the author, in speaking of Fortune, has a little bit more to say about it, because it determines all things. True it is that in the year 1400 a happy peace reigned in France, and seeing this, several princes, who had been expelled from their domains came to France to seek refuge with the king, with the hope of being supported and put back into their domains. To them the king, when he was in good health, made good cheer, and gave them good and large estates. And, by this time, the king of Armenia (who bore the arms of Lusignan, like the King of Cyprus) had arrived, seeking help against Sultan lord of Egypt and Syria, who had driven him from his kingdom; but in pursuing this end, he died in Paris and was entombed in royal habit with the Friars-Preachers (the Dominicans) most honorably at the expense of the King of France. In this season in a similar case my lord Manuel Paleologus, Emperor of Constantinople, that noble prince and handsome old man, came to France and to the king because the Prince of Turkey had taken most of his lands: to him the king made good cheer and received him grandly and lodged him in the Louvre near Bourbon. Duke Louis showed him some great signs of friendship and treated him amiably which very much pleased the emperor and his Greek chivalry. During these days when the Greek emperor was at Paris there took place the marriage of Jean, Count of Clermont, son of the Duke of Bourbon, and the excellent and virtuous princess Dame Marie, daughter of the Duke of Berry, who had been Countess of Blois and Eu, which marriage was a grand and solemn festival at the palace at Paris where the French king and the Greek emperor were present, together with the high baronage of France. There had been other such weddings: Louis the First, who no longer lived; Charles, who was Count of Clermont when his father was duke and later married the very noble lady Agnes, sister of the Duke of Burgundy, with whom he had splendid offspring; and the other Louis, of the county of Montpensier, who married the daughter of the Count Dauphin, heir to this domain, and there was a beautiful girl, her sister, Ysabel by name. To return to the subject of Fortune, it was very bad for the people of the kingdom, as I have said. For the king, who was often ill, was unable to govern well at all, from which grew up a certain hatred among the lords, who had to do all the governing. And during this dissension, without it being widely known, in the year 1407, an evil Norman servant, named Raoullet d'Auquetonville, who had a formidable power behind him, that had enough of such government, together with his allies conspired to kill the Duke of Orléans. Raoullet said to his followers that the Duke of Orléans, brother of the king, had made him lose a great office of treasurer which he had, and that he wanted to kill the duke with his own hand. Raoullet persevered to such an extent in his evil, that the Duke of Orléans and his allies one night when he went to the queen's lodgings, to dine with her, and to help her with some things that she was attending to, and the duke had hardly brought any of his people with him, on account of the queen's distress concerning the malady of the king her lord, which still persisted. And on that Saint Clemens Eve, as the Duke of Orléans was returning from the queen quite late, after matins, Raoullet d'Auquetonville, this traitorous servant and his accomplices, attacked him in front of her lodgings, and vilely murdered him, about which there was a great uproar in Paris and a terrible commotion, which lasted a long time. And this traitorous servant, along with his kin, who had done this homicide out of detestable treason, that very night were gone and out of Paris. So the Duke of Orléans was killed, about which there was an awful disturbance and great debate thenceforward, which continued long afterwards. The noble Duke of Bourbon, who was so loyal and honest, felt very great sorrow to see the death the eldest brother of the king his sovereign lord, and his own nephew, by such people as you have heard. And for this no one could know or imagine the great sorrows which the duke had afterwards. He directly witnessed the king, his lawful sovereign lord, in the grip of the malady which everyone knew that he had, for at times he was well and at other times he was ill. These were two bitter pains which the Duke of Bourbon kept in his sorrowful heart.

Chritine di Pizan presents her book to the Duke of Orleans. Maître de la Cité des dames tirée de l'Épître Othéa, c. 1419-1414.
British Library, Harley MS 4431, f.95.
Wikimedia Commons, public domain.

A 15th century depiction of the assassination of Louis of Orleans.
Maître de la Chronique d'Angleterre, *c. 1470. Bibliothèque nationale de France.*
Public Domain.

LXXXVII. How the author strongly commends the patience of Duke Louis and the good life that he led.

Duke Louis of Bourbon was mindful that the wise man ought to be cautious when in peril, fearful in prosperity, and stoic in adversity; and regarding the misfortunate events he saw befalling the kingdom, the principal ones being that of the king's state, as well as the king's brother, and his own nephew, having been killed so villainously, patiently bore his sorrow, and commended to God for everything. And hoping that God, out of his benevolence, might send the king full health, the duke remained in Paris where he often made processions and gave alms to the poor, and strove much to mediate between the lords, among whom there was much distrust, preventing quarrels between them, so that the kingdom should not worsen.

Standing in this expectation the duke held grand banquets in Paris, in his hostel of Bourbon as he had always been accustomed, and whatever people who came were well received. It happened when the king was ill that he did not hold any events at court, and all those who came to the king's court where they found nothing prepared said: "Let us go dine at the hostel of the Duke of Bourbon, and we will be welcome there." So the noble men and officers came happily, which made the duke joyful, and they were received happily. Now the Duke of Bourbon had a custom which deserves to be well known: for he wished that men should be seated and served in accordance with their honors and indeed there were officers in this hostel who knew how to do it, whom the duke delighted by recognizing each according to his rank; and gladly dined in the outer court, to be in their company. And so that none who were at table should fail to hear him and so be at his ease, he wished that none should speak and that a very great silence should be kept, when he was at table, having ordered that none should come up to him, other than those who were ordered to serve him, namely the pannetier, the cellarer, the carving squire and Baudesquin Meschin, the good master of the hostel who supervised everything. And so that none should interfere with his dining in his meal, the two ends of his table were closed off with bars, so that no one could pass behind him to distract his attention. And to have a better understanding of the great affairs he had in the kingdom, as much in council as in other things, which he knew well how to bring to a conclusion, and to improve his memory, he had read to him, throughout his dinner, the epic tales of the most renowned princes, past kings of France, and others worthy of honor, and in this he found delight second only to the divine service, which office he recited very reverently. And after dinner, grace having been said to God, they all left, and afterwards returned often. This merry round went on so long that the Duke of Bourbon found himself indebted for sixty thousand gold francs, which he owed in Paris, for the merchants delivered to him that which he asked for, because they knew him to be a gentleman and willingly gave him credit. In that time it happened that Louis, one of the sons of the Duke of Bourbon, in his young age left this world, in which the Duke of Berry during his lifetime had much cheer, for this child was a beautiful youth, polite, amiable, and like his father. And for the good love which he had for him the Duke of Berry left Nestlé, his hostel, across the Seine and entered Bourbon, the hostel of Duke Louis, in order to comfort him. And when the Duke of Bourbon recognized the Duke of Berry, he was puzzled about his arrival, for he knew that Berry had aggravated the illness of his son, but notwithstanding this, when he knew the Duke of Berry had entered his hotel, the Duke of Bourbon received him as customary, being wary of him but pretending that this great-uncle of the king had come to visit him out of respect for his nobility of character. And as soon as the Duke of Berry set eyes upon the Duke of Bourbon, he unburdened his heart to him, his eyes fluttered and he took to crying, so much that he was not able to say a word. Then Duke Louis of Bourbon had him go before him and climb up to a chamber where there were many people and he began to speak to the Duke of Berry: "My lord, I thank you for the good visitation which you have made to me and for the pity you have for your son-in-law Louis, who has gone to God. For I know that you have come here to tell me the exact truth. And to me that would suffice from a lesser lord than you, but good blood never forgets the natural love[30] which they should have for each other. Which I tell you, my lord, this present life is just a hostelry, but the life to come is the firm and proper house of the immortal soul and a good knowledge for flying to God; for my lord in my opinion the end of life is very good if the man has healthy thoughts and entire reason, and natural sentiments certain and firm, to do the duty appertaining to human life. You know, my lord, that nature, mother of all things, has given to us men lodgings to stay together, but has not given a house to live in forever. For which, my lord, if God has taken my son it is His pleasure; He has loaned him to me; He wished him for Himself, His name be blessed. Perhaps Louis has been the best of all his kin; but fortune, which puts the low high and the high low, led him to the end too early." The Duke of Berry hearing such sane words from the Duke of Bourbon was not able to abstain from tears. But the Duke of Berry ran down the steps, and went with many noble men into the chamber, where the body of the child was ready to be placed in the earth to which he did honor. And when Duke Louis of Bourbon who was in his gallery, saw the processions leaving his hotel with very great illuminations, and his son's body put in the bier the heart softened within him, and he cried tears of paternal sorrow. And quickly he went to his chapel where he called his confessor Master Pierre Chantelle, a good theologian, and other chaplains who were performing the divine offices for the soul of the newly departed child, whom together with the chivalry and officers of the hotel reflected on the constancy and patience of the duke their lord and master.

30 Good blood, natural love.

LXXXVIII. How the Duke of Bourbon took leave of the king, and went to his country, where he ordered his affairs; and how Lord Norris, by his good counsel, provided for the duke's affairs.

After the obsequies of little Louis were completed the Duke of Bourbon, his father, did not cease to keep the estate and station to which he was accustomed, until some of the governors of the finances said to him many times: "My lord, everyone comes to your hostel to eat, you are content with it, and it ought to please us, but the merchants who deliver the goods insist that we pay. So we supplicate you that you please to advise us." To this the duke answered: "My friends, you speak well; I would be disappointed if no one complained about me. But what I have done up to now was with the thought that my lord the king should return to health, so that the noble men and servants of his hotel should have some reward for their service, but since I see that it pleases God for it to be a long infirmity in his person, I thank Him. I will take into advisement what you have told me, though not one thing you have told me would separate me from the gentlemen who are accustomed to come and eat in my courts, so that they should not come there." So they told him that they would not. On this the Duke of Bourbon thought a long time by himself about three things: the first, to take leave of the king in his good healing; the second was to withdraw to his country, and think about his soul, and thank God for the good things which He had given him; the third was to pay his debtors all the expense which he had made in his life in order that he should not owe anything at the end of his days, which was good thinking for a noble gentleman. So it happened that when the King of France turned to recovery, the Duke of Bourbon went to ask him for leave to go into his country. So the king did not want to give it so said to him: "Ha, ha dear good uncle, it is by no means time for you to go!" Then the Duke of Bourbon answered: "My lord," said he, "it is time; for now I am old, alas! and it's time that I go back to live among my knights, and the humble folk who have sustained me, and ask God's forgiveness for those evils I have done, of which there are many more than I should have done. And for me to repay those whom I owe, and satisfy all those whom I might have wronged in my time." And the king said to him: "Good uncle, I pray you, remain yet, for there are many affairs in our kingdom where you can do much." Then the Duke of Bourbon told him, wishing to satisfy him: "My lord, while I am on my own lands, I can always come to back to you to do that which you command, and employ me in all your affairs for which I am able." So the Duke of Bourbon obtained leave to go from the King of France his lord, and he went to his duchy of Bourbonnois, and while staying on his lands, made some exact inquiries: the first was that he wished to know all his debts. And further he said to Lord Norris that he wished to know for how much they were able to appraise all his domains, namely Bourbonnois, Forez, Beaujolais, Combraille, Chastel-Chinon, and Clermont-en-Beauvoisin. "The reasons for which I do this," said the duke, "so they are going to be able to regulate and maintain the estate of me and my wife, and also to pay off all of those whom I owe." Then Lord Norris said: "My lord, you are taking a fine and good road for the soul and body; and when it pleases you, what you have said will be done." Then the duke said: "Norris, put in your stead three knights, who will be needed for the next month, for you are not able to be there much, for it is necessary that you be with me continually for whatever things I must do." Then Lord Norris, by the duke's command, commissioned the chamber of accounts to enroll these three knights for this position, namely L'Hermite de la Faye, Châteaumorand and Sir François de Aubrecicourt, with a clerk to record what the chamber of accounts needed to review, and the thing was so well conducted that the knights under this commission and those in the chamber of accounts [both] reported to the duke at the end of one month that he had 80,000 francs worth of domain, which was held to be a good thing by all who heard it. And then the gentlemanly Lord Norris said to the Duke of Bourbon: "My lord, you are no penniless prince, for thanks be to God you have enough to pay your debts, and uphold a great estate." Then the duke told him: "Lord Norris, for some time now you have helped me accumulate it, and wish to give me good advice concerning my expenses, and how much remains at my disposal." Then Lord Norris said to him: "My lord, the expenses of your household are in your control, for no one is able to order it, other than you, and in this you may do as you please. But allocate a sum to provide for your expenses, such as you wish, but keep in mind that these 80,000 francs of which I have told you is not cash-in-hand but is the expected revenue from the grains, wines and poultry, and many other goods, and you have, thanks be to God, in your Bourbonnois lands, enough provisions for all the necessities of life, but notwithstanding that, many other things are needed in the lodgings of a lord such as you. For there is a need for plenty of money to obtain other things, like meat, spices and other things which have their place in the hostel of a lord, as much for embassies as for messengers, and to dress you, Madame, and your son and those of your hostel. Likewise it is suitable to give particular gifts to many people who come to you with the lords." So then the duke said: "Lord Norris, you have advised us very well, and what you say is true. For this pray you to advise what sum ought to put in savings to furnish the things discussed." Lord Norris, who saw it was the will of the duke said to him: "My lord, the affairs of you great men are such as you like, and sometimes expense is so great it can't be measured. I myself think, seeing that you have enough grain, wine, poultry and wax, you have twenty thousand francs in savings for the things which ought to surround you; your estate is honorable; and further your countries of the Bourbonnois, Forez, and Combraille furnish all those goods which have been mentioned." Again Lord Norris said to the duke:

"I have advised with the people of your council that in the country of Beaujolais, and Chastel-Chinon, and Clermont in Beauvoisin, you will be acquitted inside of three years of all your debts. But your council and me further having been advised to pay down the smaller debts which the poor people are suffering, we seek with both hands the 20,000 francs to pay those debts, and the large debts assigned on the three countries, and at a certain term, which the debtors will be well content with you, so you will be quit. And yet having advised that if you wish that this estate should remain viable, that you cease to make new additions to your residence, the *Hôtel de Bourbon* at Paris, which has cost you so much to build and maintain, and all other edifices, except the convent of your Celestines, founded in your own town of Vichy, and if you do this, it seems advisable to us that before two years have passed, you'll be free of debt and your estate held in fine condition." These words greatly relieved the Duke of Bourbon and left him as much delighted as surprised by the good counsel and advice of Lord Norris. And the Duke of Bourbon said: "Lord Norris, you have liberated me from one of the great worries that has bedeviled me for more than a year, by means of your good counsel. But if I have given you, in serving me, enough trouble it is reasonable that I ought to recognize it." So Lord Norris said, "I am content with your goodwill, and always ready to obey you."

LXXXIX. How the Duke of Bourbon ordered some of his people into the bishopric of Metz, to the aid of his relative, the Cardinal of Luxembourg.

As the Duke of Bourbon was in his country of Bourbonnois, his true servants and relatives were all dismayed that they no longer saw him in court, for he was their refuge at the king's court. And one of his own cousins, Walleran, Count of St. Pol, sent a message apprising him thus: "My very honored lord, please know that our holy father, Pope Clement, has made my brother Pierre de Luxembourg a cardinal, and to hold his estate, granted his tenure of the bishopric of Metz, which is worth sixty thousand Rhenish florins, and is a grand thing. But it is true that some Germans, disobeying the Pope, cling to possession of the bishopric, and that we are not able to recover them without you, who are our defender and enforcer. If it should be your pleasure to help in this task with a contribution of four hundred men-at-arms, to assist some six hundred which I will procure from our friends and relatives, I hope, by God to make a good job of it: for my own brother the cardinal, who has a gentlemanly reputation, will then obtain his proper place, and without you, who have always been our lord and friend, we will not be able to conduct this affair. And we beseech you that, if it is to your pleasure to send them, that those who come should carry your insignia; In that way, they will be inspired, and it will be seen that we are not without a lord or allies." Immediately the Duke of Bourbon sent a herald, who announced to the Count de St. Pol the good will of the duke, that he would not fail him at all, and that concerning this he should consider it guaranteed. And not to make a long story of it, the Count de St. Pol replied immediately to the duke and requested that his men should be ready at Arc-en-Barrois within twenty-two days. So the Duke of Bourbon put his men whom he wanted to summon to be on that day in equipment, and sent his banner to Sir Jean de Châteaumorand, who always carried it. Afterwards, the duke sent the lord of Cordebuef, Sir Renaud de Roye, Michaille, the bastard of Glarins, Bellenave and the Borgne de Veulce, sending these five knights to govern his men, who were four hundred men-at-arms. So the duke paid them for a month, and they did not fail to be present on the assigned day, and they were there just as soon, or earlier than the Count de St. Pol's men, of whom there were from five to six hundred men-at-arms, and many projectile men. And when his men and the Duke of Bourbon's men assembled together, the Count de St. Pol said to the duke's men: "There is a town seven leagues from here called Commercy, which belongs to the Count de Salebruche: he is our mortal enemy and has declared against the king, and if we can take it, it will go well for us, for it is very rich." So the companions said: "Let us break camp and march through the night" so they did it, and Commercy was assaulted by the Count de St. Pol, his men and the

Bourbonnois. And so much they put their effort there that it was taken by a fine assault, whereafter the companions were well rested and restored; and the Count de St. Pol left a garrison in place to cover his withdrawal, and went from there to the abbey of Gorze, which was part of the bishopric; which speedily was taken by assault and then they went to lodge near the castle of Champillion of the bishopric, located a league from Metz. And those who were inside Champillion as guards had the custom that every evening they came out to pick cherries, for this was at the time of St. John. The bastard of Flanders, Sir Rifflard by name, was put in pursuit of these people, in the name of the count, because he was a very valiant knight, and had an eye on ruling this castle. So he set an ambush every night, by means of which, one morning, he captured the captain and his best men, who came to eat the cherries, and then Sir Rifflard ordered all his men to armor up to assault the place, for there were hardly any men remaining inside. So they went all in order and the assault was grand and fine, and took the place, and decapitated the captain, who was a German disobedient to the Pope. And from there the Count de St. Pol, the cardinal and all the companions went before Vic, where there was a saltworks worth ten thousand florins. But none of the Germans who were inside were given orders to defend themselves, but were taken, which was a great miracle for the cardinal. Then they went directly to Moyenvic, the other saltworks which likewise was taken, and from there to Marsal, more saltworks which the inhabitants never defended but also were taken, and put themselves at the cardinal's mercy, and there were there three saltworks worth thirty thousand florins and it was the advantage of the bishopric; and thus five places were taken, by right belonging to the bishop. The citizens of Metz saw the harsh war which the Count of St. Pol waged on them, and that evil should come to them from it, and thus came to render obedience to the cardinal of Luxembourg who then was blessed, and held him for their lord and prelate. From there the men of the Duke of Bourbon and the Count de St. Pol left to come to Commercy and to them came Sir Amé de Salebruche who had set an ambush to catch the men who had taken his town; which ambush was so clumsily revealed that there were, dead and taken, so many as eighty men-at-arms. From there they went before Aspremont, a very fine castle of Sir Amé, which was taken and after the taking the men retired to Commercy to refresh themselves where all the companions rested a bit, waiting so that if those of Metz rebelled against the cardinal, they would be close by to defend and maintain his right.

XC. How the Duke of Bourbon sent some of his men to his nephew the Count of Savoy, and about the terrible assault which was at Sion in Valeis.

In those days of 1408, the country of Valeis bordered on one part on Germany and on the other on Savoy and was rebelling against the bishop, prefect and lord, and by conspiracy, some of this rebellion killed him. So some prudhommes were come into Savoy to Count Amé to protest this disaster and that, by God, they had predicted it before it came to pass. And for this reason, the Duke of Bourbon sent a herald to his people and servitors, the companions still being at Commercy, proclaiming full confidence in the five knights whom he had sent out with the Count of St. Pol, that he was very joyful, and praising God that his relative the cardinal of Luxembourg had recovered his bishopric. And he had said to the knights, by means of a letter, "I have had news of my nephew of Savoy, who asks me and prays that I should wish to send him five hundred men-at-arms, to deal with whichever of his lands are revolting against him; specifically, Gruyères and Valeis, where, in a castle called Turbillon, the peasants have killed their bishop. The count, my nephew demands that I should send men-at-arms to him at Lausanne, and that I should not fail him in such great need. And the lord of St. George and the Burgundians should be able to come to his aid at Lausanne within ten days, if you ask them. So you and your company should be at Lausanne on that day, and I will send you what money I am able to pay." So the knights fulfilled their lord's orders, and had not been three days at Lausanne before the Duke of Bourbon sent them the lord of Champroupin, with enough money for a month, yet forbidding them to accept any money from his nephew in Savoy. They did not dare transgress this command of their prince. The Bourbonnois and the Burgundians went together to the Count of Savoy who awaited them at Saint Morice, in Chablais, in all his power, where they found the Count of Savoy and the Prince of Piedmont, who welcomed the companions. The next day the count, the prince, the Bourbonnois and the Burgundians went before Turbillon, there where the people had killed their bishop, which place was a very fine castle but nevertheless it was so assailed on all parts that it was taken by force and they cut off the heads of the traitors who killed their prelate. And the next day, early in the morning, the siege was put before the leading town of the country, Sion-en-Valais, where there was a great communal rebellion, of which the captains were Peter de Rarongne, the hotelier of Cheval Blanc on the mountain of Brig, from which one can cross over to Lombardy, and the other was named Haulsement from Gruyères, and they had in the town a good four thousand rebels who followed them. The Count of Savoy's and the prince of Piedmont's knights having arrived there with knights drawn from forces of the lord of Granson and others, and assaults were ordered that very day: the Duke of

Bourbon's men on the Rhône, in the gardens and from the other side of the gate, the lord of St. George and the Burgundians to attack in the morning after mass. On that morning there commenced a very fine assault, as you will learn. On the side where the Duke of Bourbon's men were, the town was very harshly assailed, with no assistance other than twenty-five of the lord Chamberlain's men, who carried similar arms to those of Bourbon. It was so fiercely attacked that seven great holes were put in the wall, and the assault lasted from morning to one hour after noon. The Count of Savoy ordered a retreat, because the Burgundians were pushed back, having been much resisted by the city folk in their assault and also the Bourbonnois in theirs. So the Bourbonnois told the Count of Savoy: "My lord, you made our assault pull back at the critical moment. We have made seven holes, and if we could make two of them into a single big one, it appears to us that the wall will fall into the town, since it looms above it." So the count was very happy, but he said to the Bourbonnois: "Many of your people are wounded." And the knights told him: "My lord, don't you worry!" Then the assault was called on stronger than before and then the Bourbonnois began that which they had proposed: so it was well assailed and well defended. And they made their holes from two into one, as was ordered. Once sundown came, the wall that they wanted to fall into the town fell directly onto the Bourbonnois men-at-arms. Of those who were on the wall, defending it with trebuchets, twenty-two fell into the trench, all of whom were killed, and also five Bourbonnois men-at-arms were killed, and thirteen valets. The one who carried the lord Chamberlain's pennon died, and that of Sir Regnault de Royce broke his arm, and Sir Jean Châteaumorand who carried the sigils of the Duke of Bourbon broke his foot, and also Michaille was severely injured. And with a great shout, the Count of Savoy's men and the Burgundians rushed through the breach, but hardly had they done this when the pennon of the Duke of Bourbon and all the Bourbonnois arrived, mightily attacking the commoners of the town, who had strung up their chains, and valiantly defended themselves street by street, but too late. There were killed in this entry by the Bourbonnois, Savoyards and Burgundians a good two thousand jaques peasants, and the town was captured, where many goods were taken. They directed the duke's pennon and the Bourbonnois, who had no intention of pillaging, made their way to the high castle of the Prince-Archbishop, where Peter de Rarogne and Haussement, leaders of that rabble, were holed up, and at sunrise the Burgundians and Savoyards climbed the steep slope. So the men-at-arms attacked the place so zealously that it was quickly captured, whereupon Peter de Raronge and others were killed; and as a result the Count of Savoy acquired the town of Sion. After his battle, the lord of St. George and the Bourbonnois asked the Count of Savoy that he should give them leave to raid the county of Gruyères, where this sedition had started. So those who were still fit went there, and did so much damage that one could not keep track of it, and they went in pursuit as far as the mountain of Brig, where they burned the hostelry, which was rather pretty, and knocked down the bridges. Then on the third day the companions returned to the city of Sion, before Count Amé, who gave to them great thanks for this incursion. And the count had found great wealth in the town: so he went to pay the duke's men for a month, but they were not willing to take anything from him, saying that they had plenty of money and their master the duke, if he knew of this, would take it badly, for he was not accustomed to serve his friends at their expense.

XCI. How the Duke of Bourbon had the intention of making many honorable expeditions.

Not long after that, in the very same year, the king sought out the Duke of Bourbon, taking him rather by surprise, saying that he wished him to head in his direction, to Chartres, where he had set aside a day to discuss what the duke might know of the dissension concerning the death of his brother-in-law the Duke of Orléans, and that the Duke of Bourbon would not want to miss it, "for the good uncles of Berry nag me persistently about it." The Duke of Bourbon acceded to the king's words, and attended that day, wherewith was proposed an accord concerning the death of the Duke of Orléans, and it was said that according to the Duke Jean of Burgundy, whom many blamed for the deed, that none should believe that he had plotted such, and that none should disbelieve him, and that he should come and go near the king as was his custom, and that if the Duke of Burgundy was able to find those who had killed the Duke of Orléans, he should have them punished. And concerning this, ambassadors of the king were sent to the Duke of Burgundy, who was two leagues from Chartres, and who concerning this held himself quite satisfied, and swore peace with the others. This treaty being made, the lords left in good peace concerning the death of the Duke of Orléans. Subsequently the Duke of Bourbon, who had a great desire to return to his country, came to ask leave of the king, who did not at all want to give it to him. It was another two days before he could get permission to leave. Also, the Duke of Berry took great pains to keep the Duke of Bourbon there, would not agree to his departure, and the duke would never have received leave unless he had said to the king: "My lord, I have promised to lead the Queen of Jerusalem to Naples and I have already sent some of my men to Valencia, where Queen Yolant, her mother, remains waiting to know when I will thus proceed. And also it is my intention, please God, to go on pilgrimage to the holy city where my Creator died, to visit his sepulcher, for after the deeds of the world, it is suitable to serve God; none can prevent me doing that, I have a firm will about it." But nothing the Duke of Bourbon said was effective, for the king was not willing to let him go. Realizing this, the Duke of Bourbon one day said to the king: "My lord, I am going to my country, and there you will find me ready at your command: and that's not so far that I cannot soon be with you." The Duke of Bourbon left the King of France, and came to Bourbonnois, where he settled all his affairs, and sent Sir Jean de Châteaumorand to Aragon to Valencia the great, to accompany Queen Yolanda, wife of King Louis, to Barcelona where the said knight demanded two ships and four galleys, and those were available; so that when the Duke of Bourbon was in Barcelona, nothing would suffice except to go by sea to take the queen to Naples. Considering this Châteaumorand negotiated with Renaud de Carillon who governed the whole kingdom of Aragon, but he was not ever able make an agreement that the queen should go to Naples, but said that one should wait for King Louis to come to Provence. So Sir Jean de Châteaumorand left Aragon and came to the duke his master and told him what had happened and that Sir Renaud de Carillon had broken the enterprise, about which the duke was very sad and angry, for he had some high thoughts of his own. The first was to bring this queen to Naples, and then, while proceeding on his intended route to the Holy Land to take possession of the principality of Morea, which some call Achaia, which was rightfully hers. For those of Morea were only waiting to receive him as their lord. And indeed the Duke of Bourbon had twice sent Châteaumorand, who had carried the seal of Achaia. And from Morea the duke went to Naples; from Naples it was the intention of the Duke of Bourbon to go to Cyprus, which ought to be his by reason, and from Cyprus to Jerusalem, to the Holy Sepulcher: so you are able to see the grand enterprise of the lord's noble heart who in his age was not willing to be idle.

XCII. How the Duke of Bourbon intended to follow the life of the Celestines of Vichy, with four knights. How at Souring news came to him that Amé de Very made war on his county of Brises, and the good remedy which the duke applied there.

When the Duke of Bourbon knew that at that time he would not able to accomplish the expeditions which he wished to, he was unhappy, but notwithstanding this delay, he hoped to accomplish and achieve them in a short time. When he was in his country of the Bourbonnois, with his barons and others, to whom he made good and grand cheer, there was not anyone who did not find aid and succor with him. Always the Duke of Bourbon had news from France which displeased him, for the king spent money excessively and it was granted to people of small estate, valets of the chamber, two or three of whom made grand palaces in and outside Paris. At that time, the king was managed by Jean de Montagu, who would later be beheaded. Although he could see that the affairs of the kingdom were still in disarray, he was reluctant to stir from his lands, and preferred to build the church of the Celestines at Vichy which he had newly founded, the most beautiful that one can see, providing it with rich and precious ornaments and more relics than anyone else had ever given them. Besides which, he wished to build a house for his estate; for he had the intention after his return from the honorable expeditions so far recounted. It was his intention to permanently remain there, with four old knights keeping him company, who would not leave the place, or at least that two or three of them were always there. And the four old knights whom he had selected for this companionship were Sir Robert de Vendac, Sir Guichard d'Ulphé, Sir Jean de Châteaumorand, Sir Jean de Bonnebaut, along with certain others of his officers. And by the time he had lived two years in this way, unfailingly, he resolved to remain there the rest of his life in the service of God. However, not a half year later, a war began against the Duke of Burgundy, at Arras in Picardy and on his lands roundabout there. Because of this conflict, the Duke of Berry retreated to Poitou and from all these disputes and quarrels which were then in the kingdom in 1409.

Duke Louis of Bourbon who was a happy and joyful man took a great melancholy in his head which advanced his death for never after did he have any joy, so that he lost sleep, which much weakened him. But he thanked God concerning that in the fullness of his days He let him see the peace of the church, of which the schism had lasted from the death of Pope Gregory who passed from this world at Rome in 1388, up to that year, 1409, by divine inspiration a man of good life and a great theologian, Master Pierre de Candy, was at the General Council at Pisa and created a sovereign apostle and named Pope Alexander V. The Duke of Bourbon rejoiced over this peace, for many times he had put great effort to do this, and for that joy which the Duke of Bourbon had for the state of the church, he went for devotion to his town of

Souvigny, where he prayed, making his oration in a place where he had built a beautiful chapel, and his sepulcher in which to rest at the end of days. And then very urgent news came to him from Beaujolais, concerning how Amé de Very, who had a good thousand horses, had come to attack his country of Brises, and had taken his town of Chalemont, and was besieging the Castle de l'Ain, having already taken and pillaged its town. The Count of Savoy had given him men, and made him do this. So the Duke of Bourbon was very hurt and angry at this news, which came to him on Good Friday at ten o'clock. So he immediately ordered his clerks to make two hundred pairs of letters, some directed to Bourbonnais, others to Forez and Beaujolais, to be carried by anyone headed there. And the duke commanded, after the service, that the lord of Châteaumorand should at once mount a horse and carry his pennon and should set off with the men of his household, who were found to number fourteen. And along the way, they were to collect such men as they were able to find. Luckily, they found a good sixty men-at-arms. When Sir Jean de Châteaumorand and his men were close to Toissé, a town of the Duke of Bourbon they were told that Amé de Very wanted to assail the town on the morrow. So they put themselves on the route, crossing the Saône at Vespers, and around midnight, arrived at the town of Toissé, which they were told Amé de Very planned to attack on the morrow at sunrise. So the companions did not sleep the whole night but prepared their watch and defense of it, so that when Amé de Very arrived he would have a fine reception. Sir Jean de Châteaumorand forbade any man to show himself until they saw the enemy at the foot of the wall, and when Amé de Very was at the peak of his assault of the bridge of Toissé, after it had been lowered, Châteaumorand would emerge with the duke's pennon conspicuous, and his company of a good eighty men-at-arms. And so it was done. Amé de Very and his company retreated to Jujurieu, among its ponds, to make a stronghold, where they stayed eight days. And at the end of the eight days there arrived at Toissé, where Sir Jean de Châteaumorand had three hundred men, as many Bourbonnois and Foréziens as Beaujolois, making altogether four hundred men, which is an adequate company, and later on, Sir Robert de Chaslus joined those at Toissé, bringing with him a good fourscore; and when he arrived at Toissé the knights made a plan to go fight Amé de Very, who was still at Jujurieu, and if he did not leave his stronghold, besiege him. So the Bourbonnois company left Toissé in battle formation. But when Amé de Very learned through his spies that so many men had come against him, he did not dare wait for them. Instead, they moved out, to the other side of the river Ain from the ponds, and went on to Rochetaillée, completely outside of the Beaujolois lands. When they realized this, the knights Robert de Chaslus and Jean de Châteaumorand, with their men, followed quickly after de Very, and camped along the river Ain. They remained there four days, waiting for whatever Amé de Very would do; but he [de Very] and his men had fled from the Brises region, and gone to Savoy. So Sir Jean de Châteaumorand and Sir Robert de Chaslus assigned all of two hundred men-at-arms to Tiercellet, a nephew of Châteaumorand, at least two hundred men-at-arms, to capture a place in Brises, where there was one of the principal houses of the Count of Savoy, which they took and burned, and then returned back to their masters. On the morrow it was reported to Sir Jean de Châteaumorand that Amé de Very and the children of Bouain were about to cross the river Ain from the other side to come fight them.

XCIII. How the Duke of Bourbon came to Villefranche, where the King of France sent him men-at-arms to aid him in his war against the Savoyards, and how the Count of Savoy surrendered Amé de Very to the Duke of Bourbon.

When the Bourbonnois learned this news they considered together what was to be done: if ordered Sir Robert de Chaslus to stay at Pont d'Ain with his people, and Sir Jean de Châteaumorand went towards Rochetaillée, with at least two hundred men-at-arms to know if they found the Savoyards or not and if Amé de Very had made preparation to cross on this side. They rode, Châteaumorand and his people, the whole night and found that Amé de Very had made a bridge wishng to cross the river against them, and indeed some thirty-two men-at-arms, Savoyards, had passed the river against them, who were all killed or taken by the Bourbonnois, and some of them drowned, and the bridge was broken and destroyed, so that they were no longer able to cross. Then Châteaumorand returned with his companions to Pont d'Ain where there were remaining four hundred men-at-arms with Sir Robert de Chaslus. So they were pleased and satisfied by the good fortune of their companions. On the morrow, all the chivalry of Bourbonnais, Forez, and Beaujolais, among whom there were many valiant men, assembled to determine what should be done, since all that remained in the Duke of Bourbon's territory to deal with was a place called Ambérieu, since all the others had been reconquered by the Bourbonnois save that one. And in Brises, the Duke of Bourbon had in the whole country an agreement that the knights and men should set out to besiege Ambérieu, which held out against them. So Châteaumorand and Chaslus affirmed that they should speak well. "But," said the knights, "if anyone is able to find a way and manner to cross into Savoy, as Amé de Very and the Savoyards crossed into Brises, this would be a fine honor to the Duke of Bourbon." So all the chivalry said that this was very true, except that someone would be able to find a passage. Then some said: "Good, let's find a way across." That night they rested and on the morrow the Bourbonnois broke camp from the Pont d'Ain very early in the morning and they went before a castle loyal to the abbot of Ambrunai, where there was a flimsy bridge, and the castle and the abbot within were taken by force. They spent a whole day repairing this bridge and after midnight they rode into Savoy right up to Ambrunai, where that morning they put themselves into battle order and found themselves to be a good six hundred men-at-arms, saying that this was enough to do great damage in Savoy. Then scouts set forth to reconnoiter the town of Ambrunai, assessing it as neither very strong nor on its guard. So these forward scouts entered it immediately, and everyone else followed with a cavalry charge. And they discovered eighty horses belonging to Amé de Very stabled there, which were confiscated. Some of those who guarded them were killed, while others who saw the commotion retreated into the abbey, which was fortified. So the town was attacked, where the companions gladly did their deed, and were well recompensed, for the loot amounted altogether to a good four thousand francs. The Bourbonnois stayed in the said town for two days to restore themselves, and in these two days attacked all the lands in the mountains, and that of the children of Bouain, who were mortal enemies; and knocked down their fences, burned down their mills, and seized a good two thousand head of livestock.

The Bourbonnois came to withdraw to Pont d'Ain, where they gained the bridge which is over the river, and they lodged in the town on this side, as they had done other times. Then Sir Robert de Chaslus and Sir Jean de Châteaumorand said to the companions: "My lords it is now time to go to Ambérieu, for you have done your affairs well. Now let's go there and not leave there until we have it. For we know for certain that there are inside a good fourscore enemy combatants." So the Bourbonnois decamped from Pont d'Ain, and they went to lodge before the castle of Ambérieu, where there was good lodging and grand, and there they remained four days, to make siege engines to attack it. During the siege the Duke of Bourbon came to Villefranche in Beaujolais with four hundred men-at-arms which he sent to the siege of Ambérieu, from which he was only three leagues away, with the others and he remained at the said Villefranche. So it happened that at the end of four days they had made the siege engines, and were assailing Ambérieu. In the low court of the castle were some little houses covered with straw, into which fire was thrown, and the low court and the priory were burned down and likewise all the provisions. And those of Ambérieu retreated into a tower, which was very strong and fine; but because they had nothing to eat, they surrendered to the Duke of Bourbon at his will; there were thirteen gentleman of Savoy. So Châteaumorand and Chaslus took all of those of the garrison, and sent them off wearing just their pourpoints, three hundred all bound in twenty-one carts, to the Duke of Bourbon at Villefranche. And when the duke saw them he was overjoyed, as were his companions. Immediately he had them eat and drink, and then commanded that they be guarded in prison; and the duke sent word to Chaslus and Châteaumorand that they had done good work, and that they should not pull back at all, but they should search out a good campsite and they should all remain together until the duke would order otherwise; and the duke ordered them to take the most beautiful lodging they could have, namely Montluel, half of which belonged to his allies and half to the Count of Savoy. And so they did. Meanwhile, the King sent six hundred men-at-arms and some men of his household from France to his uncle the Duke of Bourbon to aid him in the war he was making on Savoy, and so did the lord of Couci, all that he could summon up, and likewise the Count d'Eu, the Count of St. Pol, the Count of Harcourt and the Count of Alençon, until the Duke of Bourbon found himself with no less than four thousand men-at-arms, and everyone counseled that he should make a great effort to utterly defeat the

Count of Savoy. But the Count of Savoy who knew all this was flabbergasted and sent to the Duke of Bourbon over four days three embassies through which he disavowed Amé de Very and swore a great oath that never had he commanded him to make war, nor did he wish to. For the Duke of Bourbon was able to think that the Count of Savoy would serve him if he had need of him. So the Duke of Bourbon consulted with the knights who strongly counselled him to destroy the Count of Savoy. But Duke Louis of Bourbon who was the most honorable prince, and the most honest that one could find, responded: "Since my nephew of Savoy has excused himself, and has made so great an oath, and since he is my nephew, son of my sister, and has no quarrel with me, it appears to me that I ought to believe him." Then the lord d'Albret said: "My lord, the count sees full well that if you like, he has the power to destroy him, and to chase him out of his country. That is what makes him say what he says." To that statement the Duke of Bourbon answered: "Good cousin d'Albret, let us suppose that he has done this deed, so I would not wish to destroy him, he who is so close to me, notwithstanding he is well within my power, but I believe his denial. I will give him," said the duke "another choice, since he says that this war never has been by his commandment, and that he disavows Amé de Very, who has done it, and is his man. The count should give him into my hands, to do my will with him, to hang him or otherwise, and I will leave, I will believe what he has declared to me." So the Savoyard ambassadors were content, and reported this to the count their lord, who immediately sent Amé de Very to the Duke of Bourbon at Villefranche. Amé de Very considered himself as good as dead, and said openly that he was the man of the Count of Savoy, and that the count his lord had made him wage the war which he had made against the duke in his towns of Brises, and concerning this Amé made a great oath. These words Sir Robert de Chaslus reported to the Duke of Bourbon, about which the duke answered to Chaslus: "All that he says he says out of the fear of death, and I ought to better believe my nephew, son of my sister than him, for I have enough power with me to punish my nephew and to make this one die is a small vengeance; I will send him back to my nephew, accused by the words he has said, to see what punishment he will inflict: for it is for his master a great reproach;" and thus the duke did this, by which the count held Amé de Very banished from his country for a long time, so things remained, and further the duke returned the thirteen gentleman to Savoy free and clear, and by his generosity released the common people who had been surrendered to him at the taking of Ambérieu.

XCIV. How the Duke of Bourbon sent some of his men to Marshal Boucicault, of whom Châteaumorand was chief, and what they did, before they were at Genoa.

The Duke of Bourbon was still at Villefranche, his residence in his barony of Beaujolais, in that same year of 1408 and Marshal Boucicault, Governor of Genoa for the King of France, that the Duke of Bourbon had raised, sent Jean de Neufuis, a well-regarded squire, to the duke so that it should please him to send the Marshal twelve hundred men-at-arms, for some grand rebellion which the men of the Marquis de Montferrat had made against the King of France to the extent of slaughtering eight hundred men-at-arms from the Auvergne, whose captain was Sir Guillaume de Saigne, and they were defeated between Montovi (Mont de Vis) and St. Clare. And in addition, the Marshal sent three thousand ducats to pay the companions as far as Dauphiné and from Dauphiné he would dispense payment for one month to the men-at-arms, enough to get them to Genoa; and further the marshal prayed that the Duke of Bourbon should be willing to lend him Sir Jean de Châteaumorand to lead them, who another time had remained in Lombardy for a year with the marshal. The Duke of Bourbon agreed with him that all who wished to go should, and that Châteaumorand should be chief of their march and on the morrow the duke said to Châteaumorand: "You go to Jujurieu where there are still many men and see which of them might wish to go there both from those in my service or anyone else, as part of your company, for they have my permission, both my allies and others, to go in your company, for I am content, and I will give you my letters so that they will believe you." Then Sir Jean de Châteaumorand left and went to Jujurieu and spoke to the soldiers who were agreeable providing that they should be paid for a month or at least a part of one as soon as they arrived in Genoa. And the captains that Sir Jean de Châteaumorand first brought back included a hundred men-at-arms that the lord d'Albret had consigned to him, among whom were captains Emynion d'Albret and Gaucort who had lots of people; the lord of Jonselle, son of the lord of St. George, who had a fine company of men-at-arms, Le Barrois, Jean de Neufuis, Jean Grant of Burgundy, Leveau de Bar the lord of Mirembel, and Rauler de Tresettes. With these captains and Châteaumorand they were able to muster twelve hundred men-at-arms, and Châteaumorand made them a loan and led them into Briançonnois at the entry of Piedmont, and there Sir Jean de Châteaumorand found Le Bourgne Caqueran, and Louis Coste, who loaned him enough for a month. And Le Bourgne Caqueran said to Châteaumorand: "If you and your people wish to come with me, I will lead you to those who killed Marshal Boucicault's men." Châteaumorand was pleased with this, and from there went before Montovi, a very big town in Piedmont, where Le Bourgne Caqueran had once served. By this means, Montovi, which belonged to the Marquis of Montferrat and had been left in the custody of the noble knight Amé de Savoy, Prince of Piedmont, was taken, and from there were recovered many items of military equipment that Marshal Boucicault's men had lost the previous year. And from Montovi, Châteaumorand and the companions went to St. Clare, a fine place belonging the Marquis the Montferrat. But its houses were roofed with straw, so they set them on fire, and the place was completely burned, and a good two hundred villains were killed there. And they discovered therein the coat of arms, the standard and the harness of Sir Guillaume de Saigne, who had been defeated near there. Then the companions continued five leagues from there to a town called Les Autels, the inhabitants of which had attended the defeat of Sir Guillaume de Saigne. So it was assailed and taken, and many villains were killed, and much baggage of Sir Guillaume de Saigne was recovered. And then they went to St. Gemma, a fine fortress which was taken by assault and the villains were punished for what they had done and from St. Gemma all the men-at-arms that Sir Jean de Châteaumorand led rode out for the Duke of Bourbon to the city of Genoa, where Marshal Boucicault awaited them day and night. So he was very happy and joyful about it, and contented them and paid for another month.

XCV. How the Marshal Boucicault and the Duke of Bourbon's men defeated the Marquis of Varzi, and the brigands before Milan.

The governor of Genoa, Sir Jean le Meingre called Boucicault, Marshal of France, said to Jean de Châteaumorand and the other captains whom he had brought with him in aid of the Marshal, concerning the Duke of Bourbon: "My lords, I thank many times my lord the Duke of Bourbon, who has not in the least forgotten his servant, but has sent me so great a company as you are: you are very welcome. I have seen how you have well avenged the injury which was done over the past year to Sir Guillaume de Saigne and the country of Montferrat, and this pleases me greatly. It is thanks to that, and by God's grace, that I have retained this city of Genoa, in the name of and for the King of France, for so long. He will be greatly pleased to have his realm further enlarged. I have been told of the rivalry of the two brothers, the Duke of Milan and the Count of Pavia, and how they are no longer in accord. So I have been advised, having seen this division, and that the city is firmly in my command and also that I since have many men, it would be a good idea for the both of us to venture into Lombardy, to see if we will be able to do something which will profit the king, and our honor." Then Sir Jean de Châteaumorand said to the Marshal: "My lord, you know the subtleties of the Lombards and their factions. If you leave the city ungarrisoned, the people being mercurial no doubt will concoct a rebellion, and if you go off to Lombardy, where there is nothing but chaos, there will be hardly anything there that you can conquer." Then said Marshal Boucicault: "Châteaumorand, by my faith, you speak convincingly, but nevertheless I will go there, and I will leave some men here that I can trust." Then Marshal Boucicault left Genoa, with all his company, and he went into the territory of the Marquis of Varzi, in the high mountains between Genoa the plain of Lombardy. And the Marquis of Varzi, who knew the Marshal was coming with his men, assembled two thousand villeins and two hundred men on horse at a church, wishing to combat the [invading] company, and there was no man left there, since all had gone, they being sent into battle on a dry river bed, a fine place to fight the French coming from Genoa; and the French, seeing that they were facing only men afoot, left five hundred men-at-arms on their horses as a rearguard. They charged into their midst, and routed them, and three hundred of these commoners were killed, and the rest taken; and when those waiting in the rearguard noticed the two hundred horses ready and hidden near the church, they rode in all in a bunch, running down their masters who were trapped unmounted, and captured the horses. And all the others joined in the hunt with them in the town of Varzi, where one hundred thousand francs were gained, and the Marquis of Varzi retreated to a tower, and proposed a deal with Marshal Boucicault by which he would become a man of the King of France through fealty, if he was given back his town. The Marshal, seeing that the town was pretty much destroyed and that his people had so much loot that they were scarcely able to carry it, conceded it to the Marquis, and received him into the homage of the King of France, for which the documents are at Paris. With this done Marshal Boucicault left. The Duke of Bourbon's men and those of the other captains crossed the mountains and entered the beautiful Padan Plain, to the city of Piacenza, which surrendered to the king, and the country of Lyescot, and also the country of the Angoisseux, from which the Marshal Boucicault exacted 15,000 ducats out of the monthly income that the towns promised in Lombardy, and from there they crossed the Pô and went to Pavia, to the count, who was in no position to get help, on account of his feud between him and the Duke of Milan.

So the count did homage to the King of France in the hand of the Marshal, which he put inside his town together with his whole company. At the end of eight days, Marshal Boucicault went from Pavia to Milan with all of his company, to whom the Duke of Milan made an overture but they did not dare to enter, because it is a great town, and strong and well-peopled. Then the Marshal prayed Sir Jean de Châteaumorand that he should like to enter Milan with a full four hundred men-at-arms, to reveal if there were some men there. Châteaumorand agreed with him and at the first gate left fifty of his men-at-arms on guard and entered Milan with three hundred and fifty and went to the duke who made him a great feast, and led him through the whole town long and wide. Sir John de Châteaumorand requested from the Duke of Milan permission to enter, him and his company, to garrison his castle of Porte-Giova.* The Duke said no to this, and that none would enter it with greater strength than his own, "but if you, Châteaumorand, wish to come with thirteen companions to see inside, I am content." So Châteaumorand went to see it and found nothing but its palace guard, and returned to the Marshal Boucicault, who was in battle formation outside Milan and he made his report to him, saying that there was no real garrison and that he would be able to enter safely: "But it appears to me," he said, "that in the streets approaching each gate, we ought to position two hundred men-at-arms, so that no one can go in or out without your knowing." So Marshal Boucicault did it, and the company remained twelve days in the city, in great joy and happiness and the duke held great state. Now it happened that the third day that the French were lodged in Milan, a captain of the Ghibelline party named Pierre de Subergoine sallied from the faubourgs with twelve hundred Ghibellines, who hated the Guelfs which destroyed a good three hundred French foragers. So came the cry to Châteaumorand and to Bosredon, at their gate, who sallied out with four hundred men-at-arms, to go to the aid of their men, and they encountered these brigands who were defeated and taken; and they gained three hundred habergeons of steel, and Pierre de Subergoine was killed and his brother was made prisoner, and paid two thousand ducats and ten habergeons of steel; and never since his time was there rebellion in Lombardy; and you can be sure that Marshal Boucicault managed so well, with the help of the Duke of Bourbon's people and some other captains and companions who took their accustomed taxes in Italy—from Ravenna, Verse, Plaisance, Pavia, Milan and d'Ivrée – seventy thousand gold ducats to pay the company, and he had made a fine conquest for the king.

XCVI. How the Duke of Bourbon made his orders to aid his nephew of Orléans.

In the war that Duke Jean of Burgundy initiated in Picardy, he was driven by such rage that, in effect, he had sworn by all his power to destroy the heirs of Orléans, and all who were on their side. For he said that when the heirs of Orléans had brought the king to their own lands it was an act of war against him. So it happened that to maintain the quarrel of the young duke and of his brothers, the dukes of Berry, Brittany, and Bar allied themselves by oath and with them the Count of Armagnac, and they assembled a large number of their friends and allies at Gien on the Loire who swore by fire and sword to make war on the Duke of Burgundy. And the Count of Clermont who was there likewise swore to this alliance, in the place of his father the Duke of Bourbon as well as for himself, for which act the duke was very displeased to have it promised in his name, excusing himself to those who reported to him the treaty that the son had no power to bind the father in any oath, for which the duke said: "Once I have made an oath to my lord the king. I should do it for none other. And if brother-in-law Jean has done so, this is without my knowledge, and it very much displeases me." Now it was not long before Duke Charles of Orléans sent one of his own knights, named Sir Guillaume de Laire, as his emissary in aid of his war, to the Duke of Bourbon, and the knight said to the duke: "Most honorable prince and puissant lord, Duke Charles of Orléans, my lord and master, with his brothers who are your nephews, pray and require you, upon the affinity of lineage, that you aid them in their war, which is a just one, and take their side against the Duke of Burgundy, who wrongfully wishes to disinherit them. For the other lords, as you know, wish to do this, and they have sworn it in the presence of your son, who has agreed to it." Then the Duke of Bourbon replied earnestly: "Guillaume de Laire, you have no notion of what it means to start a war: the beginning comes quickly, but the end comes late. You are a fool, who counsels my nephews to start a war against so strong a party, as they are about to do. They have but little money, which I think you and the others want to make them spend, and they will end up poor and destitute. They are young and they don't know what it is, this kind of business. Go right back to them and assure them that I will not fail them in their need, if they face a threat. But I would prefer that they should be mature, and realize that their money should not be spent without cause." Sir Guillaume de Laire went to Duke Charles of Orléans to relate that which he had found. And the Duke of Bourbon remained at Montbrisson for a while with the duchess his wife, they returned to him from Lombardy to accompany the Marshal Boucicault, that is Sir Jean de Châteaumorand, Sir Jean des Barres, together with their companions from the Bourbonnois and Forez to whom the duke made good cheer. But thus in the end the dukes of Berry, Brittany, Bar and the Count of Armagnac and the lord d'Albret, the Constable of France wrote and sent ambassadors to Duke Louis of Bourbon and showed him that Duke Jean of Burgundy had made great plans to destroy the orphans of Orléans and indeed that Duke had defied them and that he had pity for it. So the duke thought a little, and then said: "I see that it is certain that he wishes to destroy my nephews. I have seen my flesh and blood spilled inhumanly over the paving stones, and those to whom it ought to be a sorrow are more obstinate in doing evil, so I vow and promise to God that as long as I have life, I will put body, means, and might into defending my nephews' cause, and I declare myself to be of their party." And then the duke began to speak to his wife the duchess: "Lady Anne Daulphine, dearest companion, I beg leave of you to go to the place of my devotions, for the purpose of retiring from the world in my old age, and serving God by dwelling at the convent of the Celestines of Vichy. I'm sure that the Duke Jean de Burgundy intends to destroy my fair nephews of Orléans. So I am determined to oppose all men who want to harm them. And, once this war is over, since I could not do it before, I want to undertake the voyages which I had planned to make for the sake of God. I shall spend the rest of my days at Vichy as I have arranged. So I bid you adieu, my wife, and I will soon see you again." Then the duke kissed her, and left his town of Montbrison in good company and Sir Louis de Cullant, who was then Admiral of the Sea in France, together with Ponsart de Beauval, a squire, and others from the duke's household took their leave from him and went to Granada, a Saracen kingdom, and so in a good hour they were at the siege of Antiquière, which Don Ferrant held, (who was Infante of Castile and afterwards King of Aragon) and which was taken by the Spaniards and the Saracen king was conquered, who had much fine chivalry from several countries, in 1409.

The Duke of Bourbon on arriving at Molins, commanded the count, his son, to go to Poitiers, to the Duke of Berry, to learn the details of their treaty, and where they had assembled their men. So the count left, and went to Poitiers to deal with these things, and the duke, his father, proceeded to his castle at Bourbon-l'Archambault and summoned Master Etienne de Bar, his secretary, to write letters of command in great number, which were written and sent far and near to knights, squires and men-at-arms, who heartily offered themselves, given that he was such a most-noble and valorous knight, and renowned prince, to come to defense and aid of the children of Orléans; for many noble men strongly desired to support their cause. A day was assigned at Montluçon where the duke was, who amused himself at the hunt, waiting for them, to lead them with his allies to war.

XCVII. How the good Duke Louis of Bourbon departed this life.

After the order was done each one prepared in his right, and many knights and squires came to Montluçon, which the duke was glad to see, and as he waited for the other companions, in the morrow of St. Lawrence, the duke felt a little sick, to which all day he paid no attention , but after the feast of Notre Dame in mid-August, which the duke celebrated with great devotion, he felt himself get worse and knowing the end of his days to be approaching, praised God devotedly and thanked Him for His divine will, which was to recall him. So the duke began to speak to many knights and men of good name who were close to him: "My friends, I thank God with all my heart, who has lent me life, as I have lived up to now, by his commandment. Certainly death does not displease me but if our Creator has been satisfied, I have willingly seen the health of my lord the king, the union of the princes of the fleur-de-lis and the peace of this so very desolate kingdom of France. I have worked with all my power to pacify it, and it was my wish in this expedition in which I had thought to go to employ myself in a manner that goodwill should come of it; and because I am not able to go I recommend the affair to God the all-powerful. You, my good and loyal servants, know that for a long time I have had my testament, which I wish to be kept as I have ordered to my executors, the duchess my wife, Sir Hutin le Baveux, Sir l'Hermite de la Fay, and Master Pierre de Chantelle, my confessor. Command that the pomps which are very costly for the obsequies of princes, in reverence to God, should not be done for me but the amount of money which could be employed thus should be distributed to the poor. You will love me for being praised and you will pray to God, if I have done things against his will that he will pardon me, please. The duchess my wife, I recommend to you, is not here nor Jean my son who is my heir; he is your lord. After my decease, counsel him, honor him, and love him loyally, as you have done for me; this I implore you. Tell him from me, that he should be defender of this the crown of France against all oppressors, and this I especially enjoin on him." The knights hearing the Duke of Bourbon speak such praiseworthy words wept tenderly, and promised him to do and keep what he had commanded. Then the duke requested that his hair should be cut; so it was cut and when he held the locks, he spoke in this manner: "Good lord Jesus Christ, my God, my father-Creator, of the delights of this mortal life, where so much was striven for in my locks of hair, I do not wish that their vanity should accompany me; cast them away in disdain of pride!" Then he trampled it under his feet, and each one departed, while he remained in his oratory. Notwithstanding that the duke had the custom of confessing and taking communion, throughout the illness, he performed them many times, and especially the Sunday the 17th day of August, when feeling very much worse and infirm, was absolved by a very devout confession, and reverently heard his three masses, said his canonical hours intoned lamentations and sighs for his sins, crying to God for mercy with a contrite heart and humble thought receiving the body of God his creator, from the hands of his chaplain and confessor, Master Pierre Chantelle, who wished to bring the Eucharist the Savior of the world to his prince and lord in his seat, because he was much enfeebled, but the humble lord said: "There is no reason that the worthy Creator should come to me, an unworthy one." Then he got up and tenderly weeping, kneeling before the altar, saying "My God, my father, in judgment, see here your poor creature, grant forgiveness to it, by your great mercy, so that whatever sins I might have done, about which I am very contrite to have committed, by Your lofty grace be erased. For I have truly reported and confessed them by heart and by mouth to the confusion of the enemy of fallible mankind and for the salvation of my soul, which I offer into your hands." And the noble lord took communion and during these two days, he did nothing but praise God asking him that at the hour of his passing, he should have a firm memory of His blessed passion, receive all His sacraments, as prince, true Catholic firm in the Christian faith, and obedient son of holy church. Many a time he had said that death was nothing for an honest man to fear, and continually his mouth named and praised the name of God, to him piteously, and to the glorious Virgin Mary, his advocate, in whom he put his confidence and perfect faith. He also petitioned the apostle of France, the glorious martyr Saint Denis, that he should beseech God for the health of his soul, likewise he supplicated about that to the devout confessor and patron of the most Christian kings of France, Saint Louis, formerly lord of that seigneurie, of which lineage he was descended, and he beseeched to all the saints, male and female of Paradise, angels and archangels that at the hour when he gave up his spirit they would not wish to wander. And keeping this in mind since sight was now difficult for him, and he no longer had the power of speech, it came to pass that, holding the cross lovingly embraced under his arms, and with his confessor intoning to him the Litany of the Passion of his Creator, he rendered his spirit to God, in his city of Montluçon on Tuesday 19 August, in his 63rd year, in the year of Our Lord 1410. And two cords of mortification were later found bound tightly around his waist, one of whipcord, tied with knots, the other of psaltery string, and none of his servants during his life had noticed it. And that same night, after all things proper for a departed prince were done, he was put on a litter, and carried to the church in Cosne, for his Visitation, accompanied by prayers to God for his soul. Along the route where the body was carried, there were great crowds of people, grieving for their lord, weeping and crying so loud that the voices resounded very far, and they said: "Alas!, Death, you have removed this day our champion, who has guarded and defended us from all oppressors. This is our Prince, our comfort, our duke, the most honest man of the best conscience in life that one could find, and the most pure man in his life that one could find anywhere." In this flood of tears they brought the body of this very excellent prince to Souring to the Conventional priory where after the funeral obsequies he was buried in its beautiful chapel which in his life he had founded and endowed richly with rents, sacerdotal ornaments, chalices, and books, where every day the under-prior present, accompanied by other clerics, chanting rhythmically a mass for the dead and other prayers said over the tomb for the remedy of his soul. Not much time passed before the Count of Clermont was told of the death of his father. He left the Duke of Berry and came to the Bourbonnois, much distressed by this death; his assigned duties within his lands were delegated in order to lead the men-at-arms that his deceased father Duke Louis had summoned. So there was a noble company of knights and squires which Duke Jean of Bourbon led against the Duke of Berry, to help the infants of Orléans, their cousins germain, in their war.

XCVIII. How the Duke Louis was praised.

The author tells that the virtuous man ought to be praised after his death, and glorified for his fortunate end and because the Duke Louis of Bourbon has passed from this life gloriously, he had much to praise. For they knew him and his full life, that the soul is celestial and descended from on high and the body terrestrial and low, and that the soul is immortal and the body mortal, he lived in such a way that his soul has climbed up from which it had descended and it was united with his body, as all of one will, reasonably the soul served the body and the body obeyed the soul. And the duke, in looking back on his life, realizing that the just soul rests eternally with God, ordered perpetual works be done in his memory, knowing that if his soul was in the sublime presence, they would be requesting of God the salvation of those remaining in purgatory. And if it was in the place of purgatory, he would be redeemed by such work. For this he founded masses and perpetual requiem masses for the health of his soul and those of his predecessors and successors. The first of them to be created, was a perpetual one for the soul of the deceased Duke Pierre, his father, with the Friars Preachers at Poitiers, and then for himself and his [people], one at the abbey of Cluny; one sung for the deceased at the Holy Convent of the Little Innocents; at Le Mans, one for the health of the King of France, Charles the sixth of that name; at Chartres, one to Our Lady; at Chateau-Chinon two perpetual masses; one with the Augustines of Toulouse; one at Tours in the church of St. Martin; at Notre Dame de Paris, another, and two requiem masses for the deceased. And because of the firm devotion he had for the Virgin Mary, he founded in his town of Molins a college of twelve perpetual canons, and also the hospital St. Nicholas-lès-Molins to sustain poor old officers, and that of St. Julian in the same place, for poor sick travelers; he founded also the devoted place of the Celestines of Vichy, where he had a great desire to dwell. Also at Souring, he founded perpetually a solemn choral mass in his beautiful chapel which he had had built, where he lies; and to all the places in churches founded by him, he gave rents and ornaments of his arms, surplices, chalices, and books for the performing the divine service. Every day he had heard three masses in very great devotion, weeping for his sins, asking God for mercy for his misdeeds, each Friday of the year, when none could see him, he had personally given thirteen pennies issued from his chamber to thirteen poor men, and Holy Thursday before Easter he had washed, wiped and kissed the feet of thirteen poor creatures, in reverence for God, serving them at table and giving them some money. For the sake of these acts, and many others which he did in secret, we may presume that his soul went to a good place. Duke Louis also understood that the wise man who covers himself with celestial armor against his invisible enemies, must protect fortresses against his visible enemies, and that in order that his people be more secure in time of war, he had some of his cities fortified and made ready, such as Vichy, Varennes and

Villefranche in Bourbonnois, Feurs and Thiern. And he built the castles of Molins and Verneuil, and repaired many others, like that of Belleperche, where he built the dungeon. At Bourbon, he began two fine towers; the Castle of Hericon he much improved, that of Montluçon and the tower at Billy; he raised a tower and hall at Murat, and he built the Castle of Ausance in Combraille, and that of Villeneuve in Hez, and had his beautiful house at Paris rebuilt, which cost a lot, where he put up an elegant chapel in which he hoped to establish chaplains to serve God. And truly, during all his earthly life he schooled his knights in all things honorable, saying that they should not be possessed by base greed, out of which treason grows and multiplies, and that they should prevent themselves from doing evil, and from slandering others, for these are the works which corrupt and lead chivalry astray; and he said that the envious would never be at peace; and a knight ought not to have envy in his heart except of one thing, that is to do good, more than any of his company, which should be the object of his courage, that being the root of courtesy, whereby this envy is without pride and without villainy. And Duke Louis said that his knights should deeply love their good and loyal servitors, for the greatest treasure one can have is the best men with him, who love him with a loyal and whole heart and constancy.

Duke Louis admired the practice of arms, for that was his trade, and received great honor through them and consequently he was not keen to abase himself before any and every man of nobility [because they were not all men of arms]. [In their presence] he would not change his ways. Honor did not in the least change his habits: well he knew how to receive it, and also how to hold onto it. He greatly loved his household, who were not corrupt nor of bad morals. Of great renown was Duke Louis throughout the world, as much for his clear intelligence as for his loyalty. As much as his honesty, his reputation for good counsel and noble virtues was very profitable to the house of France. The divisions he saw among the royalty demonstrated to him the evil which was to come.

Often he did his duty to pacify them; he was profitable to the whole community and he put great care to guard that which seemed to him to be the right thing. In himself he had great prudence; it would take great effort to find his equal. He was ready to defend France both in arms and in law, and France lost much with his death. Well the Good Duke was able to say in his lifetime that he saw the division growing, in these words: "I perceive that no one will be ashamed of annihilating the realm and those who more able and ought better to guard and increase it, are all one to ruin it. For each pays attention to his own advantage, not to the advancement of the people, but to their destruction." Blessed is the Duke of Bourbon who has passed from this life and soared to heaven by his merits! At least he did not see the horrible evils that have come to France, which he feared, about which those of the realm in regretting this noble prince were able say: "Ha! Ha! Good and loyal knight, discrete and wise, reliable in counsel and mighty in arms, such things are to bewail. If France had still many such defenders as you were, she would be able very long to preserve her freedom and guard and maintain it. For you ordered public affairs by counsel, by reason and by mature deliberation." For this says the author to the three estates: "He! He! lords, that you so value an honest man in great need! From among a great mob of men who were yet dismayed, a gentleman lived up to lineage, defended a kingdom, and so a thousand men were saved by one alone! God having done his part, and has left the kingdom and for men's sins in the balance of fortune according to his pleasure. Ha! Noble duke, the English invasion would not have lasted so long if you were alive, or the division of lords in France rebelling against the sovereign, to all you would have found a remedy." So conclude that the work of all workers falls and perishes, but that work of writing makes it as though the man lives and is always in the memory after his death. It appears that for the good Duke Louis of Bourbon his life endures yet because of his good renown. For one finds the place of his honorable sepulcher the writings which are written to remember his deeds which all the good characteristics we have recounted and told above that you very noble prince Charles of Bourbon Count of Clermont have commanded to describe and put down clearly. This book is compiled by the one named Cabaret a poor pilgrim but rich in pleasure and joy concerning which God and gentility which he loves so much have allowed this pleasant work to come to a good end in the year of the Maid and that is the end of the Chronicle of Duke Louis of Bourbon.

A glossary of military, religious, and technical terms useful to the reader

Fortifications and buildings

Bastide	A town, especially a fortified one.
Crenellations	Battlements.
Faubourg	A suburb, sometimes a fortified one.
Mine	A tunnel that extends under enemy fortifications to give access to a besieging army or allow the placement of fire or explosives to collapse those fortifications.
Countermine	A mine that intercepts an enemy mine.

Arms, armor and military men

Arbalestiers	Crossbowmen.
Avant-bras	Armor for the lower arm.
Avant-garde	Vanguard.
Battle	(1) A sustained fight between organized forces; (2) a major component of a large military force (cf. the later term "battalion").
Bec de faulcon	"Falcon's beak" – an object that comes to point, such as (1) a pole axe with a hammer-like head; or (2) a larger siege engine with a similar point; (3) a point of land.
Bourg	Captain of a stronghold.
Châtelet	A small fortification.
Cog	A broadly built ship with rounded prow and stern.
False brayes	A defensive fortification placed before a gate.
Garde-bras	Armor for the upper arm.
Lames	Narrow plates of armor out of which bigger pieces of armor are constructed.
Pennon (pennon); ensign	Two types of battle flag.
Piece	A type of body armor, breastplate.

Church terminology

Augustines	A religious order inspired and named after St. Augustine.
Canons	Clergy (not monks) who live according to a rule.

Friars minor; Cordeliers	The Franciscan order of mendicant (begging) friars; one tradition within the order was known as the Cordeliers.
Matins	Morning prayer service; early morning.
Miscreants	Used indifferently to describe infidels or heretics.
Notre Dame	Our Lady (the Virgin Mary).
Obit	Prayer service for a deceased person.
Orisons	Prayers.
Saint (plus name)	The churches dedicated to a saint are usually named for that saint.
Saracen	A Muslim or other non-Christian.
Solar	A private room reserved for the more important residents in an upper-class household.
Vespers	Evening prayers; sunset.

Politics, towns, and miscellaneous

Breton Brittany	The western parts of Brittany where Breton rather than French was the dominant language.
Captal	In the south of France, a lord or seigneur.
Chaperon	A hood or cap.
Cheer	Hospitality, friendly greeting, jubilation, etc.
Commune	A sworn association of (usually) townsmen or other commoners. Armed, self-governing communes were formed in late 14th-century France because of the failure of the kings and nobles to deal with the English threat. This led to conflict between nobles and commoners. The two largest communal movements were in the county of Flanders and in Paris.
Échevins	Town councilors.
Estates	A broad social and legal category or a representative body of a social or legal estate; plural, a kingdom or state considered as a group of estates.
Franc	A gold coin; a money of account.
Jacques	French for James – a nickname for peasant rebels or communards.
Maillets; Maillotins	A cudgel made of lead; rebels or rioters who used cudgels for street fighting.
Seigneur; seigneurie	A lord; a lordship.

Spain	Used in the Chronicle to designate Castile, a kingdom in the Iberian peninsula
Reise	German term for a journey or crusade, especially the regular expeditions against the Baltic pagans.
Ville	A town.
Order	Any manifestation of universal order including a social division (for instance the "order of chivalry" an organized body; an authoritative command; a plan.
Parlement (French)	A superior legal court, especially the Parlement of Paris.
Prudhomme	A gentleman, a noble or valiant man; an expert.
Siege	Today, a siege is defined as surrounding an enemy fortification to starve out the garrison; in the Chronicle the attackers would "sit" outside the gates, to the same effect.
Villein	A peasant farmer or serf.

Select Bibliography

Texts and Editions

D'Orronville dit Cabaret, Jean. *La chronique du bon duc Loys de Bourbon*, ed. A.-M. Chazaud. Paris: Société de l'Histoire de France, 1876.

Buchon, J.A.C., ed. *La Vie de Louis, Duc de Bourbon*. In Pantheon litteraire, vol. XIX. Paris, 1841.

Selected Secondary Sources

Bradbury, Jim. *The Medieval Siege*. Woodbridge: The Boydell Press, 1992.

Contamine, Philippe. *Guerre, état et société à la fin du Moyen Age: études sur les armées des rois de France 1337-1494*. Paris: Éditions de l'EHESS, 2004.

DeVries, Kelly and Robert Douglas Smith. *Medieval Military Technology*. 2nd ed. Toronto: University of Toronto Press, 2012.

Duby, Georges. *The Three Orders: Feudal society imagined*. Trans. Arthur Goldhammer. Chicago: University of Chicago Press, 1980.

Keen, Maurice. *Chivalry*. New Haven [Conn.]: Yale University Press, 1984.

Muhlberger, Steven. *Charny's Men-at-Arms: Questions concerning the joust, tournaments and war*. Wheaton, Ill. : Freelance Academy Press, Inc., 2014.

-----. *Deeds of Arms: Formal Combats in the Late Fourteenth Century*. Highland Village: Chivalry Bookshelf, 2005.

Sumption, Jonathan, *The Hundred Years War III: Divided houses*. Philadephia: University of Pennsylvania, 2009.